RENEGADES

Adrian Weale

RENEGADES

Weidenfeld & Nicolson
London

First published in Great Britain in 1994 by
Weidenfeld & Nicolson
The Orion Publishing Group Ltd
Orion House
5 Upper St Martin's Lane
London WC2H 9EA

A catalogue reference is available from the British
Library

ISBN 0 297 81488 5

Photoset in Monophoto Perpetua by
Selwood Systems, Midsomer Norton
Printed and bound in Great Britain by
Butler & Tanner Ltd, Frome and London

Acknowledgements

The author gratefully acknowledges the assistance of the following individuals, without whom the research for this book would have been considerably more difficult. Philip H. Buss, J. G. Slade, Roderick de Normann, Christopher Ailsby, Howard Davies, Eric Pleasants, Alexander Dolezalek, Hans Werner Roepke, James Donald McLeod, Shamus O. D. Wade, Kirn Rattan and Nigel West.

Additionally, the following institutions and their staff were of great assistance: The Public Records Office at Kew and Chancery Lane, London; The Imperial War Museum Library in London; The United States National Archives, Washington DC; The National Archives of South Africa; The Office of the Chief of the New Zealand General Staff; The National Archives of Canada; The Berlin Document Centre; The Bundesarchiv, Koblenz; and The Deutsche Dienstelle (Wast), Berlin.

In the summer of 1992, The Right Honourable William Waldegrave MP, Minister for Public Service, announced his intention of allowing historians to have access to public records which had hithero been deemed too sensitive for release to the Public Records Office. This decision bore fruit for me a year later when I was allowed to see material originated by the Security Service which related to several of the more prominent traitors. I am very grateful to Mr Waldegrave for this, and particularly to Mr Tony Williams and Mr David Jones of the Home Office who facilitated my access to this material and worked hard against a tight schedule to make it available. In the same context, I should like to thank Mrs Enid Smith of the Lord Chancellor's Department.

Finally, I should like to thank my publisher, Mark Crean, for his forbearance; my literary agent, Andrew Lownie, for his efforts on my behalf; Julian Foynes, Tim Lupprian and my father, Dr Ken Weale, for reading the manuscript and making helpful comments; and last but not least, my wife Mary for putting up with the mess that two thousand-odd pages of documents and notes have made of our house.

Contents

Illustrations

Introduction

By all accounts, the conduct of judicial executions in Britain in the twentieth century was dignified and humane – at least in so far as it is possible to be humane when inflicting an act of extreme violence. At the appropriate hour – normally nine o'clock – the executioner and his assistant would enter the condemned cell where they would pinion the arms of their victim before leading him a few yards to the gallows. The scaffold itself was usually sited in the room next to the condemned cell, and when the prisoner entered, he would be led to a chalked 'T' mark on the trapdoor, where the executioner would apply the noose to his victim's neck with the knot – in reality a metal eye – positioned underneath the left ear, and cover his head with a white cloth bag. As the hangman applied the noose, his assistant strapped the prisoner's ankles together and, when he had finished, the chief executioner pulled out a safety pin, pushed a lever and the prisoner fell a short distance and died instantly from a fracture dislocation of the spinal column and colossal concussion. On average the whole process, from the hangmen first entering the cell to the prisoner dying at the end of the rope, took no more than ten seconds; sometimes even less.

The last judicial executions took place in Britain in 1964, after which the death penalty was suspended and then abolished for the crime of murder. However, the death penalty continues to remain in force for a handful of crimes, most notably that of treason. At Wandsworth prison in south London, a fully operational gallows remains in existence in case a conviction is achieved. This is an unlikely prospect; the last treason trials in Britain were held in the autumn of 1945 following which three men, William Joyce, John Amery and Theodor Schurch, went to the gallows. Since then it has been recognized that the charge of high treason, and the compulsory death penalty that it carries on conviction, are too blunt an instrument to deal with the complex motives of those who betray their country, and it has, to all intents and purposes, fallen into abeyance.

Nevertheless Britain retains the extreme penalty for those who are convicted of treason and there are still men alive today who have stood in the dock and watched the judge don a black cap and pass sentence of death upon them. They were fortunate enough to have their sentences of death commuted and they survived to resume their place in society. Others were less fortunate. This book is their story: who they were, what they did, and why they did it.

In the twelve years that I have been researching this account, my surprise that the story of the British traitors who served the Nazi cause has remained largely untold has not diminished. Nobody would pretend that the traitors were of any great strategic significance to the war effort of either side – in fact, if anything they represented a net drain on German resources. Nevertheless it is a fascinating and disturbing story, and the reason that it has been neglected lies almost entirely in the picture that we British like to present of our role in the war.

Our image of Britain in the Second World War is essentially a pleasing one. We like to think of Churchill, Dunkirk and the Blitz, and our picture is of heroic resistance against the odds: of Montgomery, the Eighth Army and their crucial victory at Alamein; of D-Day and the triumphal return to Europe. Above all, we have a picture of Britain's role as being an honourable one. When Hitler controlled a European empire stretching from the Atlantic to the borders of the Soviet Union, Britain stood alone and resisted his might. It should be a source of great national pride that this picture is largely true.

However, a number of British men and women chose to reject their country at this time and follow the path of treason. When the basic facts of their treachery emerged at the end of the war they were fully reported in the press and there has been no discernible attempt by the government to 'cover up' the story. Yet, with a handful of honourable exceptions, historians have largely chosen to ignore them or, at most, to condemn them in passing. This should perhaps be contrasted with the many hundreds of thousands of words expended on the subject of the secret pro-Soviet treacheries of Burgess, MacLean, Philby and Blunt and their fellow spies.

In 1949, the novelist and journalist Rebecca West published *The Meaning of Treason*, a book that has often been hailed as a masterpiece of reportage. It was based on West's coverage, for the *New Yorker* magazine, of a number of the trials, civil and military, of the British traitors in the year after the end of the war. As an account of what happened at the trials and their atmosphere it is an admirable work; as a description of who the traitors were and what they did it is much less reliable. Despite a review in the *Sunday Times* when the book was published which suggested that 'the thoroughness of her investigations is superbly professional', the content of *The Meaning of Treason* was almost entirely derived from what was read and said in the courtrooms during the proceedings. As a result there are a considerable number of errors of fact and inference throughout the text. More dangerously, *The Meaning of Treason* is characterized by the author's attempt to draw conclusions about its subjects from the statements read out in their defence and, importantly, by their physical appearance and demeanour as she observed them in the dock. This is certainly an acceptable practice in journalism but not in history. Whatever West's intentions were, the book is seriously flawed as the basis of our view of the British traitors in the Second World War. Unfortunately, that is what it has become.

By way of example, I should like to quote West on William Joyce: 'His destiny was to be honest; to be wrong; to have his habitation "south of the river". Wormwood scrubs lay on the scabbed edge of London, but nevertheless on the same side of the Thames as the imperial city, so his place was not there. The prison was seized by a spasm of madness and ejected him. The news that Joyce was within its walls spread amongst the other prisoners and they raged against his presence.'[1] This one paragraph sums up what is wrong with the book as a work of history. Rebecca West managed to combine perception and great sensitivity with brazen snobbery and a tendency to flights of fancy that were simply wrong (Joyce was removed from Wormwood Scrubs to Wandsworth because 'the Scrubs' did not possess a gallows with which to hang him). Nevertheless, as an attempt to explain why some Britons chose to side with Hitler *The Meaning of Treason* deserves to be treated seriously.

The best published account of treason in the Second World War is J. A. Cole's *Lord Haw-Haw and William Joyce*. It is a reasoned and meticulously researched book which greatly extended our understanding of that complex and unlikeable man. Cole's intention was to create an account that balanced what Joyce actually did with how he came to be perceived by the public at the war's end. In his foreword Cole wrote: 'A desire to take literary revenge on Joyce was . . . natural enough in the immediate post-war period, but what was written in anger soon came to look spiteful and even absurd.' In writing *Renegades* I have attempted to do the same thing on a wider canvas.

Joyce and his fellow traitors represented a blot on Britain's otherwise largely honourable escutcheon. A palpable anger at their conduct, as represented by Rebecca West in 1949, is still present in works written in the last few years. This book is not an attempt to excuse their treason; simply to show what they actually did and why. Sufficient time has now elapsed for us to extend our understanding of the circumstances in which the renegades found themselves, even if we cannot forgive them.

1

Oswald Mosley, William Joyce and Fascism in Britain: The Background to Treason

2 May 1945 was a warm spring day in Berlin but few people in the city were of a mind to enjoy it. A great pall of dust and smoke hung over the ruined heart of the capital of the 'Thousand Year Reich' and, in dug-outs constructed amongst the devastated buildings, the last few active defenders of the city took shelter despite an uneasy ceasefire which had settled on the government quarter. In most cases they were down to their last few rounds of ammunition and their last few mouthfuls of food. The only area of the city held by the German forces were around the Tiergarten, the great wooded park in the centre of Berlin; the Zoo bunker, on the southern boundary of the Tiergarten; the two almost indestructible 'Flak Towers' at the western end of the park; and a couple of streets of wrecked government buildings along the south-eastern edge. Two days had passed since word had spread amongst the defenders of Hitler's death. As the morning wore on, the exhausted soldiers, dressed in the traditional field-grey uniforms of the German Wehrmacht and Waffen-SS, emerged from their hiding places and threw down their weapons ready for the long march into Soviet captivity. The victorious Russian troops began the process of searching and registering their captives against the bizarre backdrop of the cries of the frightened, wounded and starving animals still resident within the zoo itself, where an old

keeper, oblivious to the human suffering which surrounded him, wept over the body of a dead hippopotamus, killed by a Soviet mortar barrage.

But most of the last defenders of Berlin were not German. Although they were dressed in the uniforms of the German Army, they wore badges identifying them as Frenchmen of the 'Charlemagne' division; as Scandinavians of the 'Nordland' division; as Latvians, Estonians and Spaniards. One slightly older soldier, blind in one eye, came from an even stranger organization: although himself German – but born in China – Wilhelm August Rössler wore on the right arm of his SS uniform the Union Jack badge of the smallest of the foreign contingents of the German Forces: the British Free Corps. As Rössler went into captivity, his erstwhile comrades – supposedly the vanguard of Britain's contribution to Europe's crusade against Bolshevism – were desperately trying to cover the traces of their membership of the Waffen-SS; ingratiating themselves with the advancing Allies and attempting to submerge themselves into the mass of the 160,000 newly liberated prisoners of war. It was too late; the Allied intelligence services had long known the identities of the majority of the British renegades and the manhunt had begun.

Even before the guns fell silent on 11 November 1918 it was clear that the 'war to end wars' had exacted a terrible toll on the political culture of Europe. Together with the millions of young men who had been killed, the Great War had also put paid to the monarchies of all the defeated powers. In Imperial Russia, Austria-Hungary, Germany and Ottoman Turkey the established governments had been, or were in the process of being, swept away by a new order of politicians who were no longer prepared to accept the leadership of their supposed social betters. For the governments of the victorious powers, and more particularly for those attempting to assert authority amid the wreckage of defeat, a new menace had arisen. The Bolshevik faction of the Russian Communist party had succeeded in seizing power in Petrograd by a bold *coup d'état* in October 1917 and, even as civil war raged within their own country, provided inspiration for similarly-minded groups throughout Europe. Revolution was in the air!

The passing of the old order affected different people in different ways.

At the end of November 1918, a 29-year-old corporal of the German Army called Adolf Hitler, who had just been discharged from a convalescent hospital at Pasewalk following his temporary blinding by a British gas attack, was attempting to make his way back to his adopted home town of Munich. Very much inspired by the conservative nationalism of the front-line soldier, he was shocked by the spectacle of 'Social Democrats, Bolsheviks and Jews [he did not distinguish between them] – as Germany's new masters and, finding that his regimental barracks had been taken over by a 'Soldiers' Council',[1] volunteered for service as a guard at a prisoner-of-war camp.

Britain, the most stable of the victorious European democracies, was spared a great deal of the tumult heralded by the end of the war. Even so, seizing on the maxim that 'Britain's difficulty is Ireland's opportunity', a group of Irish nationalists had already declared the Irish Republic and occupied Dublin's General Post Office during Easter 1916. The rebellion was not popular, but the government backlash was even less so and succeeded in creating martyrs for the Republican cause. Subsequent British dithering exacerbated the situation and inculcated the realization amongst Irish nationalists that they were only likely to achieve a measure of independence by the use of force.[2]

As peace broke out in Europe, but with nationalist resentment continuing to fester in Ireland, David Lloyd George, prime minister of the coalition government since December 1916, called a general election. The problems which faced Britain were numerous, but revolved mainly around the colossal cost of fighting the war. Lloyd George campaigned on the basis of creating 'a land fit for heroes to live in' and his previous record as a social legislator appeared to hold promise. In reality the majority of new members of his National Liberal and Unionist coalition that swept to power on 14 December 1918 were 'hard-faced men who looked as if they had done well out of the war',[3] who supported Lloyd George for his record as a war leader and had little interest in social reform – despite their fears of the emergence of Communism in Britain.

However the youngest amongst the 260 new members who entered the Commons in 1918 was somewhat different. Oswald Ernald Mosley was just twenty-two years old when he began his political odyssey. Born on 16 November 1896 into a wealthy family of landed gentry, he had experienced an upbringing common to many of his class. He was educated at Winchester (where he showed little taste for academia but was a noted sportsman) and the Royal Military College at Sandhurst before being commissioned into the 16th Lancers in October 1914. In common with many young men of his background he was eager for war: finding his regiment stationed in Ireland, Mosley volunteered for the Royal Flying Corps (forerunner to the RAF) as an observer. His explanation was simple: 'How to get to the front was the burning question of the hour. One service alone supplied the answer'.[4] But in his eyes an additional attraction of the RFC lay in its glamorous, buccaneering reputation. To fly in the flimsy contraptions of wood and canvas required versatility and daring, characteristics which he possessed in abundance, but it was also an individualistic way to wage war. As observer, his task was to mark enemy troop deployments and topographical landmarks on to gridded maps for use in future ground operations but after four months he was posted back to Britain to train as a pilot. He gained his pilot's certificate in May 1915, but shortly afterwards crashed his aircraft whilst showing off in front of his family and badly broke his ankle. After convalescing he returned to his original regiment, the 16th Lancers, who by then were serving in the trenches. Pressure on manpower had meant that he was called back to active duty before his leg had properly recovered; in the appallingly unsanitary conditions that prevailed his injuries became infected and his health collapsed. Mosley was invalided home in March 1916. For the rest of the war he worked in the Ministry of Munitions and the Foreign Office.

Mosley's emergence as a political animal can be dated to his period in hospital in 1916. It was there that he began to read history and politics seriously and it was from hospital that he went forth into society as a man of good social position and considerable financial means.[5] His experience of the mass slaughter on the Western Front had left him profoundly convinced that there should be no more war. It also persuaded him that blame for the sacrifice of a generation lay with the old men of the establishment. Describing Armistice Day 1918, he wrote: 'Smooth, smug people, who had never fought or suffered, seemed to the eyes of youth –

at that moment age-old with sadness, weariness and bitterness – to be eating, drinking, laughing on the graves of our companions.'[6] Determined to follow a career in politics, his entry into parliament was smooth enough. His money, family connections and military background were sufficient to see him adopted for the safe Tory seat of Harrow and, in the Commons, he sat on the coalition benches.

Despite his conventional background, however, Mosley, and many other young politicians of his generation, quickly became convinced that the politicking of the 'old gang' of pre-war statesmen could not hope to solve the social and economic problems that were threatening to engulf Britain and the Empire. Mosley himself was far too individualistic to submit himself to party discipline and was gripped with a powerful sense of his own destiny; within six years of entering parliament as, effectively, a conservative, Oswald Mosley and his wife Cynthia, the daughter of Lord Curzon, had joined the Labour Party.[7] His transformation from conservative to socialist, which encompassed two years as an independent MP aligned with the Liberals, was initially precipitated by his opposition to the methods being adopted to suppress the continuing Irish rebellion. Horrified by evidence of torture and reprisals against the civil population, Mosley crossed the floor of the Commons on 3 November 1920.

The brutal suppression of the Easter rising of 1916 had directly led to the election of seventy-three Sinn Féin MPs in November 1918. They had constituted themselves as a separate parliament in Dublin and organized the Irish Republican Army in an attempt to take power from the British by force. On the fourth anniversary of the Easter Rebellion the IRA struck, seizing the tax offices in Dublin and burning down 315 police stations.[8] The British government countered by meeting terror with terror. Numbers of ex-servicemen were recruited for duty with the Royal Irish Constabulary (known, because of their mixture of RIC and Army uniforms, as the 'Black and Tans'), and a force of auxiliaries was raised from amongst ex-officers of the 'gentleman-adventurer, *Freikorps* type'[9] (one of their 'agents' was the 14-year-old William Joyce).

The activities of the irregular forces on both sides during the Irish rebellion horrified Mosley for two reasons. In the first place, he was disgusted by the dishonour brought upon the British Army – of which he saw himself as a champion – by the use of torture, rape, murder and looting against a civil population (equally he had no sympathy for the IRA 'murder gangs'). Secondly, he regarded the method by which the insurgency was being fought as inefficient; he strongly believed that an effective intelligence system would allow the government to round up the murderers and nip the troubles in the bud. His stand was probably naive – he certainly allowed himself to be misled by Sinn Féin propaganda – but it was also pragmatic. He recognised that Britain would have to leave Ireland to govern itself and that it would be better to do so generously and with honour intact. In any event his opposition to his own party's Irish policy undoubtedly secured his reputation as a great parliamentary orator and a man who would stick to his guns despite considerable opposition. By the time the government called a truce in July 1921 (to the amazement of the rebels who were on the point of collapse), Mosley was sitting with the Liberals on the opposition benches.

Although he loosely followed the Liberal line in parliament, Mosley in fact remained an independent. He had realized that the Liberal Party alone was in no condition to bring down the mainly Conservative coalition. Instead he advocated forming an alliance of liberal Tories and 'patriotic' Labour supporters as a 'confederation of reasonable men' to govern the country; in this he was disappointed. In the two years after leaving the coalition benches, Mosley became more and more convinced that his future lay with the Labour Party. He fought a final election at Harrow as an independent in December 1923, winning by a margin of 4646,[10] before finally applying for membership of the Labour Party on 27 March 1924. He immediately found himself on a political fast track that was much more to his liking.

Ramsay MacDonald became the first Labour prime minister on 18 January 1924, leading a minority party with only 191 seats. His government fell on a vote of censure in September of the same year and a general election was called for the end of October. Mosley realized that he would not be able to hold Harrow and, instead, took on Neville Chamberlain in his supposedly safe Ladywood constituency. The first count showed an astonishing two vote victory for Mosley, although a recount gave it to Chamberlain by 77.

Losing his seat after six turbulent years gave Mosley time for reflection. For the next two years he travelled widely and applied himself to understanding economics, the science which, as far as he was concerned, underpinned the realities of everyday life. In the United States he saw, for the first time, production-line manufacturing which could produce complex artefacts with virtually unskilled labour; in India he was convinced that 'political independence [is] less pressing than "a mogul with a tractor and a deep plough" '.[11] His experiences, and his reading, told him that the free-market doctrines of the *laissez-faire* economists were profoundly wrong. He had become convinced that the job of government was not to secure the free market but, instead, by careful planning and centralized control, to manage the economy to produce stability and employment.

Mosley returned to the Commons in December 1926 as the Labour member for Smethwick after a by-election, having by then established a firm power-base in Birmingham. Despite his two years outside parliament he was elected to the party's National Executive Committee in October 1927; clearly he was becoming a force to be reckoned with in the Labour movement. In the aftermath of the general election of May 1929, fought largely on the issue of unemployment, MacDonald was once again asked to form a minority government; Mosley was an obvious candidate for ministerial office. However, after considering him as a possible Foreign Secretary,[12] MacDonald bowed to pressure from more senior Labour men and gave him a post outside the cabinet. At the age of only thirty-two Oswald Mosley was appointed Chancellor of the Duchy of Lancaster as a member of MacDonald's 'Economic General Staff', which had responsibility for looking for solutions to the unemployment problem under the former railwayman, the Lord Privy Seal J. H. Thomas. Thomas was a poor choice; he was far too narrow-minded to consider options outside the existing structures and he lacked the ability to stand up to his fellow cabinet members in argument. Additionally, he was the classic example of a socialist for whom social acceptance had become a goal in itself and he was not prepared to rock the boat by involving himself in political controversy. By contrast Mosley – confident in his own social status and sure of his political ability – was seething with ideas.

His first effort was a plan to tempt older workers into retirement by raising the state-funded old-age pensions, thus creating vacancies for younger men. This was rejected by the Cabinet. His next offering was a public works scheme, but this too fell by the wayside. His final move was to produce a four-point memorandum outlining a complete strategy for dealing with unemployment and the slump. Broadly speaking, Mosley was arguing in favour of detailed state intervention in the economy. The first plank of his memorandum was that the Government should establish an executive committee under the prime minister which could mobilize all necessary resources towards solving the unemployment crisis, just as Lloyd George's Supreme War Council had done during the war. Secondly he argued that the government should distinguish between long-term planning for economic revival and short-term relief of unemployment, rather than simply hoping that long-term revival would sweep up the problems in its wake. The long-term measures that he proposed included the setting up of a state financial corporation to fund the rationalization of industry, and in the short term he argued in favour of public works schemes. Mosley knew that his proposals would be anathema to the Treasury, but he believed that the Treasury's policies were those of the Government's opponents; he did not appreciate the thrall in which the comparatively inexperienced Labour cabinet was held by its civil servants. Opposition to the 'Mosley Memorandum' was led by the Chancellor of the Exchequer, Philip Snowden, and Mosley's proposals were rejected by the Cabinet in May 1930. Mosley resigned from the Government in disgust shortly afterwards.

Mosley's experience of government office lasted for barely a year, yet arguably it profoundly influenced public opinion about him during his career. For the conservative British, it is difficult to imagine that an aristocratic ex-minister could be so profoundly 'unrespectable'. Much of Mosley's support in his early days as a Fascist came from people who believed that, by rejecting Labour Party socialism, as he was to do by February 1931, Mosley was somehow advocating a muscular con-servatism. Despite his political radicalism, Mosley continued to move in the milieu of the wealthy élite that he had been born into, and his immediate social circle included, amongst others, Harold Macmillan,

Bob Boothby, Cyril Joad and Oliver Stanley; it was primarily amongst his friends that he found support in the early days after he renounced Labour socialism.

Together with his wife Cynthia (also a Labour MP) and a group of like-minded associates, Mosley left the Labour Party amidst a great deal of acrimony during the period February–March 1931. They embodied themselves as the New Party and, as a test of their strength, decided to field a candidate in the forthcoming by-election at Ashton-under-Lyne, a seat once held by Lord Beaverbrook. Support for the New Party was heterogeneous to say the least. Most of the members followed Mosley from the Independent Labour Party but he also attracted intellectuals like the philosopher Cyril Joad and the writer and diarist Harold Nicolson. From the other side of the political spectrum came a collection of young upper-class hearties. Inheritors of the violent tradition of the auxiliaries of the Irish rebellion, they came together in an attempt to break the mould of British politics that was to leave many of them bitterly disillusioned.

The Ashton by-election, on 30 April 1931, was bound to be fought as an attack on the Labour government. Labour had held the seat since 1929 with a majority of 3407, but with unemployment in the constituency at 46 per cent their grip was weakening. The New Party, though, was still in its infancy and Mosley had been ill with pleurisy since its foundation; nevertheless they fought a creditable battle against overwhelming odds. The enraged Labour Party picked the New Party as its chief target and deployed its heaviest artillery in support. The result was predictable: Allan Young, the New Party candidate, polled 4472 votes, Labour received 11,005 and the Conservatives 12,420. As the results were announced, Mosley and his collaborators stood on the steps of the Ashton Town Hall listening to the shouts, jeers and insults of the infuriated Labour supporters. He turned to John Strachey, one of his closest political associates and remarked: 'That is the crowd that has prevented anyone doing anything in England since the war.' Strachey was later to claim that was the moment when British Fascism was born.[13]

With the New Party, Mosley had hoped to hold the centre-ground of British politics. In fact he found that most of his support was coming from the radical right and from his admirers in high society. It never attracted a mass membership of ordinary people, and he, together with Harold Nicolson and Robert Forgan (an MP who had left the Labour Party with Mosley), began to seek support, financial and moral, from big business and the social élite. Despite this, the left-wing leadership of the party – Strachey, Joad and Young – continued to proselytize trade union and socialist groups in the hope of attracting recruits for the New Party as a left-wing grouping. They were to be disappointed; within a few months all three had left the New Party (Joad declared that he had detected 'the cloven hoof of Fascism').

The final test for the New Party was the general election of October 1931. Fielding twenty-four candidates they did disastrously: only two, including Mosley, retained their deposits, and eighteen polled fewer than 1000 votes each. For Mosley this was the end of the road in mainstream politics. During the months that followed his defeat, his mind turned more and more to Fascism. A visit to Rome, where he met Mussolini at the height of his power, confirmed his instincts: Britain needed Fascism and it needed Mosley to implement it.

But Oswald Mosley was by no means the first Briton to turn to this comparatively new ideology. In the 1920s a number of groups had sprung forth beneath the banner of Fascism which would later provide Mosley with some of his most assiduous recruits; among them a young teacher of Irish descent, William Joyce.

Notwithstanding his reputation as the most odious British traitor of the twentieth century, William Brooke Joyce was, in fact, born on 24 April 1906 at 1377 Herkimer Street, Brooklyn, New York. His father, Michael Joyce, a native of Mayo in Ireland, had naturalized as a United States citizen in October 1894. Thus William, by any standard of law, was born, and indeed remained until the last five years of his life, a United States citizen.

As a builder and landlord in turn-of-the-century New York, Michael Joyce was able to enjoy a reasonably prosperous life-style. Despite this he decided, in 1909, to return to the land of his birth to enjoy the fruits of his labour amongst his own people. His wife Gertrude and three-year-old son followed shortly afterwards. At first the Joyces lived in Ballinrobe, County Mayo, where Michael kept a pub, but in 1913 the family moved to Salthill in Galway. At this time Michael Joyce had acquired some property, including the local police barracks, and the family appear to have had a comfortable middle-class existence. William was sent to be educated at the Jesuit Ignatius Loyola College where it seems that he excelled at Latin, French and German, but he was also known as a gang leader and for his fiery temper. In later life William Joyce praised his Jesuit education, but it had left several marks on him. His mother was a Protestant and he was distressed to discover that the Catholic church consequently regarded her as being damned. This led him to turn his back on Catholicism at an early age; he also acquired a strong guilt complex about sex.

Michael Joyce was too old to be involved in the First World War and his son too young, but the entire family were to become embroiled in the political tumult sweeping through Ireland. The burning of police barracks at Easter 1920 caused severe financial losses to Michael Joyce for which he never received compensation. The young William, a middle-class schoolboy, witnessed incidents which 'haunted him all his life'.[14] In the first he came across the body of a local policeman, whom he knew, lying dead with a bullet in his head, and in the second he witnessed a Sinn Féiner being cornered by the police and shot dead. Even though Michael Joyce had renounced his British citizenship in 1894, he was a firm partisan of the British Crown and, with the arrival of members of the Auxiliaries in Galway in August 1920, William decided to take part by becoming an informer. There is no record of his service with the *Auxies*, if indeed it was ever more than a figment of his schoolboy imagination, but his father was unwilling to remain in Ireland after the Anglo-Irish Treaty of December 1921 and took his family to live in Lancashire in the same month.

William Joyce's first significant act after arriving in England was to enlist as a recruit in the Worcestershire Regiment, although he was not yet sixteen. When his birth certificate was demanded he claimed that he had never had one, and he was able to survive for four months before his real age was discovered while he was recovering from rheumatic fever in hospital. After this first rebuff he remained set on following a military career, but determined to do so as an officer. His chosen method was via the London University Officers Training Corps, to whom he wrote in 1922 claiming to be 'of pure British descent'. In the same year he passed his London University matriculation examination and registered as a student at the Battersea Polytechnic in London to continue his studies. He passed from Battersea Polytechnic to Birkbeck College in September 1923, following the 'intermediate BA' course (the equivalent to modern A-levels) in Latin, French, English and History, but at the same time he was becoming interested in politics. In December 1923 he joined a curious group called the 'British Fascisti' which had been set up by an eccentric member of a military family, Miss Rotha Lintorn-Orman, as an 'organized force to combat Red Revolution'.[15]

The British Fascisti were not Fascists in the radical sense; the official party line was that they were defending King and Parliament. Instead the movement was a collection of reactionary conservatives who felt that their way of life was threatened by the rise of trade unionism and socialism and had determined to use force to oppose it. Joyce was attracted to the movement because of the militancy of its views and its willingness to get physically involved, but, like most of the rest of the membership, he remained a Conservative Party supporter (he was President of the Conservative Society at Birkbeck College). For the rank and file of the British Fascisti, enjoyment was to be had from the strong-arm stewarding of Conservative political meetings. On 22 October 1924 Joyce was in charge of a squad of Fascisti stewards at the Lambeth public baths, defending Jack Lazarus, Unionist parliamentary candidate for Lambeth North. The meeting developed into a rough and tumble during the course of which Joyce received a vicious razor cut from the corner of his mouth to behind his right ear. According to his own account, he did not at first realize what had happened until people began to draw back from him in horror; he was also to claim that his assailant had been a 'Jewish Communist', but there is no evidence that this was the case. Whoever had actually attacked him, Joyce was to carry the scar to the end of his life.

Even during the General Strike of 1926 there was no hint of a 'Red Revolution' in Britain, and support for the British Fascisti began to fade away. Joyce was a successful student, maintaining himself as a part-time tutor, and it seems that he allowed his political enthusiasms to wane whilst he applied himself to his studies. He gained a first-class honours degree in English in June 1927 and started desultory research for a Master's degree whilst looking for a job as a secondary-school teacher. He was not successful in either aim; on the other hand, having got married just after his twenty-first birthday and now having a full-time job at the Victoria Tutorial College, he appeared to be settling down.

His last attempt to follow a conventional career came when he applied to join the Foreign Office in 1928. He sat the Civil Service board on 1 and 2 May but was turned down. Subsequently he was to claim that he had passed the examination but was rejected because he had no private income and would not have been able to fulfil his duties as a result. This fantasy explanation is an important indicator to his psyche. Despite his high intelligence (evidenced by his first-class degree) Joyce was unable to rationalize failures and setbacks without reference to some outside source, particularly Jews, Communists and the 'Establishment'. He blamed his severe facial scarring on 'a Jewish Communist'; he blamed his failure to complete his MA on a 'Jewish woman tutor'[16] who had 'stolen his research' (his tutor was a woman but she wasn't Jewish); and he attributed his failure to join the Foreign Office to the fact that he was not a moneyed member of the bourgeoisie. In this, Joyce exhibits the classic characteristics of an outsider trying to explain to himself why he is not fully accepted by society. Although he rigorously concealed it, he wasn't a British citizen, so he tried to make up for it by adopting an excessive patriotic fervour. During his upbringing in Galway, as a child of loyalist parents in a nationalist area, he appears to have developed a fantasy notion, that he was unable to shake off, of what life in England really was. In consequence he cast around for reasons that explained his predicament; as many have done before and since, he found his answer in conspiracy theories.

It is not possible to explain precisely why Joyce hit on the Jews as his particular enemy. The most likely explanation is that he simply fell in with the views of his contemporaries in the right-wing circles in which he moved, where casual anti-Semitism was the norm. His fantasies allowed him to translate Jews from being merely an identifiable, and apparently disliked, out-group into something more sinister. Anti-Semitism is, of course, no more rational than any other brand of racial hatred. At about the same time that he sat the Foreign Office exam, Joyce seems to have decided to give Conservatism a last chance. Within the party he advocated a brand of isolationist nationalism that won him few friends, and at the same time he began to inveigh eloquently against the imagined conspiracy of Jews which included Wall Street financiers, Communists, economists, psychoanalysts, artists and musicians. This was too much even for the most extreme Conservatives, and he left the party in 1930.

Oswald Mosley's first move on deciding to create his own Fascist movement in Britain was to contact the existing Fascist organizations: the British Fascists (who had changed their name from 'Fascisti' as it sounded too foreign), the National Fascists (a splinter group from the British Fascists), and the Imperial Fascist League,* to suggest amalgamation. The proposal was couched in predictable terms: Mosley was to be leader in the 'full Fascist sense'[7] with power over organization and policies. The Imperial Fascists rejected it outright but a member of the British Fascist Grand Council, Neil Francis-Hawkins, negotiated with Mosley for a while until Miss Lintorn-Orman found out. She regarded Mosley – as an ex-Labour minister – as a near-Communist and firmly banished his proposal from discussion. Unabashed, Francis-Hawkins resigned from the British Fascists, taking with him a few friends and the organization's membership lists.

Mosley and thirty-one others inaugurated the British Union of Fascists at the New Party headquarters in 1 October 1932, publishing 'The Greater Britain', Mosley's manifesto for a Fascist state, on the same day. Mosley's perception of Fascism centred on his detailed critique of Marxist

* The Imperial Fascist League had been set up by a retired vet, Arnold Leese (1877–1956), in 1929 from his Stamford branch of the British Fascisti. Leese was a virulent anti-Semite, probably because he had developed a horror of the Jewish method of ritual slaughter, but he developed a coherent ideology similar to German National Socialism. Despite the fact that his organization never achieved a membership greater than 200, Leese and a fellow Fascist, Henry Simpson, were the only two avowed Fascists ever to win an election in Britain when they successfully stood for the council in Stamford in 1924 (Simpson was re-elected in 1927).

economics which, he believed, failed to take account of the changing nature of capitalism; the solution was a corporate state, ruled by strong-willed young pragmatists, such as himself.

The initial impact and immediate success of the BUF was based to some extent on the misapprehension that it was, like the British Fascisti, a young, aggressive but essentially conservative movement. This fallacy was fostered by the organization's confrontational approach to Communism and Socialism, by Mosley's energetic but essentially aristocratic grandeur, and also by its relatively non-violent methods, at least compared to the Italian Fascists and the German National Socialists. The BUF were certainly aggressive in defending their own meetings, but at the outset they were circumspect about physically attacking their opponents.

The British Fascisti, and the other groups of that ilk, had been bizarre and reactionary offshoots of the old order which seemed to offer little hope for the future, but the BUF, as a dynamic political party led by a young man of thirty-five who had already held high office, seemed to promise much. In the first two years of its existence it grew to a strength of over 40,000 and was able to set up its own drinking clubs, football teams, gymnasia and social activities, providing a disciplined, regulated life that many of its members hankered after. The BUF consciously promoted itself as the party of the 'war generation' and its quasi-military organization reflected this, offering rank and status to the dispossessed and those who feared that they might become so. 'Those who identified with the "war generation" expected the values of war, the comradeship, the disciplined life, the responsibility, the danger and excitement, the freedom from the usual sexual inhibitions, to be carried over into civilian life,'[18] and despite the essentially socialist nature of much of the organization's doctrine, a majority of the recruits were identifiably members of the middle classes. The BUF became a closeted existence for many, from which they could observe the outside world whilst living out their fantasy roles, and it also seemed to offer a quick and 'military' solution to the problems that beset the nation. Such was the organization that William Joyce joined in early 1933.

It was clear from an early stage that Joyce was a cut above the average Fascist recruit. Highly intelligent, he had an individual and magnetic speaking style which was to rank him with Mosley and 'Mick' Clarke (who controlled the BUF in the east end of London) as one of the top three speakers in the movement. Soon after joining he resigned from his post at Victoria Tutorial College to become the West London Area Administrative Officer, and shortly after that, within a year in fact of joining the movement, he was made the full-time Propaganda Director at a salary of £300 per annum (a respectable sum in 1933). But Mosley's corporate state Fascism was not enough for Joyce; he, and others, were determined to drag the BUF along the path of full-blown anti-Semitism.

The anti-Semitic tendency within the BUF received a strong impetus as a consequence of a mass rally held at Olympia in London on 7 June 1934. At the time Olympia was one of the largest indoor venues in Europe, with a seating capacity of 13,000, and Mosley's plan was to fill it to capacity during the penultimate meeting of a series designed to culminate in a huge outdoor rally at the White City stadium in August. At this stage the BUF was receiving strong support from Lord Rothermere, owner of the *Daily Mail*, who viewed the party as a bulwark against Communism and organized labour. Rothermere's support for Mosley – in January 1934 he had written an article for the *Daily Mail*, entitled 'Hurrah for the Blackshirts', in which he praised Mosley's 'sound, commonsense, Conservative doctrine' – not only raised the profile of the BUF, it swelled membership numbers as well. Communist and anti-Fascist groups viewed the success of Mosley's campaign, and the support that he was receiving, with some alarm and decided to make a determined effort to stop him. The battleground that they selected was Olympia.

In the capacity audience at Olympia on 7 June were over 2000 invited (non-Fascist) guests and 1000 black-shirted stewards. Opposition was provided by 2000 anti-Fascists outside and about 500 who had managed to penetrate the audience. At 8.40 p.m., in a scene which presaged the later Nuremberg Rallies, Mosley marched down the main aisle to the speaker's dais, preceded by fifty-six blackshirts carrying Union Jacks. As he started to speak anti-Fascist protesters began to chant slogans. Mosley paused, warning the hecklers that they would be thrown out, before attempting to continue. Anti-Fascist taunts resumed and he ordered his stewards into action. During the disturbances that followed, approximately fifty protesters were violently ejected, several of whom were beaten up by the blackshirts (in fairness, a number of the stewards were injured as well). Nobody died and no-one was seriously injured but the outcry was enormous.

The most serious outcome for the BUF was the withdrawal of Lord Rothermere's support. Like many others he had believed that the BUF was essentially a conservative organization, and he was unprepared for the violence that the party appeared ready to embrace. With Rothermere went considerable numbers of the BUF's other fair-weather supporters, causing a drop in party membership from which it never recovered. Casting around for a scapegoat to explain the Olympia débâcle, Mosley and his advisers took note of the number of Jews arrested for disrupting Fascist meetings. Until 1934 anti-Semitism had been banned within the BUF (although many members held violently anti-Semitic views), but from December of that year it became official policy. As far as William Joyce was concerned the BUF was on the right track.

As Propaganda Director Joyce was a driven man, and his first marriage did not withstand the pace. During the course of his hectic schedule, whilst attending a meeting in Dumfries he met a young woman Fascist who strongly attracted him. Margaret Cairns White was a secretary in a textiles company and the daughter of a factory manager; she had joined the Carlisle branch of the BUF after hearing Mosley speak locally, and fairly quickly had joined the circuit of minor Fascist speakers. Joyce courted her in a whirlwind romance and married her at Kensington Register Office on 13 February 1937, only five days after his divorce became absolute. The couple did not have time for a honeymoon because William was already involved in a campaign for election to the London County Council for the Shoreditch constituency. As a Labour stronghold the result was regarded as a foregone conclusion but Joyce, together with another BU* member, J. A. Bailey, campaigned intensively. The result surprised everyone: Labour won as expected, but the Fascists came in a

---

* At the prompting of Joyce, amongst others, Mosley had renamed the party 'The British Union of Fascists and National Socialists', abbreviated to British Union (BU) in 1936.

strong third, with Joyce polling over 2500 votes (he managed to mar this comparative triumph by flouting the traditional 'good loser' speech and declaring, in front of his opponents and the press, that it had been a 'thoroughly dirty fight'[19]).

Despite his good showing at the election, Joyce's days as a member of the BU were numbered. He was becoming increasingly critical of 'The Leader' because of Mosley's apparent reservations about anti-Semitism (in private Joyce referred to Mosley as 'the Bleeder'), and he felt that Mosley was keeping him in the background. His close friends, John Beckett (a former Labour MP) and Angus MacNab, agreed. However, before they could do anything concrete Mosley struck first. The BU was a very top-heavy movement, employing 143 staff, and funds, in a party with no prospect of power, were always short. Mosley's solution was to cut the staff to thirty; amongst those dismissed, only two weeks after the LCC elections, were Joyce and Beckett; MacNab, an ex-schoolteacher and the editor of the *Fascist Quarterly*, resigned in protest.

Almost immediately Joyce, Beckett and MacNab started the National Socialist League, with headquarters in Vauxhall Bridge Road, Victoria. To earn money Joyce and MacNab set up 'MacNab & Joyce, Private Tutors' from a flat that they shared in Onslow Gardens, South Kensington, offering instruction for university entrance and professional examinations, together with English language tuition for suitable (i.e. not 'Jewish or coloured') foreign students. The National Socialist League was even further out on the political fringes than the BU and never amounted to more than a hundred members. Funds were supplied by an elderly admirer of Joyce's named Alec Scrimgeour, a retired stockbroker who lived in Sussex, and were supplemented by takings from the bar that Joyce started in the League's office (he registered the League as a club to do so).

Freed from Mosley's restraining influence, Joyce was able to do and say what he wanted. In a pamphlet, *National Socialism Now*, he gave full vent to his racial hatred: '– International Finance is controlled by great Jewish moneylenders and Communism is being propagated by Jewish agitators who are at one fundamentally with the powerful capitalists of their race in desiring an international world order, which would, of course, give universal sovereignty to the only international race in existence'.[20] The programme of the League was the predictable mix of half-understood corporatist economics, anti-Semitism and support for a pact with Hitler. Its theories were propagated at poorly attended street-corner gatherings.

To understand the resistance of the average man in the street to Mosley's Fascists and Joyce's National Socialists, one had only to look to Europe. However modern, dynamic and appealing Hitler and Mussolini might seem to the hard core of British Fascists, the practical results of their brand of politics had become all too apparent. The trickle of refugees from Nazi Germany was turning into a flood, Italy had invaded backward Abyssinia and was suppressing lightly armed tribesmen with bombs and poison gas. In Spain the Nationalist revolt was providing the Fascist states on one side, and the Soviet Union on the other, with an opportunity to fight a brutal war by proxy. In Britain and the rest of Europe, not fully recovered from the effects of the First World War, there was a rising tide of fear that reawakened German expansionism was about to plunge them into a second. It was clear where the British Fascists stood: they were undoubtedly anti-war, but equally obviously they were all for allowing Hitler and his allies a free hand. Memories of 1914 were far too recent for the average Briton to stomach that.

Had the war not intervened, it is likely that Joyce would have remained one of those bizarre characters that are to be found on the fringes of politics. He positively enjoyed speaking at tiny, open-air meetings to hostile crowds, and he had very little interest in material things. All he required were 'books, cigarettes, alcohol and agreeable companions',[21] but as the storm-clouds gathered he felt himself forced to plan for the future. As international tension grew during the Czechoslovak crisis of 1938, Joyce decided that if war with Germany became inevitable, he could not fight against a National Socialist regime. He decided that he, Margaret and MacNab would go to Dublin, and then perhaps seek a way of getting to Germany. To this end he renewed his fraudulently obtained British passport (he was still a US citizen).

The crisis passed when the British and French prime ministers, Neville

Chamberlain and Edouard Deladier, signed away the Sudetenland at Munich in September 1938, prompting Joyce to take his wife for a celebratory holiday on the Isle of Wight. After Munich, Joyce's speeches in praise of Hitler were not well received by his London audiences and his meetings became increasingly rowdy. He was twice charged with assault, after incidents at meetings in November 1938 and May 1939, and although he was found to be innocent on both occasions, he was convinced that he was the victim of police provocation.

It was soon obvious that the Sudetenland was not Hitler's last demand. As the summer of 1939 wore on the Joyces were again faced with the prospect of war between Britain and Germany and the dilemma of whether or not to stay in London. William had cultivated several German contacts and his thoughts were turning towards a move to Berlin in the near future. In August he asked Angus MacNab, who was planning a holiday in Berlin, to sound out Christian Bauer, a young official of Dr Josef Goebbels' Propaganda Ministry, as to whether Joyce would be welcome in Germany in the event of war. Margaret Joyce was of the opinion that logic demanded they go to Germany and 'let fate decide the rest'.[22] In the event Bauer assured MacNab that there would be no problem and that Goebbels would oversee the Joyces' application for naturalization as a matter of priority.

On the same evening that MacNab left Berlin, the German government announced that it had concluded a non-aggression pact with the Soviet Union. The news left Joyce momentarily dumbfounded: for years he had been praising Hitler as a bulwark against the menace of 'Jewish Bolshevism'; now he found that his hero was making friends with a regime that had, hitherto, been regarded as his most implacable foe. Joyce had, in the past, shown a marked readiness to discard parties and personalities that did not live up to his rigid standards of ideological purity and the Nazi–Soviet Pact could have given him an opportunity to dump Hitler; but he did not. Instead, he rationalized the German move, arguing that as the Western powers had failed to take advantage of the possibility of alliance with the Third Reich, it was proper for Hitler to safeguard Germany by reaching agreement with the nation which, above all others, presented the greatest threat. At the far end of the political spectrum, many Communist supporters were reaching precisely the same conclusion.

As Joyce dithered about fleeing to Germany, the security authorities in Britain were gearing up for war. A meeting held in November 1933 between representatives of the Home Office, Metropolitan Police, Special Branch and MI5 had agreed that Fascist groups should be monitored by MI5 and Special Branch in the same way that Communist organizations were.[23] In July 1939, as war appeared to be approaching, it was decided that the close association between British Fascists and the Nazi regime might lead to individual Fascists being used for espionage and sabotage. Contingency plans were drawn up for the detention of individuals whose activities might be damaging to public safety or the defence of the realm; Joyce would have undoubtedly featured amongst this category. On 24 August, still undecided about their ultimate destination, Joyce renewed his British passport for the last time, leaving on it an expiry date of 1 July 1940. All through that day he failed to make up his mind and, around midnight, he received a telephone call. Years later he was to claim that it was from an intelligence officer for whom Joyce had occasionally informed on Communist activities, warning him that the government's Emergency Defence Regulations were to come into force on 26 August and that he would be arrested and interned. The Joyces debated the pros and cons of Dublin and Berlin through the night before finally making the decision around breakfast time: Berlin.

The next day passed in a frenzy of activity as Joyce withdrew all his funds from the bank, wound up the affairs of the National Socialist League and started packing. Margaret travelled to Sussex to say farewell to the Scrimgeours, William's financial backers for several years, and to dispose of a pistol that he illegally owned (she buried it under a tree). Making their final preparations that evening the Joyces held open house for William's family and Angus MacNab, who was apprehensive for the couple. The next morning, 26 August, they rose early without having slept and, still accompanied by MacNab, made their way to Victoria Station where they bought boat-train tickets to Berlin. Nobody questioned them there, and nobody made any attempt to detain them as they passed through immigration at Dover.[24] In fact, those parts of the

Emergency Regulations which interfered with civil liberties were not brought into effect until 1 September, when they were already in Berlin. From the stern-rail of the ferry, the Joyces were able to look back at the English coast; it was a sight that they were not to see again for nearly six years.

2

Germany Calling: British Traitors and White Propaganda

William and Margaret Joyce reached Berlin on 27 August 1939 under the firm impression that their arrival was eagerly awaited by the Government of the Third Reich; they had, after all, been assured by Christian Bauer, a man whom they thought to be a senior official of the Propaganda Ministry, that Goebbels was personally aware of their decision to throw in their lot with Germany. Instead they were greeted with indifference and embarrassment. Bauer, it emerged, had none of the influence that he pretended and was, anyway, called up for military service the day after their arrival, having admitted that the most likely fate for the Joyces would be internment. Faced with this prospect, they seriously contemplated returning to Britain but found that they had closed this avenue by changing their British pounds for Reichsmarks; they could not buy rail tickets for travel outside Germany. Instead, resigned to their fate, they sought out cheap rented accommodation and waited to see what would happen. Their contacts in Berlin were few, consisting of Mrs Frances Eckersley, a Fascist friend, and her young son James Clark who had come to live in Berlin in anticipation of war, travelling via Hungary.

As matters turned out, Mrs Eckersley's presence in Berlin proved to be very valuable to the Joyces. An acquaintance of hers, Dr Schirmer, was an official of the Foreign Office and she felt sure that he would be able to help them. Sure enough, on 30 August Joyce was called to a villa which housed a Foreign Office translation unit and was given the German text of a recent Hitler speech to translate into English. He finished the task quickly (not realizing that he was being paid by the hour) and returned to his hotel.

Time passed slowly during the next few days, as Europe simmered in anticipation of events to come, until on 3 September Britain and France declared war on Germany in response to Hitler's attack on Poland. That afternoon William and Margaret Joyce had tea with another pre-war friend, a member of the von Bülow family, and his American wife, who had just arrived from London. Joyce was beginning to sink into a mood of despair; in his fantasies he was the leader of the British National Socialist movement who had come to Germany to fight for the leader and the ideology that he worshipped, but, unusually for him, the reality of his situation was beginning to penetrate and he was sure that he was going to be interned.

But Dr Schirmer had not been idle on his behalf. He organized a series of interviews with officials of the Foreign Office in the hope of finding him a niche in the department specializing in British affairs. Not unnaturally the diplomats were suspicious of Joyce and he was wary of them, but eventually it was suggested that he talk to Dr Erich Hetzler, a member of Foreign Minister, Joachim von Ribbentrop's personal staff. Hetzler, then approaching thirty, had received part of his education at the London School of Economics and was an admirer of the British way of life. He had joined the Nazi party in the early 1930s after his father's business had gone bankrupt during the slump, and he had travelled in Britain in 1936 as an envoy of Ribbentrop. He had even, on one occasion, been at a party at the same time as Joyce though the two had not met.

Hetzler's mildly pro-British outlook evidently caused him to look favourably on Joyce when they did meet. He had previously met several British Fascists at a Nuremberg rally and had not been impressed, finding them 'cheap and anxious to please',' but he quickly realized that Joyce was a different proposition entirely. Joyce opened by explaining that, as a National Socialist and anti-Semite, he supported Hitler's policy towards the Jews and consequently felt constrained to leave England when war seemed inevitable. He had hoped that in Germany there would be some form of useful employment for a sympathizer 'who knew Britain and the British mentality'.[2] He had no clear idea about what he wanted to do and Hetzler realized that there was no possibility of finding him full-time work within the Foreign Service or even on Ribbentrop's personal staff. Instead he suggested that Joyce might like to work for the German Radio Corporation (Reichsrundfunk) external service as an English language broadcaster. Joyce was hesitant but Hetzler made an appointment for him to meet Walter Kamm, at that point the head of the overseas short-wave services.

The Reichsrundfunk's overseas service bore a superficial resemblance to the World Service of the BBC. Apart from English language broadcasts to Britain, North America and the Far East, it also produced programmes in French, Polish, Italian, Spanish, Portuguese and Afrikaans. The difference lay in the content of the broadcasts; the BBC took (and still takes) pride in the independence of its programming from government control, whereas the German output was strictly supervised by Goebbels' Propaganda Ministry, in association with the German Foreign Office, the Armed Forces (Wehrmacht) and any other state body with an interest. During his interview with Kamm, Joyce was shy and reserved but agreed, none the less, to take a voice test despite the fact that he had a troublesome cold. Unfamiliar with broadcasting technique, he read his test piece poorly and would have been rejected but for a technician who claimed that he had 'possibilities'. With nothing to lose, the English service producer decided to allow him to read a real bulletin later that day. Thus was Joyce's fate decided; had he not gone in front of the microphone that evening, he might never have done more than translation or scriptwriting. As it turned out, he was to become known and hated by millions as the English mouthpiece of Nazism.

The staff of the English language service when Joyce first arrived consisted mainly of British and US-educated Germans, with a few individuals of mixed parentage. The only other 'Englishman' amongst them was going by the name of Manfred von Krause; his real name was Norman Baillie-Stewart. Joyce and Baillie-Stewart were of much the same age but came from markedly different backgrounds. Born on 15 January 1909 as Norman Baillie Stewart Wright, he had in 1927, at the age of eighteen, passed out tenth in order of merit from the Royal Military College, Sandhurst, and been commissioned into the Seaforth Highlanders. (He was a contemporary at Sandhurst of the actor David Niven, who remembered him as a 'singularly unattractive piece of work'.³) He showed promise as an officer and appeared set for a sound, if not necessarily distinguished, military career. In 1929 he changed his surname by deed-poll to Baillie-Stewart, claiming that this was his mother's maiden name and as the last 'heir-at-line' it had been 'thought advisable that he should carry on the name'.⁴ In reality this was only part of the truth; his mother's name had been Stewart but Baillie was actually one of his father's Christian names. However, he found that life in an upper-crust regiment of the British Army was not to his liking. He later said that 'the Army I knew was a world in which a doctor looked down on a dentist and an infantryman looked down on the air force and so on "ad infinitum". I myself had the misfortune to join a regiment with a famous name but with a set of officers unrivalled for their snobbishness. These officers looked down on everybody, including each other – a man who rode a motorcycle was a "cad", an air force officer a "shit".'⁵

Baillie-Stewart's fame, or rather notoriety, resulted from his conviction in 1933 for an offence against the Official Secrets Act. In 1931 he had been travelling on holiday in Germany and had become involved with a young German woman named Marie-Louise, with whom he had apparently had sexual intercourse in a park. Subsequently he appears to have passed her some relatively trivial classified information for which he received a payment of £90. It became clear to those investigating his case that this was simple sexual entrapment although Baillie-Stewart was probably too infatuated to realize it. In any event, he caused great hilarity at his trial by claiming that the £90 had been payment for his performance *en plein air*. He was sentenced to five years' imprisonment.

In August 1937, eight months after his release from custody, Baillie-Stewart travelled to Vienna and applied for naturalization. He had hoped to be able to work for the Austrian Tourist Board but found that his conviction in Britain continued to dog him and he was unable to obtain work. He also learnt that to gain Austrian citizenship he needed to have been a resident of at least seven years' standing. He then found himself summoned to the Vienna police headquarters where he was confronted by two officials who believed him to be a Nazi agent. In February 1938 he was given three weeks to leave Austria as an undesirable alien. He immediately turned to the British Embassy for help in appealing against his deportation, but when the diplomats found out who he was they refused to assist him. This decision enraged Baillie-Stewart – from then on he felt that he had no duty of loyalty to Britain – and he was forced to travel to Bratislava for three weeks to comply with the deportation order.

Baillie-Stewart was only able to return to Austria as a result of Hitler's Anschluss on 13 March 1938. The German government was more favourably disposed towards him than the Austrians and he was permitted to apply for German nationality in September of the same year, though the process was delayed slightly when he was found by the Vienna police to have been helping Jews escape overseas. He later stated: 'I helped these Jews as individuals and human beings although I was opposed, in principle, to the general question of Jewry, but was more than opposed to the Nazi Jewish policy.'[6]

Baillie-Stewart made a modest living for the next year by running a small trading company in Vienna as he waited for his naturalization papers to come through. In July 1939 he was listening to the German radio's English language service with some of his Austrian friends. As the broadcast went on, he made a few derisive criticisms of the style and content, thinking it stilted and insulting. Amongst the group he was with was an employee of the Viennese radio station who mentioned Baillie-Stewart's criticisms to his boss the next day. This was passed on to the Propaganda Ministry, and shortly afterwards Baillie-Stewart was summoned to Radio Vienna for a voice test. He passed and was soon ordered by the Propaganda Ministry to report to the Reichsrundfunk in Berlin. A week before the war broke out, Baillie-Stewart made his first broadcast on the 'Germany Calling' service. Joyce claimed that, when the two first met, Baillie-Stewart lugubriously remarked, 'I suppose you've come to take our jobs away'.[7]

Other broadcasters on the English language service included Eduard Dietze and Roderick Menzel, both the sons of German fathers and British mothers with the ability to speak public-school English. Dietze was to become the editor of the English language service and Joyce's immediate superior, as well as taking regular stints at the microphone. They were joined in November 1939 by Mrs Eckersley, who became a continuity announcer, and her son, 17-year old James Clark, who read the news.

When Joyce joined the English service its output was uninspiring, to say the least. It consisted of news and commentary with a heavily anti-British bias, compounded by exaggerated claims and outrageous lies. Despite this, listening to the 'Germany Calling' programme became quite popular in the early months of the war simply because, with little real combat activity taking place as both sides geared up for battle, there was a distinct dearth of news. The broadcasts themselves were made in the course of the Reichsrundfunk's normal output of domestic programming: an announcer would state that the station would now broadcast the news in English, and by the end of September 1939 at least nine daily broadcasts were taking place, consisting of a news bulletin followed by a commentary written and delivered by one of the English speakers. It was during this period that the myth of Lord Haw-Haw grew up.

Amongst the listeners to 'Germany Calling' were a number of newspaper columnists. On 14 September 1939 'Jonah Barrington' (a pseudonym) of the *Daily Express* wrote: 'A gent I'd like to meet is moaning periodically from Zeesen [the site of the English service transmitter]. He speaks English of the haw-haw, damit-get-out-of-my-way variety, and his strong suit is gentlemanly indignation.'[8] On 18 September Barrington wrote for the first time about 'Lord Haw-Haw'. The butt of his humour was not, then, William Joyce, who spoke standard English with a slightly nasal accent, but Baillie-Stewart, the Sandhurst-educated 'officer and gentleman'. Nevertheless there was much speculation in Britain about the identity of this broadcaster, who certainly appeared to be of British origin. Other journalists took up Barrington's nickname and one, Lord Donegal, who wrote a column for the *Sunday Dispatch*, made an earnest endeavour to identify him. Donegal had heard it suggested that a likely candidate was the founder of the National Socialist League, who appeared to have left the country; he visited Joyce's former partner MacNab in order to find out. MacNab agreed that he would listen to the broadcasts and 'tell him no lies'.[9] When they met, they listened together to

'Germany Calling' on an unearthed short-wave radio and MacNab could quite clearly hear Joyce reading the news through the static; before he could comment, however, Donegal said 'That's not the man I'm talking about', and invited MacNab to visit his country house where reception was better. The next day they listened to Baillie-Stewart's clipped tones and Donegal asked if it was William Joyce. MacNab, quite truthfully, replied that it was not.

Even if Haw-Haw remained an enigma, his broadcasts began to get under the nation's skin. During the phoney war it was possible to laugh off his more ludicrous claims, but as the action began to heat up during the spring of 1940 'Germany Calling' became more menacing. After the invasion of France and the Low Countries in May and the miraculous escape of most of the British Expeditionary Force from Dunkirk, and with the Luftwaffe's aerial blitz of British towns and cities in full swing, the British people themselves were directly threatened with attack and invasion. Fear of invasion brought with it anxiety about spies, saboteurs and fifth columnists, intensified by the regular German bombing raids. Stories about the Haw-Haw broadcasts began to proliferate, in particular commenting on the amazing local knowledge that he seemed to possess. The most memorable rumours centred on town clocks; it was frequently claimed that Haw-Haw had remarked during his broadcasts that such-and-such a clock was running fast or slow, or had stopped altogether. He was supposed to have had a detailed knowledge of factory conditions in numerous locations, as well as chapter and verse on troop and shipping movements. Haw-Haw seemed to be not only the spokesman of the overt foe but also, perhaps, of Britain's enemy within.

These rumours were, of course, without any foundation in fact, being merely a symptom of the hysteria generated by the invasion scare. None the less, they caused sufficient concern in official circles for two pros- ecutions to be made against people accused of spreading rumours (contrary to the Emergency Regulations). The first was of a civil servant in Mansfield who admitted that he had fabricated a story about Haw-Haw broadcasting information concerning schools in his area from Hamburg, only one hour and forty minutes after it had become public in Britain. The second was a Birmingham businessman who had told his employees that Haw-Haw had broadcast news of a fire before it had become generally known in England. Unofficial measures to counter Haw-Haw also began, with the *Daily Mirror* taking the lead by organizing the 'Anti Haw-Haw League of Loyal Britons', members of which were pledged not to listen to the broadcasts or mention his name. However, more sinister than the activities of rumour-mongers were those of the British Fascists who remained at large. Emergency Defence Regulation 18(b) allowed the Home Secretary to order the detention of individuals who presented a possible security risk, but little use had been made of it before the invasion of Denmark and Norway (two Special Branch officers visited MacNab in search of Joyce just two days after he had left Britain). During the spring of 1940, Joan Miller, a very beautiful young MI5 agent, had been planted in the 'Right Club', a crypto-Nazi group headed by the Conservative MP Captain Maule Ramsay. She had managed to become close to Anna Wolkoff, an extreme anti-Semite daughter of a White Russian refugee admiral who owned a Russian tea-room in Harrington Gardens, South Kensington in London. Miller discovered that Wolkoff had a friend in the Italian embassy through whom she was able to contact Germany; she was also in touch with Tyler Kent, a cipher clerk at the American embassy who was passing her copies of correspondence between Winston Churchill and President Roosevelt. Wolkoff was arrested after giving Miller a letter addressed to Joyce at the Rundfunkhaus, Berlin, commenting on the effectiveness of his broadcasts (she had known and admired Joyce before the war as a fellow anti-Semite and a near neighbour). The text of the letter ably illustrates the fantasy world in which anti-Semites like Wolkoff existed:

Talks effect splendid but news bulletin less so. Palestine good but IRA etc. defeats object. Stick to plutocracy. Avoid King.

Reception on mediums fair but BBC 376 tends to swamp, while BBC 391 and Toulouse try squeeze Bremen and Hamburg off air at times. Why not try Bremen at 500? Bremen 2 on longs very weak. Needs powerful set to get.

Here Krieghetze [war-fever] only among Blimps. Workers fed up. Wives more so. Troops not keen. Anti-Semitism spreading like flame everywhere – all classes. Note refujews in so-called Pioneer Corps guaranteed in writing [not?] to be sent into firing line. Churchill not popular – keep on at him as Baruch tool and war-theatre extender, scarificer Gallipoli, etc. Stress his conceit and repeated failures with expense lives and prestige.

Butter ration doubled because poor can't buy – admitted by *Telegraph* – bacon same. Cost living steeply mounting. Shopkeepers suffering. Suits PEP.

Regret must state Meg's Tuesday talks unpopular with women. Advise alter radically or drop. God bless and salute to all leaguers and C. B.

Acknowledge this by Carlyle reference radio not Thurs. or Sun. Reply same channel same cipher.

She added as a postscript:

If possible, please give again sometime in the week, the broadcast which the German radio gave in German about three months ago, namely:
The Free Masons' Meeting in the Grand Orient in Paris, 1931 (?) where Lord Ampthill was also present. It is now more important that we hear more about the Jews and Freemasons.

P. J.[10]

Meg was, of course, Margaret Joyce; 'Leaguers' were the members of the National Socialist League who, Wolkoff assumed, had gone to Germany with Joyce; C. B. was Christian Bauer and P. J. stood for 'Perish Judah', a prep school-style slogan used amongst anti-Semites. MI5 did actually allow the letter to go to Germany, from where its receipt was acknowledged with a Carlyle reference in a broadcast, but Joyce himself never actually saw it.

The Wolkoff case, and that of Tyler Kent, provoked the Government to begin the great round-up of British Fascists, starting with Mosley and thirty-three others, which finally broke the back of the movement. Prominent members of the British Union and the National Socialist League knew that, even if they weren't actually interned, they were under surveillance, and their campaigns, which included fly-posting and chalking anti-war and anti-Semitic slogans on walls and in telephone boxes, began to die out.

After Dunkirk Lord Haw-Haw had changed from being a joke figure to a public enemy. In Germany propaganda officials were startled by the impact that they achieved: at first they were unsure who Haw-Haw actually was – after all, a number of their broadcasters seemed to be making the broadcasts attributed to this one mythical figure. But it soon became clear that Joyce was their most effective weapon in the psychological war, and from May 1940 the Reichsrundfunk had taken to announcing him as 'Lord Haw-Haw'.

The decision to promote Joyce as their main 'English' mouthpiece prompted the Germans to seek other ways of exploiting his notoriety, and the Foreign Office commissioned him to write a book. *Twilight Over England* was published in September 1940 by the Internationaler Verlag in Berlin with an English edition of 100,000 copies. It was another *tour d'horizon* of Joyce's anti-Semitic fantasies, anti-Bolshevik remarks having been struck out at the insistence of the Foreign Ministry, and as such is of only marginal interest. However, his introduction included remarks which were to assume a certain piquancy five years later:

> The preface is usually that part of a book which can most safely be omitted. It usually represents that efflorescent manifestation of egotism which an author, after working hard, cannot spare either himself or his readers. More often than not the readers spare themselves. When, however, the writer is a daily perpetrator of high treason,* his introductory remarks may command from the English public that kind of awful veneration with which £5000 confessions are perused in the Sunday newspapers, quite frequently after the narrator has taken his last leap in the dark.''

He also set out the reasons for his hostility to the Jews, a matter that he normally regarded as self-evident. They possessed, he claimed, the following inherent tendencies:

1. An incapacity to avoid forming a state within a state.
2. Complete inability to view their Gentile hosts as possessing equal rights with their own.
3. Predetermined specialization in all those processes which bring high profit. Hence, in capitalism, almost exclusive preoccupation with finance, distribution, and exchange as distinct from productive industry. Professional work undertaken either for profit or for the sake of social advancement.
4. A natural tendency to utilize social and economic advancement for the purpose of gaining political power.
5. An unholy dread of nationalization as a factor which would draw attention to their racial nature and expose their operations.

---

* Joyce was, of course, aware that he was a US citizen but his propaganda value rested in his being apparently British. In any case, he was fully aware that he was committing moral treason.

6. The deliberate debasement of the standards of culture in the land of their sojourn.
7. The elimination by competition of the Aryan who merely wants to get enough for himself and not more than anybody else.[12]

The life-style enjoyed by the early traitors was quite comfortable. Shortly after Joyce signed his first contract, he and Margaret moved into an apartment in the Kastanienallee in the Charlottenburg district of Berlin, close to the Rundfunkhaus. They had freedom of movement through the city and were able to socialize with whomsoever they wanted, frequently meeting journalists from neutral countries in Berlin's Foreign Press Club. Joyce was paid enough money to ensure a comfortable home life and he was, additionally, given an extra ration of cigarettes as a privilege because, he felt, they helped him to concentrate. Baillie-Stewart and the Eckersleys, *mère et fils*, enjoyed a similarly carefree existence. For Joyce, revelling in the triumphs of the Third Reich through the winter of 1940 and the spring of 1941, the only cloud on his horizon was his increasingly difficult relationship with Margaret.

William Joyce's first marriage had broken up in the 1930s because his work as a Fascist agitator always took precedence over his wife and children; in 1941 his second marriage began to go the same way. When relaxed Joyce could be capable of kindness and tenderness towards his wife and friends, but when under pressure he alternated between haranguing Margaret and ignoring her. She naturally found this difficult to cope with and eventually left him for a young German army officer; they formally divorced in August 1941. The pressure created by Joyce's heavy workload – he was recognized as the senior commentator and scriptwriter for 'Germany Calling' – was probably exacerbated by his discovery that his idols had feet of clay. Although he was naturalized as a German citizen in 1941, he never actually joined the Nazi Party; the reason for this was his discovery that it had, like so many conventional political groups, abandoned revolution for the comforts of bureaucracy and graft. Disgusted by what he saw, he reached the conclusion that the Germans were not the ideal race to carry the National Socialist torch; nevertheless, he continued his work for the wider cause.

Baillie-Stewart, on the other hand, fell out with the Reichsrundfunk at quite an early stage. He was no Nazi – simply an immature and embittered authoritarian with a chip on his shoulder – and he found the content and grammar of many of the broadcasts that he was required to make, ridiculous. He wasted no time in telling the Propaganda Ministry officials his opinion, and their response, now that they had found Joyce, was simply to sack him. He made his last broadcast for 'Germany Calling' on Christmas Eve 1939.

The Reichsrundfunk's English language service continued to be broadcast until the fall of Hamburg at the end of April 1945 and Joyce remained the principal speaker throughout, although Dietze would always take the microphone when the situation demanded a subtle or tactful treatment of the news. Other broadcasters came and went. Frances Eckersley and her son continued until late 1941, when both became disillusioned with the Nazi regime (James Clark later said: 'By then all my moral reserves were used up. I owned up to my mother that I couldn't carry on'[13]); by the end of the war both had been incarcerated in internment camps. Baillie-Stewart's successor was an actor, Anthony Cedric Sebastian Steane, who used his stage-name, Jack Trevor, in Berlin. He was joined by a succession of people whose brief radio careers served to brand them as renegades at the war's end, including Ralph Baden-Powell, nephew of the famous Boy Scout founder, and an Irishman named Edward Bowlby who was one of the few, apart from Joyce, to broadcast under his own name. Bowlby, a member of the BUF, had been a cinema manager in Stockport until 1938 but had then moved to Budapest to start a language school; he was arrested by the Germans whilst trying to flee to Sofia in 1941 and volunteered to work for them after eighteen months in the interment camp at Tost.

Baillie-Stewart's broadcasting career languished for a while and he spent his time in Berlin producing translations for the German Foreign Office and lecturing in English at Berlin University. This highlights an interesting split which appeared amongst the British traitors who broadcast radio propaganda. Although the German Foreign Ministry took a close interest in the material that was broadcast on the 'Germany Calling' service – and later by the so-called 'secret stations' – the broadcasters themselves were almost all employees of the Propaganda Ministry of which Joyce was the senior British member. However, as time went by a number of the renegades fell out with Joyce, or with Hetzler who controlled the secret stations, and they were then often taken directly on to the staff of the Foreign Ministry, employed by the England Committee under Dr Fritz Hesse, the former press attaché at the German Embassy in London and a supposed propaganda expert. The England Committee itself was a body that had been set up within the German Foreign Ministry in order to supervise all policy relating to propaganda operations against Britain, although it was placed under the auspices of Ambassador Paul Schmidt, Hitler's interpreter, who organized the Foreign Ministry's languages service.

Baillie-Stewart's naturalization came through in the spring of 1940 – too late to save him from treason proceedings at the war's end – but there was never any question of his being called up for military service even though he tried to volunteer on one occasion. Instead, he passed his time as the senior member of the small group of British men and women directly employed by the Foreign Ministry. Although it later included propaganda celebrities like John Amery and the RAF officer Railton Freeman, at first it was mainly composed of minor academics who had been interned at the outset of hostilities. One such was the self-styled 'Professor' Noel Mac-Kintosh. Born in 1885, MacKintosh had been the Registrar of Hong Kong University between 1919 and 1924 but had then moved to England to work as a schoolmaster. He had fled from England to France in August 1939 to avoid a court case resulting from his homosexuality (which was then, of course, illegal), and had wound up as an internee at the Tost internment camp where a fellow inmate was the writer P. G. Wodehouse. On 21 June 1941 MacKintosh and Wodehouse were summoned to the commandant's office and told that they were being taken to Berlin to inspect a work camp for internees; both were mystified. They were then taken to the German Foreign Ministry where they were separately interviewed by Ambassador Paul Schmidt and Professor Haferkorn, the head of the radio propaganda department. It became apparent to MacKintosh that he had been taken by mistake (in fact an internee named McKenzie had volunteered to broadcast), but he was told by the two Germans that he would have to work for them anyway and was given a job as a translator.

Wodehouse had been living in Le Touquet, on the French north coast, since 1934 where he spent his time entirely submerged in creating the fictional upper-class England of his brilliant comic creations, notably Bertie Wooster, Jeeves, Psmith and Lord Emsworth of Blandings Castle. When Germany invaded France in May 1940 he was a rich man of fifty-eight, cocooned from the realities of the outside world by his protective wife Ethel and by a small army of agents, advisers and accountants who directed most aspects of his life outside his work. Like many other British residents in France, the Wodehouses were taken aback by the speed of the German advance and, initially at least, they followed British military advice to stay put. When they realized the danger they were in it was too late; the vehicle they were travelling in broke down and they felt forced to return to their villa and await events. On 22 May Le Touquet was occupied by the German Army and the Wodehouses, along with other British residents, were ordered to report to the German authorities in Paris-Plage on a daily basis. For two months Wodehouse continued to live at Le Touquet, working on his novel 'Money in the Bank'; then on 27 July he was informed that, along with all other British residents of military age, he was being taken into custody. His wife, Ethel, was not detained; she stayed first in Le Touquet and then moved to a hotel in Berlin.

Wodehouse was held first in Lille, then moved via Liège and Huy in Belgium before arriving at Tost in Upper Silesia in September. Even though he was an internationally renowned author, he received no special privileges in internment other than space to continue writing and a typewriter; otherwise he lived in a dormitory with other internees, ate the same food and took part in the normal routine of camp life, including his share of the chores. Nevertheless, despite his unworldliness and naïvety, he was in a far more secure position than most of his fellow inmates. He had no worries about money, being very wealthy in his own right, and as probably the most celebrated internee, with a large following in the still neutral United States, he received many letters of support from friends and admirers outside. In early 1941 the Germans permitted him to write an article for the *Saturday Evening Post* entitled 'My War with Germany', and this brought him even more correspondence. The final reason for Wodehouse's buoyant attitude in captivity was the knowledge that when he reached the age of sixty, and thus was deemed to be past 'military age', he would be released in accordance with the then German policy (which was not rescinded until 1942).

The suggestion that Wodehouse might broadcast from Germany came from the head of the Büro Ribbentrop – the German Foreign Minister's private secretariat – who was keen to use any means to reinforce American neutrality. In May 1941 Wodehouse was guardedly sounded out by a German officer who enquired whether he might like to make a broadcast to thank his many American correspondents for their letters (regulations did not permit him to write to anyone other than his close family). Naïvely he jumped at this idea; he had become distressed at the thought that his fans in America might think him rude for not replying to their messages. Even so, the matter was not at that stage pursued.

Wodehouse was playing cricket when he was summoned to the camp office with MacKintosh before their move to Berlin. His arrival at the Adlon Hotel was given full publicity in the German press – it was leaked that he had been released as the result of American pressure and because his sixtieth birthday was approaching – and no direct approach was made to ask him to broadcast. However, two men who had known him in Hollywood, Major Raven von Barnikow and Hauptmann Werner Plack, both spoke to him during that day and the subject of broadcasting came up. He told Plack that he would like to broadcast to his fans and the German agreed to arrange the details.

Wodehouse made a total of six broadcasts from Berlin. The first was an interview with a journalist called Harry Flannery who worked for CBS in the German capital. The interview was recorded the day after Wodehouse had recorded his first talk for the Reichsrundfunk but the day before it was broadcast, and Flannery, who held strong anti-Nazi views, found it difficult to conceal his disgust with Wodehouse who he assumed was either a dupe or a collaborator. The interview, which was scripted by Flannery, included the phrase 'I'm wondering whether the kind of people and the kind of England I write about, will live after the war – whether England wins or not, I mean',[14] which was taken by many listeners to be utterly defeatist. But in fact it is impossible to find anything anti-British in any of Wodehouse's five later talks: they were, if anything, mildly anti-German, describing his life in a succession of internment camps in typical Wodehouse style: 'An Associated Press man who came down to interview me later wrote in his piece that Tost Lunatic Asylum was no Blandings Castle. Well, it wasn't, of course, but still it was roomy. If you had a cat, and had wished to swing it, you could have done so quite easily in our new surroundings.'[15]

During this time Wodehouse and his wife lived at the country home of a relative of von Barnikow during the summer months, and at the Adlon Hotel in the winter. He had been shocked to find that his well-intentioned broadcasts had caused him to be branded a traitor in England, and he resolved to do no more broadcasting on behalf of the Germans. In September 1943 they were given permission to move to Paris and stay at the Hotel Bristol, where they were liberated with the rest of the inhabitants of the city just under a year later. A detailed investigation by MI5 showed that Wodehouse had acted naïvely and foolishly, but it cleared him of being a traitor.

Norman Baillie-Stewart returned to the microphone in the spring of 1942 under the pseudonym 'Lancer', to deliver commentaries on current events which were then broadcast by the Reichsrundfunk and by Radio Luxembourg. But he wasn't a convinced Nazi and he spent the last two years of the war trying to avoid doing the propaganda work that his masters demanded of him. At the beginning of 1944 he managed to be sent to Vienna for medical treatment, and thereafter he sent his commentaries by post for someone else to read. By the end of the war he had managed to get himself away to Altaussee, in the heart of the so-called 'Alpine Redoubt', although he had by then severed his connections with the Third Reich.

Joyce, however, continued as a loyal servant of the Third Reich, both as broadcaster and as scriptwriter for the secret stations (see next chapter) until the end of the war, and is rightly identified as the central figure in German propaganda towards Britain throughout the conflict. Despite their divorce he was reconciled with Margaret and they remarried in February 1942, and although the marriage went through several difficult stages thereafter, they stayed together until his capture in 1945.

3

Black Propaganda:
G-Senders and V-Men

Specialists in psychological warfare classify propaganda in three ways. White propaganda is the acknowledged broadcasting and publishing of information by one side in a conflict aimed at the other; in this it can take the form of, for example, Joyce's 'Germany Calling' broadcasts, leaflets dropped by aircraft, or loudspeaker messages broadcast at front-line troops. Grey propaganda is material published or broadcast which is given no overt attribution, leaving the recipient in doubt as to where it was originated. Black propaganda directly and falsely purports to be from a source with which it has no actual connection. All sides in the Second World War eventually took to using black propaganda but Germany actually opened the conflict with it.

The first German black propaganda operation of the war was a cack-handed affair undertaken by the intelligence service of the SS – the SD. Hitler had announced his plan to invade Poland to a secret meeting of the Third Reich's military and political élite on 22 August 1939. After reviewing the situation in Europe, he had concluded, 'No-one knows how long I shall live. Therefore, better to have the show down now!'[1] But before Germany could actually invade, they needed a pretext. The solution was supplied by Reinhard Heydrich, head of the SD, an embittered, cashiered naval officer who had drifted into the Nazi Party and then the SS. Quick-witted, highly intelligent and utterly ruthless, he was selected by Himmler to form and lead an intelligence and security service within the SS. Heydrich proved an ideal man for the job, expanding his service quickly and efficiently so that, by the time war broke out, he was effectively competing with the Abwehr, the intelligence arm of the Wehrmacht, as the principal supplier of intelligence to the Nazi leadership. His idea was to fake attacks on several German border installations so that they appeared to be the work of Polish troops; the main target was to be the Gleiwitz radio station.

Under the command of SS-Sturmbannführer Alfred Naujocks, a detachment of SD men dressed in Polish uniforms launched an attack on the Gleiwitz transmitter during the evening of 31 August 1939. They rounded up the staff and locked them in a cellar before interrupting the broadcast, using a Polish speaker to harangue the audience via the airwaves and firing pistols into the ceiling. On their way out they dumped the body of a concentration camp inmate, who had been given a lethal injection that afternoon and then shot, outside the main gate. As this was taking place, other apparently Polish troops were attacking a customs post and a forestry station; more prisoners, cynically killed on Heydrich's orders, were scattered about at these locations to add verisimilitude. Only the committed few really believed the Nazi lies about Gleiwitz but the operation served its purpose; the modern, highly sophisticated Wehrmacht could justify rampaging through Poland, using its tactical and technological superiority against an enemy still partly reliant on horse-mounted cavalry. The High Command of the Wehrmacht (OKW) had got the message that Hitler had long learnt: black propaganda could be a useful tool.

The next experiment came in the spring of 1940. The German Propaganda Ministry authorized the setting up of a radio station 'La Voix de la Paix' (the voice of peace) to beam defeatist propaganda at French troops and civilians. This station claimed to be not only run by Frenchmen concerned for the security and well-being of their country but also actually operating as an underground station in metropolitan France. During the German invasion La Voix de la Paix was integrated with military operations, broadcasting messages designed to cause panic amongst the civil population in the hope of getting refugees to flood the

French Army's lines of communication, hindering troop movements and resupply efforts. In this the station was so successful that, at the close of the campaign, the OKW officially thanked the Propaganda Ministry and the Reichsrundfunk technicians for their part in the invasion.

As the first broadcasts of La Voix de la Paix were being heard in France, the Propaganda Ministry decided that Britain would benefit from a similar service and decided to set up a special department within the Reichsrundfunk to control it. Named the 'Büro Concordia', the man chosen to head it was none other than Dr Erich Hetzler, the former Büro Ribbentrop official who had suggested Joyce as a possible broadcaster. Hetzler's most pressing requirement was to find people capable of manning his new station. Native speakers of English (and Britain's other major languages, Welsh and Gaelic) were thin on the ground in Berlin in the early months of 1940, and those that there were, and who more importantly were willing to undertake propaganda work, were already involved in the overt propaganda effort. Hetzler realized quite correctly, that to use the very recognizable voices of Joyce, Baillie-Stewart and company for 'black' transmissions would be to nullify their effect.

Despite the manpower problem, the first and most important of Hetzler's 'secret stations' (in German they were called Geheim Sender, normally abbreviated to 'G-Sender') went on the air on 25 February 1940. The men selected to make the broadcasts, in a programme called 'Between Ourselves', were Leonard Banning, using the alias John Brown, and Kenneth Vincent Lander. The station was called 'The New British Broadcasting Station', known to the Germans as Büro N, and it was to continue operating until 9 April 1945.

The broadcast on 25 February was actually made by Kenneth Lander, although the script was written by William Joyce. Lander was born in London on 29 May 1904 and had been educated at Ampleforth, the Roman Catholic public school in North Yorkshire, and at Pembroke College, Oxford, where he had taken a degree in modern languages. He had been living in Germany since May 1933, teaching English at the Hermann Lietz Schule at Schloss Bieberstein near Fulda. In 1934 he had made a visit to Munich, spiritual home of the Nazi Party, and, as he later said, 'Whilst there, I found that National Socialism rather appealed to me.'² Happy in Germany, he stayed there until August 1939 when he returned for two weeks holiday in England and Northern Ireland. Undeterred by the threat of war, he made his way back to Germany at the beginning of September and, when the war actually broke out, he reported himself to the Gestapo in Kassel as an alien and made an application for German nationality, largely in order to avoid internment. His well-known pro-German views stood him in good stead and he remained at liberty, continuing to teach in the Fulda area.

It is not clear how Lander came to the attention of Büro Concordia but he received a telephone call in early February 1940: 'I was surprised, asked what it was about, and demurred, saying that I had work to do at the school. They then said they would wish very much to speak to me if I would come to Berlin and this I agreed to do.' At his interview Lander was anxious to make clear that he would not broadcast what he considered anti-British propaganda, and it seems that Hetzler, who conducted the interview, gave him this assurance because he was soon at work at the Concordia office in Berlin, reading scripts into the recording microphones and, on occasion, writing them himself.

Banning, another English teacher though a Berlin resident, joined Lander at the NBBS in March 1940. He had been a BUF member in the early 1930s but his political affiliation had latterly been with the Conservative Party for whom he was a paid organizer. After his arrival, he and Lander alternated as speakers and writers for the NBBS, occasionally appearing together as a form of cross-talk act.

As a 'black' station, the impression that the NBBS was attempting to convey was as the mouthpiece of an underground Nazi movement based in Britain. The themes for the daily broadcasts were decided at the morning meetings in Goebbels' Propaganda Ministry before being passed down to Hetzler, who would then discuss them with Joyce and the other English writers. They would go away and produce scripts for Banning and Lander, using as much topical material as they could cull from the English news media (British newspapers were available in Berlin, a day late, throughout the war, via neutral Sweden). Joyce felt strongly that the scripts should be produced with as little German interference as possible, in order to make them seem realistic; even so he was unable to avoid using the terminology of his pre-war street-corner meetings and the broadcasts bore his unmistakable stamp. As fears of a German invasion increased in June 1940, Banning and Lander began to broadcast material designed to have the same effect as 'La Voix de la Paix', flooding Britain's lines of communication with refugees; this caused Lander some disquiet – he still had serious qualms about his work – and, combined with a reference to the King in a Joyce script as 'that stuttering imbecile',[3] he decided that he had had enough and voluntarily went to the internment camp at Tost in Silesia at the beginning of August.

Even though the German authorities had no direct means of monitoring the effect of their secret broadcasts, they decided to persevere. The fall of France gave them access to thousands of British prisoners, from amongst whom, it was assumed, it would be possible to recruit a quantity of Fascist or Nazi sympathizers to man further stations. In consequence, in June 1940 Joyce was despatched to Stalag XXA at Thorn in the Warthegau district of East Prussia to trawl for potential recruits. At this time, he had seen little of Germany outside Berlin and he enjoyed the change of scenery and the opportunities for exercise that his mission gave him. He decided that he liked the area around the camp and thought the Stalag itself 'rather nice',[4] though it was later to feature amongst the most notorious POW camps. He was given an office in the Kommandantur (the administrative area of the camp) and a number of pre-screened prisoners were brought to him.

Joyce's recruiting brief stipulated that no pressure was to be applied to potential broadcasters, but he was able to offer them a move to Berlin, accommodation in a private house, a change of identity, the opportunity to wear civilian clothes and a salary. For a prisoner with a Fascist outlook the offer must have been very tempting; by this time, the end of June 1940, the British soldier's experience of war with Germany was only of defeat. They had seen the British Expeditionary Force in France humbled by the numerically inferior but technically far superior Wehrmacht, and had then been humiliatingly force-marched across all of France and most of Germany by their contemptuous captors. Joyce, at his most articulate and persuasive, managed to attract eight volunteers, the largest haul of renegades by an individual recruiter during the entire war.

The second station to go on the air was 'Worker's Challenge', known by the Germans as Büro S. The first broadcast was on 7 July 1940 and it purported to be the mouthpiece of a Communist faction in Britain. The main themes of 'Worker's Challenge' were attacks upon capitalism in general and Churchill and his Cabinet in particular; workers were urged to bring the war to an end by withdrawing their labour from vital industries. In fact the real appeal of the station for listeners in Britain lay in its frequent recourse to foul-mouthed invective against its principal targets, including the first broadcast use of the word 'fuck'. Manned at first by two of Joyce's recruits, Guardsman William Humphrey Griffiths of the Welsh Guards and a Sergeant MacDonald who both spoke with working-class accents, the Worker's Challenge produced such gems as: 'We know bloody well one reason why Churchill wants the war to go on. He's afraid that if he isn't kicked out by the Germans, he'll be kicked out by us'.[5] MacDonald only lasted until October 1940 before he was replaced by William Colledge, alias Winter, a member of the North Somerset Yeomanry who continued to broadcast until 1943.

The third station of the original quartet, and the first to disappear from the airwaves, was Büro P, otherwise known as the 'Christian Peace Movement'. This purported to be the output of an underground organization of pacifists agitating against British involvement in an immoral war. The principal speaker and writer of the Christian Peace Movement was Rifleman Cyril Charles Hoskins of the King's Royal Rifle Corps, who had been recruited by William Joyce at Thorn and was assisted by a Corporal Jones. The station continued to broadcast until the middle of 1942 when it disappeared from the airwaves; by then Corporal Jones had returned to his POW camp and Hoskins was used to monitor British broadcasts.

The last of the original four stations was 'New Caledonia', alias Büro NW. This station was specifically aimed at Scotland and represented itself to be broadcasting on behalf of an organization of separatist nationalists protesting against England's involvement of Scotland in an unwanted war. The chief speaker on the station was Donald Grant, alias Palmer, who was assisted at first by a Sergeant Beasley (one of Joyce's recruits from Thorn), and later by Susan Hilton. The station closed down late in 1943.

The impact of all the black stations was severely hampered by poor reception in Britain. Even the BBC who monitored German transmissions on behalf of the government often had difficulty in receiving them clearly; for ordinary listeners with domestic radio sets these problems were multiplied several fold. Nevertheless the Propaganda Ministry and the radio propaganda department of the German Foreign Ministry were sufficiently confident in them to persist in efforts at black radio propaganda throughout the war.

A problem that the German propaganda authorities failed to recognize, however, lay in the themes and messages that were being broadcast. It is by far the most difficult task in constructing propaganda of all types to present it in a way that will persuade the target audiences without alienating them. The overt 'Germany Calling' service on which Joyce was the mainstay broadcaster did not claim to be anything other than a German station and naturally adopted a fiercely pro-German stance, although of course it attempted to couch its message in acceptable terms. But in employing Joyce as, effectively, the script supervisor for the 'black' stations the Germans made a crucial mistake. For all Joyce's undoubted intelligence, he only retained a tenuous grip on reality. It should not be forgotten that he was a man who sincerely believed that a Jewish conspiracy was behind the evils of communism and capitalism, who thought, when he was leader of the tiny National Socialist League, that he had a genuine chance of persuading Britain to adopt his policies; and who was convinced that he was the victim of police persecution in London. His contact with the British masses was limited to his experience of street-corner political meetings where he was subject to relentless barracking and physical attacks, and he was never able to raise the quality of his propaganda and speechmaking above that level. The broadcasts of the first four secret stations all bore the unmistakable stamp of William Joyce's soap-box invective and his peculiar brand of imaginary working-class English. The only sure evidence that the secret stations had any real effect was in the small number of stickers which appeared in Britain advertising the broadcasts, and these were all the work of convinced Fascists in any case.

The renegades who worked on the G-senders lived a strange existence.

The first group of military traitors recruited by Joyce were given an apartment near the studios at the Olympic Stadium, where they lived under the watchful eyes of members of the SS Funkschutz (radio protection unit). They were allowed to wear civilian clothes, given an allowance of tobacco and alcohol, and escorted, once a week, to a nearby brothel if they wanted to (some didn't). As time went by and they became more trusted (in German parlance they became *Vertrauensmänner* or V-men) they were given more freedom, being allowed to rent their own apartments, travel unsupervised within the confines of Greater Berlin, as well as form relationships with German women. Even so, Gestapo surveillance of their activities was onerous – a fact that they were well aware of – and even within the somewhat cosmopolitan atmosphere of the Concordia Büro, which as the war dragged on added a considerable number of other languages to its repertoire, they were usually careful to keep their views to themselves.

From its start in the spring of 1940 the German black propaganda effort ground on relentlessly, and a surprising number of people were recruited. The second phase of recruitment came in 1943 when a further three stations were inaugurated under the auspices of the Concordia Büro. The most important of these was 'Radio National', a station that was originally intended to exploit the impact of John Amery, the renegade son of Churchill's Secretary of State for India. Its purpose, and that of its two sister stations, Interradio and Radio Metropole, was no longer the promotion of defeatism and dissatisfaction in Britain. Rather, in recognition of the changing tide of the war, they were directed at the promotion of a disruption of the British alliances with the United States and the Soviet Union. Despite this, the tone of the broadcasts was only a little different to that adopted by the earlier black transmitters. Instead of making direct attacks on Britain *per se*, the stations now attacked Britain's two major allies, levelling the standard Nazi accusations of Jewish domination of their governments, whilst at the same time attacking Churchill for being in league with them. As before, reception of this message was hampered by the technical problems associated with long-distance broadcasting, and there is no evidence to suggest that the stations gained a significant audience.

The early secret stations were manned by a mixture of military and civilian renegades but the second group were largely drawn from the forces. The most prominent amongst them was a Merchant Navy officer who was serving as a sublieutenant in the Royal Navy on an emergency commission. Roy Walter Purdy was a native of Barking in Essex where he was born in May 1918; he qualified as a naval engineer before the war and also became an active member of the Ilford branch of the BUF. In June 1940 he was captured by the Germans when the armed merchant ship HMS *Van Dyck*, on which he was the engineering officer, was sunk by enemy action off Narvik. He was a POW at several camps in Germany before ending up in 1943 at Marlag/Milag, a special camp for naval personnel. Whilst there he bought a copy of Joyce's *Twilight over England* from the camp shop and soon after was asked by a German Sonderführer* if he would like it autographed. Purdy presumed that this offer was made because Joyce remembered him as a Fascist.

Purdy decided to take up Joyce's offer and the Sonderführer then made him a more tempting proposition: if he agreed to make ten broadcasts from Berlin, he would be allowed to escape to a neutral country. At this stage Purdy demurred, but when the offer was put to him again a few weeks later in June 1943, after he had been taken to Berlin to meet Joyce, he decided to accept. He began to broadcast in August on Radio National, using the pseudonym 'Pointer' and reading scripts provided by Peter Adami, the German controller of the station, and his British associate, V. N. Q. Vernum. After he had given six talks of an anti-Semitic nature he was switched to newsreading duty which he continued for a few months.

However, in March 1944, after going temporarily absent without leave from Berlin, Purdy was arrested and sent to the notorious special camp for officers at Colditz. There he was subjected to a detailed interrogation by his fellow prisoners, who had heard an account of some of his activities on the POW grapevine, and he was removed from the prisoners' section of the camp at the insistence of the Senior British Officer, who informed the German commandant that Purdy's safety could not be guaranteed.

* Sonderführer were English-speaking NCOs seconded by the Abwehr for work in POW camps, ostensibly as interpreters but actually to monitor the prisoners. In POW parlance they were generally known as 'Ferrets'.

By this stage he had already acquired enough information to denounce J. H. O. Brown, a British prisoner in Berlin who was gathering intelligence by the pretence of co-operating with the Germans,* in the hope of restoring his own position in the Germans' confidence. In the event the Germans did decide to continue to use Purdy, but only as a translator for the SS 'Kurt Eggers' propaganda regiment, and he was always kept under armed guard.

Another serviceman to play a significant role in the secret stations was Raymond Davies Hughes, an RAF air gunner from Mold in north Wales. He had been shot down in August 1943 and taken to the Luftwaffe interrogation centre at Dulag Luft, where he quickly broke down under interrogation and agreed to co-operate. Transferred to Berlin at the end of October 1943, he broadcast for some time on Radio National before switching to Radio Metropole in April 1944, from where he made broadcasts in Welsh. Hughes appears to have enjoyed considerable freedom in Berlin, during the early days of his career at least, and he was able to make the acquaintance of many of the other renegades, including the early members of the British Free Corps of the SS, to whom he lent money at the instigation of an RAF squadron leader called Carpenter, who spent some months in the latter half of 1943 pretending to collaborate with the Germans, presumably in the hope of gaining intelligence from them.

Others who took part in the secret stations included: Reginald Arthur Humphries, known on air as Father Donovan; Arthur Perry; Peter Kosaka, who was half-British, half-Japanese, Sergeant Arthur Chapple, alias Lang; and Frank Maton and Roy Courlander who both subsequently joined the British SS unit. Several of the personnel from the early black stations transferred into the second wave, and of course the NBBS continued broadcasting until almost the end of the war. A number of others who are known to have made broadcasts under duress also served in the secret stations but it is not my intention to embarrass them or their families by detailing their roles.

* Fortunately for Brown, Purdy was not believed. An account of Brown's activities is given in Chapter 7, p. 99.

From the little that is known about reception in Britain of the G-Senders it is possible to deduce that their impact was negligible, certainly when compared to the effect that Britain's parallel effort had in Germany, where such stations as 'Soldatensender Calais' achieved a remarkably wide audience. The reason for this almost certainly lies in the high reputation of the BBC who, whilst enjoying a monopoly in broadcast news in Britain, nevertheless largely succeeded in avoiding becoming perceived as a propaganda tool of the government. For the average radio listener the BBC could be relied on to provide a news service that was reasonably reliable and entertaining, and they therefore had little reason to make the effort to listen to the weak signals of the German propaganda stations. As with the Haw-Haw phenomenon, those who did listen almost certainly did so out of curiosity rather than any particular desire to hear the Nazi viewpoint, and in the final analysis that is simply not enough to achieve propaganda success.

4

John Amery: Facing England

One of Karl Marx's better-known remarks appears in *The 18th Brumaire of Louis Napoleon*, published in 1852: 'Hegel says somewhere that all great events and personalities in world history reappear in one fashion or another. He forgot to add: the first time as tragedy, the second as farce.' Although a statement of dubious general validity, it is unmistakably echoed in a comparison of the careers of Sir Roger Casement, the anti-slavery campaigner and Irish Nationalist patriot executed for his role in forming an 'Irish Brigade' in Germany during the First World War, and John Amery. Both men came from distinguished backgrounds and both went to the gallows for their principles; that Casement's career was tragic there is little doubt, that Amery's was a farce is equally clear.

John Amery was born on 14 March 1912, the first son of Leopold Amery who had, the year before, been elected as the Conservative MP for Birmingham South (later Sparkbrook). Leo Amery had graduated with first-class honours from Balliol in 1896 and shortly afterwards was elected a Fellow of All Souls before embarking on his first career as a journalist and lawyer. He then enjoyed considerable success in politics: in 1916 he was appointed to the cabinet secretariat as a special adviser on European affairs, and he achieved cabinet rank himself in 1922 as First Lord of the Admiralty, and then as Secretary of State for the Colonies and the Dominions from 1924 to 1929. However, his further political career was held back by two significant factors: in the first place his enthusiastic advocacy of British imperialism and protection of the 'Imperial Preference' was perceived as being reactionary; and secondly, it was felt that 'though able [he was] a long-winded bore'.[1]

Thus John Amery found himself growing up in the shadow of a father of great distinction; it was to prove to be too much for him. His youth was pock-marked with incidents which can be characterized as the desperate attempts of a young man anxious to make his mark in the world independently of his family. At the age of fifteen his parents were asked to withdraw him from Harrow school (where he was remembered by Churchill's private secretary, Sir John Colville, as 'intelligent') because he was attempting to launch a film company and had solicited, and received, money from investors with which to do so. It almost goes without saying that this venture stood no chance of success and the foolish investors inevitably lost out. He persisted with attempts to become a film producer during the early 1930s and made a precarious living from doing so, but throughout this period his propensity for disaster continued, and at the end of 1936 he was declared bankrupt. At the same time he had managed to acquire seventy-four convictions for motoring offences which were 'not just breaches of regulations but quite unforeseen embroideries on the commonplace process of travelling from point to point aided by an internal combustion engine.'[2] In 1932, much against the will of his family, he had married Una Wing, a woman somewhat older than himself, having the ceremony conducted in an Orthodox church in Athens in order to circumvent the legal measures to which the family had resorted in order to prevent the union.

The flaw in John Amery's personality which eventually took him to the gallows is a common one. His inability to emulate the success of his father led him through a succession of ridiculous exploits that became increasingly outrageous. His milieu – London café society of the 1930s – gave him the spurious glamour and celebrity which he craved, but at root he knew that he was regarded as a failure and this spurred him on to even greater excesses in his attempts to prove himself. There was an element of hysteria in his speech and in his actions that survived through to his eventual work for the Germans during the war and the broadcasts that he made for them; his desperation led him to disregard moderation and compromise in his approach to life and he was ultimately to suffer the consequences.

Following his bankruptcy he decided that he needed to make a fresh start. Already inclined towards Fascism and the right, in October 1936 he went to Spain to fight on behalf of the Nationalist insurgents. Despite his father's opposition he was provided with an allowance from family funds. His wife did not follow him but continued living in Chelsea, also on an allowance provided by the family.

The period between 1937 and 1940 was to have a profound influence on Amery. For much of the time he acted as a volunteer with Franco's Nationalists, one of a handful of Britons who followed this path, serving as an intelligence and liaison officer, running guns from France provided by the Fascist 'cagoulards', and as a combatant officer with the Italian 'volunteer' forces who decorated him with their medal of valour. As a result of this he came into contact with Jacques Doriot, leader of the Fascist 'Parti Populaire Français' (PPF).

Doriot had originally been a Communist – and Mayor of Paris – but he had quarrelled with Moscow in the early 1930s and swung towards the extreme right. As a Fascist leader he achieved considerable success – by 1939 his movement claimed 250,000 members[3] – and he took the young Englishman under his wing. When Amery was not otherwise engaged in Spain, they travelled together to Austria, Czechoslovakia, Italy and Germany. It was during these journeys that Amery's political outlook crystallized. Despite the undoubted fact that he was, in many ways, an immature and reckless adventurer, his political beliefs were sincere and strongly held. At their root was a profound fear of the rise of Communism in Europe which, in common with many others, he identified with a Jewish conspiracy. Under Doriot's tutelage, he came to believe that the only way to counter Communism and preserve the British Empire was by launching a social revolution of the right, appropriating the means of production and exchange in the national interest and mobilizing the working class against Bolshevism. In the fevered demonology of Fascism, capitalists are generally regarded as being in league with Communism, or at least duped by it, and the fact that many successful capitalists happen to be Jewish is regarded as confirmatory evidence. Amery had no difficulty in accepting this strange and contradictory view, perhaps because by associating himself with it and with the leaders of political parties who espoused it, he gained a sense of self-worth which overcame the feelings of inadequacy engendered by his early exploits. Leo Amery later wrote: 'His failures in the film world, and his unfortunate experience with money lenders . . . inclined him to accept current Nazi and Fascist doctrine of the Jews as the prime instigators of Communism as well as the evils of international high finance.'[4]

Amery was demobilized by the Italians in July 1939 but continued to live in Spain in the town of San Sebastian, where he remained for several months after the war broke out. His purpose in this was not to avoid military service but instead to return to film production. In March 1940 he travelled to Paris to meet his father and discuss his future plans with him. He later wrote:

I told him that I considered that the French Army did not want to fight and would be very rapidly defeated and this gave me cause for the greatest anxiety. He did not share this view but suggested that I should, in one form or another, political, intelligence etc. join up (*sic*). I agreed to this, but departed first to the south of France to wind up some business matters; while I was thus engaged the French Army collapsed, the Armistice was signed and I found myself virtually trapped in the free zone of France, where by the terms of the Armistice visas outgoing were not granted to British subjects of military age.[5]

In fact he had been contracted to make three short films in Nice which he felt would turn his fortunes around. This was not to happen. In May 1940 he suffered a complete breakdown of his physical health and was found to be suffering from tuberculosis; he thereafter spent several months confined to a sanatorium in the Grenoble area, refusing an offer of repatriation in July because, according to a consular official named Wilfred Brinkman, he was unable to take 'his dog or his common-law wife'.[6]

For the year after the fall of France Amery lived a comparatively quiet life in the unoccupied zone. He was a source of occasional irritation to the staff of the American consulate in Nice, from whom he drew his 'relief grant', because he always wanted more than they could give him and because they suspected that he was involved in illegal currency dealings, facilitated by a British diplomatic passport that he possessed (how he obtained this is unclear; possibly his father was able to use his influence to supply it). But he was not involved in political activity, which was in any case banned in the Vichy zone. The event that stirred him to action was the German invasion of the Soviet Union in June 1941.

In the explanatory statement that he made to MI5 at the end of the war, Amery wrote: 'It came as a very great shock to me when I heard that England and Soviet Russia had become allies. So much so that I thought that the people responsible in London were acting in a manner that no longer coincided with British imperial interests.'[7] It was this attitude which underpinned all of his subsequent activities in occupied Europe; it also starkly highlighted his own political naïvety.

In the wake of the invasion of Russia, Amery was able to visit Vichy, the new French capital, with the intention of ascertaining how France was reacting to what he saw as a momentous development. He was disappointed to find that there was 'no intention whatsoever of carrying out any social revolution, that, in a word, Vichy was an ultra-reactionary government, of priests, the worst type of French industrialists and militarists'.[8]

Amery's outspoken views and his friendship with Doriot made him the object of considerable suspicion within the free zone, and in the months after his visit to Vichy he found himself increasingly isolated, both from his French friends and from home as restrictions on communication increased. Finally, in November 1941 he was arrested and imprisoned by the Vichy authorities in retaliation for the British arrest of a French diplomat in Syria. It took nearly a month for his common-law wife, Jeanine Barde, and Jacques Doriot, who was by now serving as a volunteer in the Légion des Volontaires Français (LVF), to obtain his release. At this point Amery decided that enough was enough and applied for repatriation on health grounds at the start of 1942.

His application was turned down by the Vichy government on the grounds that, although he was not fit to serve as a combatant, he might be fit enough to be an 'auxiliary'. In desperation he sought other ways of leaving Vichy France. His first attempt was made via Count Grandi, the

Italian Minister of Justice, whom he had met when the Count was serving as ambassador to London during the 1930s. He wrote a letter outlining his predicament and his political views in the hope that he could be found some form of employment in Fascist Italy – but he received no reply. His next approach was to the Finnish embassy in Paris, through whom he hoped to be able to obtain a commission in the Finnish Army to fight against the Soviets. He did receive a response but, to his disappointment, it was a polite rejection of his offer of help. By now lonely and miserable, Amery was forced simply to remain in the Grenoble area, to which he was officially restricted, and await his fate.

At some point during the summer of 1942, Amery was surprised to receive a visit from Graf Ceschi, the German armistice commissioner in Savoy, suggesting that he might like to go to Berlin in order to discuss his possible employment in political work. Flattered by this, Amery was nevertheless cautious enough to seek a guarantee of safe conduct from Ceschi. Unable to give one, the German undertook to transmit this requirement to Berlin and left Amery in a state of considerable excitement. On 26 September he received his answer personally from Hauptmann Werner Plack of the England Committee. Amery was guaranteed safe conduct to travel to Berlin for 'political discussions' with the German Foreign Ministry and would be permitted to return to his home in France at their conclusion, whatever the outcome. Plack himself had been appointed as Amery's aide-cum-minder.[9]

Amery, Plack and Jeanine Barde left for Berlin together at the beginning of October 1942. Amery and Barde were lodged at the Kaiserhof Hotel and, shortly after their arrival, Amery was summoned to a meeting with the chairman of the England Committee, Dr Fritz Hesse. The question in Hesse's mind was: what was Amery prepared to do? Amery quickly enlightened him. He later told MI5:

It was, in my view, quite insane to carry on as they did, calling the British 'the enemy' and so forth, as was their custom, if we wished to get together. I told Dr Hesse perfectly frankly that I was not interested in a German victory as such, that what interested me was a just peace where we could all get together against the real enemies of civilization, and that the British Empire as it was, intact, must be a part of this and not a dependant of such a regroupment. That I was perfectly aware of the enormous losses of the Germans of the preceding winter in Russia as also the folly of their policy in Vichy, in Croatia and elsewhere.[10]

He went on to suggest to Hesse that he be allowed to broadcast a 'British' hour, uncensored by the Germans, during which he would call for peace negotiations on the basis of Hitler's offer of July 1940, and that the Germans should consider founding a British anti-Bolshevik legion along similar lines to the French LVF.

Not surprisingly, Hesse was somewhat surprised by Amery's bold stance, having imagined that he was simply going to meet yet another of the cheap traitors that made up the bulk of his English staff. He frostily replied that Amery was asking a great deal and that, in any case, he did not control radio broadcasting. He went on to ask what material reward Amery was seeking: '. . . and when I told him that far from wanting anything I was not disposed to accept anything other than that he consider me as a guest having no resources of my own available, he seemed quite taken aback'.[11]

Hesse's report of the meeting had such far-reaching implications for the framework of the German propaganda effort towards Britain – hitherto, as we have seen, a stilted and crude operation at all levels – that it was reported by Ambassador Walter Hewel, the Foreign Ministry's representative at the Wolfsschanze, to Hitler himself for a decision. Only fourteen days after their first meeting, Hesse was able to inform Amery that he was, henceforth, to consider himself a guest of the Reich and that the Führer had personally approved the proposal that Amery could make a series of *uncensored* talks on the overt Reichsrundfunk 'Germany Calling' service, from which the announcer would dissociate the German government. Hitler was also enthusiastic about founding a British anti-Bolshevik force although Hesse does not seem to have passed this information on to Amery at the time.

Amery's arrival in Berlin and the concessions that he had extracted from the German government caused a certain amount of resentment amongst the established traitors. Joyce, in particular, felt that Amery's fairly well-publicized past would nullify the effect of any propaganda that he broadcast, and he warned Dietze, his immediate boss, to this effect. Amery, on the other hand, had made a valid point about the impact of

Joyce's brand of sneering invective: only the confirmed Nazis amongst his listeners – and there were very few – would listen with any sympathy at all. Amery saw that Joyce and Baillie-Stewart – the 'leaders' of the two factions of British propaganda broadcasters in Berlin – had come to identify themselves completely with the German cause, whereas, he maintained, he remained a British 'patriot' whose views happened to vary markedly from those of the government of the day: 'In consequence their views and outlook differed widely from mine.'[12]

The first of Amery's seven talks was transmitted on the 'Germany Calling' service on 19 November 1942. It caused a certain amount of publicity in the British press and deep anguish to his family in England (Leo Amery had been appointed Churchill's Secretary of State for India and Burma in 1940 and was still a member of the Cabinet), but the impact of the talks was limited simply because few people in Britain now bothered to listen to German radio propaganda. Nevertheless Hesse and his colleagues in the German government were pleased with the reaction that they had caused.

The theme of Amery's broadcasts was only slightly different to the general run of German propaganda at that period. He talked at length about the supposed folly of Britain's alliance with the Soviet Union; the effects of the American 'occupation' of Ulster; Jewish domination of the British, American and Soviet governments; and about the geo-political necessity of a 'Nordic Bloc' under Anglo-German domination. The first broadcast gave a clear indication of his main ideas:

Listeners will wonder what an Englishman is doing on the German radio tonight. You can imagine that before taking this step I hoped that someone better qualified than me would come forward. I dared to believe that some ray of common sense, some appreciation of our priceless civilization would guide the counsels of Mr Churchill's Government. Unfortunately this has not been the case! For two years living in a neutral country I have been able to see through the haze of propaganda to reach something which my conscience tells me is the truth. That is why I come forward tonight without any political label, without any bias, but just simply as an Englishman to say to you: a crime is being committed against civilization. Not only the priceless heritage of our fathers, of our seamen, of our Empire builders is being thrown away in a war that serves no British interests – but our alliance with the Soviets! What is that really? Is it not an alliance with a people whose leader Stalin dreams of nothing but the destruction of that heritage of our fathers? Morally this is a stain on our honour, practically it can only lead sooner or later to disaster and Communism in Great Britain, to a disintegration of all the values we cherish most.

It is not the Government, the members of Parliament to whom the ultimate decision belongs, it is up to you to go forward sure of your sacred right of free opinion, sure of your patriotism. It is up to you to decide that this has lasted long enough, that our boys are dying to serve no British interest but for the interests of a small clique of utterly unscrupulous men. There is more than enough room in the world for Germany and Britain. Your leaders say Germany seeks world domination. Did it ever enter your mind that this is but another trick of that long-planned strategy of Jewish propaganda, expected to thwart Germany's commanding position on the continent, to which she is, after all, entitled? However fantastic it may sound, the German Army is at this moment the only thing that stands between Communism and you, the only protection that exists for private property. If that rampart collapsed your liberties would be a vague souvenir of a happy past.[13]

With a disingenuous flourish, each broadcast finished with the following disclaimer from the continuity announcer: 'You have been listening to John Amery, son of the British Secretary for India, the Right Honourable Leopold Stennet Amery. We should like to remind you of the fact that Mr John Amery spoke in his own name and that the German government bears no responsibility for what Mr Amery has said.'[14]

Amery continued his broadcasts until the beginning of January 1943, but he became infuriated because they were all followed by Joyce, or another propagandist of the same ilk, launching into the standard anti-British tirade. In consequence he decided that he should return to Paris for consultations with his political associates. To his slight surprise, Dr Hesse raised no objections and arranged the necessary permits for travel. Amery, Barde and Plack – who continued in his role as the England Committee's watchdog – returned to Paris in mid-January, to find that Amery's mentor, Jacques Doriot, was there on leave from the LVF on the eastern front. Following the reverses sustained by the Germans at Stalingrad and in North Africa, Doriot – and his fellow collaborationist leader Marcel Déat – were gloomy about the prospects for ultimate victory. The two Frenchmen were both disillusioned with the German policy in occupied Europe, believing that, with the exception of Norway which was 'governed' by Vidkun Quisling, the Germans were happy simply to install 'reactionary puppets'[15] to carry out their will. They both believed that the future of Europe lay in unification and a Fascist social revolution, and they were disappointed to find that their idol, Adolf Hitler, had no such thoughts in mind. Nevertheless both reasoned that as Germany was the only country fighting the Soviet Union, it was better that they continued to offer their support. Doriot thought that the best way of achieving recognition was through combat as an ally on the eastern front; Déat argued for a diplomatic approach to sympathetic Germans.

The chief result of his meeting with Doriot and Déat was to reawaken Amery's enthusiasm for the idea of raising a British anti-Bolshevik force for service on the eastern front. His idea was that a group of fifty to a hundred volunteers should be gathered together for propaganda purposes and used as a nucleus to attract individuals from prisoner-of-war and internment camps. At the same time, he reasoned, a British force would attract volunteers for the other national contingents being raised from the countries of occupied Europe to fight the Russians. Considerably excited by this scheme, Amery decided at the beginning of February to return forthwith to Berlin to place it in front of Dr Hesse and the England Committee.

In fact Hesse had already prepared a brief feasibility report for Hitler at the end of December and received instructions to proceed in the matter. On 28 December he had received the following message from the Führer's headquarters deep in the pine forests of Rastenburg: 'The Führer is in agreement with the establishment of an English legion . . . The only personnel who should come into the framework should be former members of the English fascist party or those with similar ideology – also quality, not quantity.'[16] As a result Hesse had initiated desultory discussions with both the OKW and the Waffen-SS to begin to make administrative arrangements for a propaganda campaign amongst British POWs and internees.

Hesse listened to Amery and then briefed him on what the Foreign Ministry required from him for the British legion project. Amery agreed with Hesse that he would write a book as a companion volume for his collected radio talks – which had been released with the title *John Amery*

Speaks in January – and that he would undertake a recruiting tour once the necessary arrangements had been made. In return he suggested to Hesse that the British unit be called 'The British Legion of St George', which he thought sounded suitably patriotic. At the end of this discussion, he returned to his quarters at the Hotel Kaiserhof in order to start work.

Amery spent most of February and March 1943 working on the manuscript of his book, *England Faces Europe*, whilst the POW administration of the OKW geared up for the recruiting campaign. When he wasn't writing, Amery managed to incur the displeasure of his sponsors with a series of riotous drinking parties held at the Kaiserhof and the Foreign Press Club, but this came to an abrupt halt on 7 April when he was celebrating the completion of his book. After a particularly heavy session that evening, Amery had a loud argument in the Press Club with Jeanine Barde which ended with him roughly bundling her into a car and taking her back to the Kaiserhof. He put her to bed and then retired himself but, whilst he slept, she appears to have vomited and asphyxiated herself; when Amery woke the next morning he was horrified to find that his companion was dead.

After a panicky phone call to Hesse and an interview with the police, Amery was allowed to start preparations for returning to France with Jeanine's body. He left Berlin accompanied by Plack on 15 April, bound for Bergerac where Jeanine was to be buried. By coincidence his first scheduled recruiting visit was planned to take place at the St Denis internment camp in the north of Paris a week later, and it was decided that he would go ahead with this. Consequently he took with him a quantity of recruiting material that he planned to use.

After burying Jeanine, Amery journeyed to St Denis with Plack on 20 April in order to begin his recruiting campaign. On the orders of the OKW, the commandant of St Denis, Hauptmann Gillis, had been ordered to separate forty or fifty of the inmates who were thought to be particularly susceptible to an appeal from Amery. They comprised representatives from many parts of the British Commonwealth, including South Africa and Australia, but their selection was far from systematic – they included at least one veteran of the Boer War and several others were well above military age. Gillis himself evinced considerable irritation at having the normal calm of camp life disrupted by his unwanted visitor, but he was duty-bound to assist Amery as far as possible.

On the morning of 21 April the small group of 'guinea pigs' were assembled in the St Denis camp theatre and given a leaflet headed 'British National Representation. Proclamation to all British Subjects Interned' (for the full text see Appendix 3, p. 209). After being given a few minutes to digest this, Amery himself took to the stage and began to speak. What he said contained elements that were to become a constant refrain for those who became subject to the German effort to subvert British POWs, and was a model of mendacious eloquence. According to Royston Wood, an internee who was present at the first meeting, Amery said:

You mustn't think that everybody in England is in favour of continuing this war. Three days ago a British plane flew over from the RAF and joined the Legion of St George. In the British POW camps in Germany we have already got several hundred (I forget the exact number!) to join the British Legion of St George. Should you wish to join the Legion you will leave the camp immediately and you will never come into it again. You will have to wear German uniforms and you will have German officers, but you will have NCOs who are English or British. You will never be called upon to fight in any sector where British troops are.[17]

Amery continued to speak in this vein to his bemused audience for the best part of an hour. Then he asked if there were any questions. Immediately a man named Wilfred Brinkman stood up and asked: 'Good morning, Mr Amery, do you remember me?'[18] Brinkman was a British businessman who had been resident on the French Riviera until the fall of France, after which he had been employed by the American consulate in Nice as an assistant dealing with British interests. Whilst working in the consulate Brinkman had had a number of dealings with Amery, upon whom he looked with considerable disfavour. When Brinkman had ascertained that Amery did know who he was talking to, he forcibly pointed out that Amery, and anyone else who joined him, were committing treason and that they would surely be punished for their actions after the war. Embarrassed and perturbed, Amery brought the meeting to a close and allowed his audience to leave. By this time, as word of Amery's appearance had spread around the camp, a crowd of hecklers had gathered outside the theatre to jeer and catcall at the audience as they filed out, mistakenly thinking that they had voluntarily attended Amery's peroration.

Inside the hut Amery was doing his best to mollify Brinkman, telling him he appeared to be under a misapprehension as to his motives and asking him not to say a word about him in the camp. Repeating this request, Amery told Brinkman that he was acting on behalf of the Vichy government and held out his hand in farewell. Brinkman responded by telling Amery, 'I am not in the habit of shaking hands with traitors',[19] turned on his heel and left.

Despite this setback Amery and Plack remained at St Denis for the next two weeks, supervising the distribution of propaganda material and interviewing any inmates who showed the slightest interest in his proposition. In the event, only four men offered themselves: Professor Logio, an elderly academic of Italian ancestry who wanted to study Plato on one of the Greek islands under Axis control; Maurice Tunmer, the son of the owners of a large Central Paris sporting goods store; Oswald Job, who had been born in London of German parents but had lived in Paris since 1911; and Kenneth Berry, a 17-year-old who had been captured at the age of only fourteen when the SS *Cymbeline*, the ship on which he was serving as a deck-boy, was sunk by a German raider.

Amery and Plack quickly obtained permission to remove the four men from the camp and got them lodged in Paris under the auspices of the German embassy. At this stage matters went a little awry. Tunmer took Berry under his wing and lodged with him at an apartment on the Avenue Exelmanns whilst apparently waiting to go to Berlin. In fact Tunmer, through contacts in the French resistance, was organizing a journey across the Pyrenees so that he could travel to Britain and join de Gaulle's Free French forces in England. After a week or so two civilians appeared and spirited him away from Paris. On the same day Amery visited the flat to see how the two were getting on, and on hearing the news from Berry called in the Gestapo, who immediately arrested his young protégé for questioning. Berry was held in detention for eight weeks.

Deemed harmless by the authorities, Logio was apparently allowed to remain at liberty in Paris. Job meanwhile was recruited by the Abwehr.

They gave him some rudimentary intelligence training and instructions to deliver some jewellery to another agent in Britain and attempted to infiltrate him into England via Lisbon in November 1943. The agent that he was to deliver the jewels to was 'Dragonfly', an MI5-controlled double, and Job was caught when he landed at Poole in Dorset. He was hanged as a spy in March 1944.

Thus Amery's one and only systematic attempt to recruit for the renegade legion ended in comparative failure. The only one of the four who actually served in the legion, Kenneth Berry, had only attended school up the age of thirteen and a half and was under the confused impression that Amery was actually the British Foreign Secretary. After his eight weeks in detention, he went to Berlin in August where he was lodged in a boarding house and given a small amount of money to subsist on; he actually joined the legion in November 1943.

Amery remained bullish about the prospects for the legion and in July he returned to Berlin to report back to Dr Hesse. He was disappointed to find that the project was proceeding only slowly but received the consolation from Hesse of being offered his own 'secret' station with which to propagate his views. 'Radio National' was discussed in the previous chapter and needs little further explanation but it was originally intended that it should be a mouthpiece for Amery's own pro-German viewpoint. Amery did work for several weeks through August and September as a sort of news editor for the station, but he showed little aptitude for the work and the Germans swiftly moved him on to more congenial tasks.

At the end of September he returned to Paris where on 4 October he went through a form of marriage at the German embassy with Michèle Thomas, a young woman he had met earlier in the year after the death of Jeanine Barde. The recruiting brief for his British Legion of St George had been passed to the Waffen-SS a few days before and they had decided to dispense with Amery's services. Instead, his task was now to travel through the towns and cities of occupied Europe preaching his particular brand of National Socialist pan-Europeanism. He set off for the first of these tours in November, travelling via Berlin to Belgrade where he addressed an audience of Serbian Fascists and collaborators. Returning to Berlin on 23 November he was just in time to be caught in a massive air-raid during which the Kaiserhof Hotel was destroyed. He joined in the rescue operation, for which he subsequently received a German bravery decoration, but almost all of his personal possessions were destroyed.

Although the British volunteer legion, which by then had been officially named the 'British Free Corps', had been taken out of Amery's hands, he still regarded it as his baby. In a report for the German Foreign Office after his return from Belgrade, he wrote:

Throughout Europe both in talks with German diplomats and local sympathizers, the idea that Dr Hesse, Werner Plack and myself hatched out of the British Free Corps, that at long last we have so laboriously brought to life . . . is considered by far the BIGGEST PROPAGANDA IDEA that anyone has EVER thought out.

For my part I respectfully request to be allowed to continue my action that has given such enormous proofs of success throughout Europe until such time as the British Free Corps has finished its training and then as political officer to that Corps be allowed to take it through Europe to consecrate the success of our joint creation.[20]

In fact John Amery was never allowed to have more than social contact with members of his legion. Instead he existed as a peripatetic lecturer, travelling in the first five months of 1944 through Czechoslovakia, Norway, Belgium and France, speaking to local collaborators about the iniquities of the Churchill government and exhorting them to further efforts against Communism. Despite his initial protestations to Hesse about not wishing to be paid, he received a salary of 650 Reichsmarks per week for his efforts – vastly more than any other traitor – as well as having his usual living expenses covered. In May he returned to Germany, where he was given a dressing down by Hesse because his speeches were so far at variance with the official German line on the treatment of the occupied territories. With the Allied invasion of Normandy imminent, Hesse argued that it was best for Amery to keep out from under the feet of the Wehrmacht and stay away from Paris. Amery reluctantly agreed, and after a brief trip back to the French capital to collect personal belongings, he returned to live in a lakeside villa in Gatow in the south-west of Berlin.

Amery and Michèle Thomas stayed at Gatow throughout the difficult months of June and July 1944, during which the Allies landed in Normandy and the German resistance launched their failed *putsch* against Hitler. Hesse called upon Amery's services only once, in August, asking him to speak on the 'Germany Calling' service to disprove a British newspaper rumour that he was a prisoner of the Gestapo; otherwise, he simply idled his time away. His last active role as a servant of the Axis came in September when he received an invitation from Mussolini to visit him at his Lake Garda headquarters. During discussions at the end of October, Amery learnt from Mussolini that he felt he had made a mistake by not launching a true social revolution in 1922 but that he felt he was now on the 'right road'.

Mussolini explained to Amery that, having brokered the Munich agreement in 1938, he felt that he had sufficient prestige and experience to attempt to make peace between Germany and the Western powers, and he wanted Amery's help in doing so. Amery agreed to assist him, and so spent the last six months of the war in northern Italy, travelling from town to town, speaking in public and broadcasting on the Italian radio service. At the end of January 1945 he was briefly recalled to Germany at the instigation of the German ambassador to the Mussolini government, but there was nothing for him to do apart from attend the funeral of Jacques Doriot in February. He met Mussolini for the last time on 23 April 1945 in Milan. Seemingly unconcerned by the imminent collapse of the German armies in the area, Mussolini offered him a commission in his 'Black Brigade' but Amery felt unable to accept, explaining to the dictator that he would not want to find himself in the position of having to fire on his fellow countrymen. Instead, he offered to dress in Fascist uniform as a demonstration of his continued support. It was in these clothes that he was captured two days later by a unit of Italian partisans.

5

The Lost Boys: Thomas Cooper and James Brady

In December 1942 *Verordnungsblatt der Waffen-SS* (the Official Gazette of the SS) published a special supplement requesting information on the current whereabouts of a young NCO whose services were required in Berlin for a special project. The soldier in question was SS Unterscharführer Thomas Haller Cooper, who had been born in Chiswick, West London, on 29 August 1919.

His father, Ashley Cooper, was a self-employed photographer and commercial artist. Born in Cheltenham in 1881, he had served in the British Army in the Boer War; in 1908 he had travelled to Berlin to start a photography business. There he met and fell in love with Anna Maria Simon, who had been born in Leipzig in 1886, and in 1910 they married in Weston-super-Mare. Returning to Germany, Ashley Cooper continued with his career until August 1914, when war broke out and as a British national he was detained at the huge civilian internment camp at the Ruhleben racecourse in Berlin, where he remained throughout the war. Anna Maria managed to keep the business going, but when he was released in November 1918, with Germany in turmoil, the reunited couple used the opportunity to return to England and try to rebuild their lives together. Thomas, their only child, was born almost exactly nine months after the Armistice. (Ashley Cooper eventually died in Devon in 1978; Anna Maria died in 1977.)

Anna Maria's pregnancy had been fraught with complications – short rations in Berlin in the latter stages of the war had severely weakened her – and Thomas Cooper was deemed lucky to survive his infancy. Nevertheless within a few years he was attending the local primary school on the same terms as the other local lads in the Hammersmith area of London. At school he proved to be a bright pupil and, after passing his Eleven Plus examination, he gained a place at the Latymer Upper School in King Street, Hammersmith. Latymer Upper was founded in 1624 by a Lord Mayor of London who wanted to create an institution where 'poor lads' from London could receive a first-rate education. By the time that Thomas Cooper went there, it had evolved into a direct-grant grammar school – in effect, an institution where those who could afford to pay fees did so whilst others were subsidized by their local authorities. Cooper was remembered by his headmaster, Frederick Wilkinson, as 'a clever boy who was interested in modern languages and, whilst still at school, was endeavouring to teach himself Japanese. He was regarded at school as having a somewhat eccentric mental outlook but his character appeared quite sound – he was known to need careful handling to obviate his resentment to discipline.'[1]

Cooper does not appear to have acquired any close friends at school and remained a rather solitary youth. He was very much under the influence of his mother, who still regarded herself as a German (by marrying Ashley Cooper, she had acquired British nationality but she does not appear to have realized this), and in his spare time he retreated into the world of books and fantasy. He left school in December 1936 after matriculation because his parents could not afford to support him through to university.

In the economic situation of 1937, Cooper was unable to find a job that he considered suitable and, after much searching, he became a clerk at the firm of W. J. Bush & Co., importers of 'essential oils', in Hackney, East London; as he was being paid only 18/6 per week, he continued to live with his parents. At the same time he decided to try to find employment in the public service. He made three applications to join the Metropolitan Police with the hope of joining CID and going to Hendon Police College; they were all refused. After enquiring why he had been turned down, he was told that because his mother was German he was ineligible. Frustrated by this, he applied for the Royal Air Force and the Royal Navy, but again was refused because of the nationality question. His final throw was an application to join the Foreign Office but it appears that he did not pursue this; his father later suggested that 'for [the diplomatic service] one needs power and influence, we had neither'.[2]

Embittered by his failure to get employment that he thought worthy of his talents, Cooper joined the Hammersmith Branch of the British Union in September 1938. Like many other well-educated, middle-class young men of his time he was piqued and embarrassed by his failure to obtain suitable work and he looked for a scapegoat to explain his troubles; he found it in the Jews. He remained a member of the BU until he left England.

Unable to join a middle-class profession in Britain because, as he thought, of his mother's nationality, Thomas Cooper decided instead to seek his fortune in Germany. From his upbringing he spoke German well and was in contact with a number of relations there. At the beginning of 1939 he contacted the German Academic Exchange Organization in Russell Square, London, which organized working visits under the auspices of the German Labour Service or Reichs Arbeits Dienst (RAD). After a short period of negotiation, the Coopers were told that arrangements had been made for Thomas to enter an exchange camp and that he should report to the RAD Office in Stuttgart during the summer.

On 9 July 1939, together with his mother, Cooper travelled to Chemnitz to stay with her family, and a week later they moved on to Stuttgart where they stayed with more relatives. To their disappointment they discovered that the paperwork from London was incomplete and that Thomas could not enter the camp. After a few wasted days in Stuttgart they returned to Chemnitz, and five days after that Anna Maria left for London. Thomas stayed on, hoping that the RAD would complete the paperwork that would allow him to start work, but nothing appeared to be happening and after a few days he decided to return home.

The day before he was due to start his journey back to London, he received a message from the RAD offering him a job teaching languages at a school in the Taunus mountains. He accepted immediately and started work there on 20 August. Cooper was seemingly oblivious to the events taking place in Europe; he was certainly surprised to be dismissed on 5 September because he was a British subject. He travelled to Frankfurt am Main to register as an enemy alien and was ordered by the police to report to the head office of the Exchange Organization in Berlin; he did so on 8 September. Three days later he was arrested by the police, who intended to intern him until he produced a certificate that his mother had obtained, classifying him as an 'ethnic German' (Volksdeutsche), which gained his release.

Just over twenty years old, never having left home and from a sheltered, protected background, Thomas Cooper now found himself alone in Berlin at the start of the war. With no means of looking after himself, he found work for a few months as a farm labourer in Liebenwalde. Cut off from his family, he kept in touch with the official of the exchange group who had sent him to Germany in the first place, Hans Neithar Wagner. Wagner took pity on the young Englishman and found him a post as a private tutor of English to the 17-year-old son of a senior civil servant called Wiesemann; Cooper wasn't paid but he did receive bed and board, and earned pocket money by tutoring other children in his spare time.

In November a friend of Wagner's, Georg Nebbe of the Volksdeutsche Central Administration, suggested that Cooper should join the German Army. As Cooper later said, 'I didn't accept his offer . . . as it was my object to try and maintain my freedom without adopting such crass measures if possible.'[3] But he was actually running out of options. In January 1940 Wiesemann dispensed with his services and Cooper was back to square one. He visited Nebbe again and the official repeated his offer; this time Cooper accepted. Nebbe quickly dictated a letter to his secretary outlining Cooper's background and circumstances, and sent the young man with it to a nearby office. There it was read by a man wearing the uniform of a Brigadeführer of the SS – Gottlob Berger, who ordered Cooper to return to the office at six o'clock the next morning. Cooper did not know it but Gottlob Berger, a Swabian veteran of the First World War and close colleague of Himmler, was at that time head of SS recruiting. He was always pleased to gain new recruits for his organization and was aware that Cooper could not actually serve in the Wehrmacht because of his British nationality. Largely as a result of his own efforts, Berger knew full well that no such barrier to recruitment existed in the SS.

The next morning Cooper arrived at the office as instructed. He was given a medical examination and was then interviewed about his family background. This was standard procedure in the SS: theoretically, all recruits were required to show that they had 'pure Aryan' antecedents back to 1750. Finally he was told that he would be called up in due course. Some days later he was again seen by Nebbe, who informed him that he could not be accepted by the Wehrmacht but would be going to the Waffen-SS instead, 'which according to him was exactly the same, only had more scope for attending to the needs of foreigners such as myself'.[4] Cooper did not appreciate the significance of this.

On 1 February 1940 Cooper reported for duty at the famous Berlin-Lichtefelde Barracks, the home of the training battalion of the senior unit of the SS, the 'Leibstandarte Adolf Hitler'. There he was kitted out with his field-grey SS uniform and equipment, and had his blood group tattooed under his left arm. Recruit training is never an enjoyable experience and Cooper, whose resistance to discipline had already been noticed at his liberal grammar school, particularly disliked it. After three weeks he approached his Rottenführer (squad corporal) to tell him that he had received a letter from his parents saying that his father was now serving in the British Army and that he did not think he could continue as a member of the SS. (This was at least partly true: his girlfriend had an uncle who lived in neutral Sweden and Cooper had written home via him, telling his parents of his straitened circumstances; they had replied by the same means, sending him some money.) The NCO reacted by placing Cooper under arrest and having him interviewed by his platoon commander. He was given twenty-four hours to think about his position and then allowed to go back to his billet. Talking to his comrades, they warned him to be careful as he was likely to land himself in a concentration camp. When he was sent for to announce his decision the next evening, he agreed to soldier on.

At the end of February Cooper was posted to the Leibstandarte's artillery training battery, but he remained for only two weeks before being moved on to a new unit entirely. This was the infantry training battalion for the notorious SS Totenkopf (Death's Head) Division (1/T. Inf. Ers. Bat. 1) based at Radolfzell near the Bodensee, not far from the Swiss frontier. Totenkopf units were started by the SS for the specific purpose of guarding concentration camps, but in a move that many SS commanders regarded as 'an insult to any soldier,'[5] they were made available in August 1938 by order of Hitler to reinforce other parts of the Waffen-SS in time of war. The Totenkopf Division was formed in November 1939 in preparation for the German attack on France.

At Radolfzell Cooper had to go through his basic training over again although he does seem to have shown some aptitude. Any thoughts that he might have had about escaping over the border to Switzerland were dispelled, however, after a conversation with his Stabsscharführer (Company Sergeant Major) during a drinking session. The NCO proposed the theory that Cooper might be a British spy, but if he was he wouldn't get away with much because both he and his mail were under Gestapo surveillance. Cooper decided to keep his head down.

In July 1940 Cooper received yet another transfer, this time to the 8th Company of the newly formed 5th Totenkopf Infantry Regiment (8/T.Inf.Regt.5) based at Oranienburg to the north of Berlin. His task was to train recruits in indirect fire from tripod-mounted machine-guns and he received temporary NCO status as an instructor. He remained with the 5th Totenkopf Regiment until February 1941. By that time the unit had moved to Plock, near the River Vistula, in Poland and he had been promoted to Rottenführer. He left the regiment to go to the SS NCO School at Lauenburg in Pomerania, where he underwent a course which finished in May 1941. Thereafter he was moved to yet another Totenkopf unit, the Wachbataillon Oranienburg (Oranienburg Guard Battalion), from which he was detached to a subunit based at the Debica training area near Krakow.

Later in the war Cooper was to boast widely of his exploits in occupied Poland which, he claimed, included the liquidation of Jewish and Russian prisoners; Roy Futcher, a member of the British SS unit, later stated that

Cooper had told him that '[he] had been in the parties that had rounded up Jews in Poland and thrown women out of top storey buildings (*sic*)',[6] whilst John Brown, a highly educated and articulate POW, remembered Cooper telling him that '[he] had taken part in atrocities against the Jews, and had himself killed several Jews'[7] and, according to Brown, 'He used to boast about this openly at Genshagen'.[8] Thomas Freeman, a commando who joined the British SS unit in order to disrupt it, also remembered Cooper's claims: 'He had himself shot over 200 Poles and 80 Jews in one day – by merely lining them up against a wall and shooting them down. This was in Warsaw.'[9]

The duties of Cooper's detachment at Debica basically centred around the permanent security and administration of the training area, which was designed for use by visiting units, whilst the 5th Totenkopf Infantry Regiment (with whom Cooper served between July 1940 and February 1941 – latterly in Poland) had a garrison role. With Germany involved in a war with Russia from May 1941 onwards, manpower was short and could not be easily spared for manual labour in the occupied territories. The solution adopted throughout the Nazi Empire was to use press-ganged local civilians, prisoners of war and slave labour from concentration camps, all of whom were in plentiful supply in occupied Poland. It is highly likely that these people were used for heavy manual labour at Debica and that they were supervised by members of Wach-bataillon Oranienburg, including Thomas Cooper who was promoted to Unterscharführer in November 1941. It would be entirely unsurprising if the SS men had treated their charges brutally. Additionally, many Waffen-SS garrison units were called in to assist in anti-Jewish pogroms in Poland as Hitler's 'final solution' progressed and it is possible that Cooper participated in these actions.

Not surprisingly, the statement that Cooper gave to MI5 at the end of the war bears no mention of any atrocities that he might have been involved in, despite his earlier claims. Indeed, after D-Day in June 1944 he instructed John Brown to 'forget what he had told me about his Jewish atrocities'.[10] The evidence against Cooper rests on what he told his associates during the course of the war (there were enough reports of his remarks to warrant a comment in the MI5 report on Cooper's case[11]);

but the possibility that Cooper was a participant in war crimes must remain speculative.

It was not until January 1943 that Cooper was moved from Debica. In that month he and all the other NCOs in his unit were transferred into a transport unit of the SS-Polizei-Division (an infantry division of the Waffen-SS made up partly from ex-members of the German Police) which was working up at the training area. At the beginning of February, they were loaded on to cattle-trucks and transported east. Passing through Riga in Latvia, they began to get an idea of where they were going, the Leningrad sector of the eastern front.

They reached their destination, the small Russian town of Schablinov, on 7 February. Three days later the NCOs were called to their company commander's office for a briefing. He informed them that, due to the collapse of the Spanish Blue Division, they were being sent to the front line; they reached their dugouts the same day. The situation remained confused for some three days, before the Soviets resumed their attack on the 13th. In the face of a heavy artillery barrage, and an attack by tanks and infantry, Cooper collected his men together and began to retreat. They had got no more than 500 yards when Cooper fell, severely wounded in both legs by shell splinters. He was picked up from the snow by his men and carried back to Schablinov, now only eleven kilometres behind the front line. From there he was evacuated via Narva, Riga and Königsberg all the way to Bad Muskau, a small town not far from Görlitz. As a result of his injuries Cooper was awarded the Wound Badge in Silver, becoming the only Englishman to receive a German combat decoration during the war.

In contrast to Thomas Cooper, who had a relatively secure lower-middle-class background, James Brady hailed from an agricultural family in rural Ireland. He was born in Roscommon on 20 May 1920, his mother dying when he was young, and he followed a path familiar to many young Irishmen at the time by enlisting in the British Army in Liverpool in December 1938.

After he completed his basic training, Brady was posted in May 1939 to join the Royal Irish Fusiliers, who were then stationed on the Channel

Island of Guernsey. He did not have long to enjoy this comparatively peaceful posting because, in the same month that he was taken on to the battalion strength, he and another Fusilier, Frank Stringer, got drunk in a local pub, broke a few windows and then made the mistake of punching the policeman who came to deal with them. For this offence Brady received a sentence of eighteen months' hard labour (Stringer, the more experienced soldier, got twenty-one months); both were to serve their sentences in the local prison.

Neither Brady nor Stringer was discharged from the Army and, had the war not broken out, it is likely that both would have been released after their sentences were completed and returned to their regiment to serve out their contracts. When war was declared in September both men requested permission to return to their battalion but were refused, and they made the same request, and received the same answer, in June 1940 as the Germans approached the Channel coast and the RIF were evacuated. Thus in July, when the Germans took control of the Islands, Brady and Stringer remained, to their considerable indignation, languishing behind bars; disgracefully abandoned by the Army to become prisoners of war. They remained in prison until the end of September when they were removed by the Germans to a temporary POW facility near Saint-Lô in Normandy. There they remained until December when the entire camp was shifted to Luckenwalde and, shortly afterwards, on to Lamsdorff, where they joined a road-making gang.

In the early stages of the war, the Germans were very much aware of the opportunities that Irish independence had given them as a means of creating trouble for Britain. Even before war broke out the Abwehr had established channels of communication with the IRA with a view to co-operating in sabotage attacks in Ulster and the British mainland, although as events turned out their efforts were farcically inept. The IRA Chief of Staff, Sean Russell, who had fled to Germany from the USA, died of a perforated ulcer on board a U-boat only 100 miles or so from the coast of County Galway in September 1940, during an operation designed to land him and an IRA companion, Frank Ryan, in Eire to start a sabotage campaign in the North. The U-boat returned to Germany without landing Ryan, and instead the Germans concentrated their efforts on dropping spies, such as Captain Hermann Goertz, to attempt to co-ordinate the IRA's spasmodic activities. As Goertz later said to a senior IRA officer: 'You know how to die for Ireland, but of how to fight for it you have not the slightest idea.'

Nevertheless, despite the failure of their operations in Ireland itself, the Abwehr felt that it might be possible to raise a unit of Irishmen for service in the German Army from amongst the ranks of Irish prisoners of war (as they had attempted in 1916 through the good offices of Sir Roger Casement), and accordingly in the spring of 1941 they began to trawl through the POW camps for suitable candidates. Since the end of the war there has been considerable speculation about the existence of an 'Irish Brigade' in the Wehrmacht or Waffen-SS, but in truth the operation never really got off the ground. In May 1941 about fifty Irish POWs, including Brady and Stringer, were segregated in a camp at Friesack under the supervision of the Abwehr as the nucleus of the 'Irish Brigade'. They were a mixture of officers and other ranks, whose common feature apart from their nationality, it should be noted, was that they were all volunteer soldiers in the British Army. Initially under the command of a Lieutenant Bissell as 'Senior British Officer', they were shortly joined by Major John McGrath of the Royal Engineers. On the German side, the camp was run by Leutnant Rheinherst of the Abwehr who quickly earned the sobriquet 'Gestapo Joe'.

The Abwehr men set about propagandizing the prisoners, attempting to persuade them that Germany was the natural ally of Irish Republicans, but much of their work was subverted by McGrath who was much liked by his fellow Irishmen. Nevertheless Rheinherst and his colleagues succeeded in establishing that a few of the POWs did indeed hold republican sympathies, and amongst this group were Brady and Stringer, who no doubt greatly resented their treatment by the British Army. In September 1941 Rheinherst suggested to Brady and several others that they might like to consider working for Germany 'to help further Ireland's cause'. Brady was not averse to the idea but he discussed it first with McGrath, who told him that the only possible justification for working for the Germans was to gain intelligence for the British (McGrath's actions throughout his period in captivity were entirely beyond reproach), and then with Sergeant Cushing, an Irish-American who seemed to be thinking along similar lines to Brady. Eventually Brady and four others told Rheinherst that they would work for Germany.

The five supposed renegades – James Brady, Sergeant Cushing and individuals named Walsh, O'Brien and Murphy – were taken from Friesack to an Abwehr safe-house at 208 Hohenzollerndamm in Berlin in December 1941. The Abwehr's scheme to recruit a 'brigade' of Irishmen to fight against England had simply degenerated into the recruitment of spies. During their journey the five were given civilian clothes, a quantity of money and, when they arrived in Berlin, the Abwehr threw an all-night drinking party for them.

The next step was training in the tradecraft of spying. They were taken to a house somewhere in Brandenburg, known to them only as 'Quintz', where they received two weeks of intensive instruction in bomb-making and sabotage techniques from a pair of secretive German chemists, and then they were returned, in mid-January, to their Berlin safe-house. For the next four months they underwent a course in secret radio transmissions, learning encoding and decoding, high-speed Morse and the skills necessary to build a transmitter/receiver from scratch. They also began to form into teams; Brady paired with Walsh. In May 1942 they were separated from the rest and taken to Stettin for field training. By now Leutnant Rheinherst had left the scene and they were under the control of Dr Kurt Haller, section leader of Abwehr (II) Amt 1 West, responsible for espionage operations in Britain and Ireland. Haller increased the pay that Brady and Walsh were receiving but demanded high standards – they were required to transmit eighty Morse letters per minute – and he also had a proposition to put to them. Whilst they were still training in Stettin, Haller suggested to Brady that he should be sent by parachute or submarine to Northern Ireland or England in order to gather information on American forces and to build espionage networks. Brady and Walsh both agreed to this and they were moved on to the next phase of their training – a return to Quintz for refresher explosives training.

By this time Brady was conducting, for training purposes, a radio schedule with the Abwehr base in Hamburg, using a transmitter that he carried about with him. He took the transmitter with him to Hamburg in August 1942 when he was being instructed in the use of secret inks, and to a bungalow in a wood near Hamburg when he was taught the procedures for extreme long-range radio work. It was there that he began to receive his operational materials: a book code based on Jack London's '*Call of the Wild*', a small coding machine and a special emergency code. He briefly went back to Stettin with Walsh and then, on 15 September, he was taken to Berlin for a mission briefing.

At the Berlin safe-house Brady learnt that he was shortly to parachute into Northern Ireland, carrying an ID card in the name of Charles de Lacy, £8,000 in sterling and $3,000 in US currency. His task was to report on the activities of US troops in the province. Four days later he was flown, with Walsh and Haller, to Trondheim in Norway, the jumping-off point for the operation. There he was told that he was to leave on 23 September and Walsh on the 24th.

Had Brady and Walsh actually been dropped, the chances are strong that they would have been arrested almost immediately. All German espionage in Britain was, by then, under the control of MI5, and the Abwehr 'ISOS' codes were being routinely broke by the Government Code and Cypher School (GC & CS, forerunner to GCHQ). MI5's penetration of the Abwehr's British networks was so complete that in almost all cases they received plenty of warning of the impending arrival of an intelligence agent and no spy escaped the net after 1941.[12] Captured spies were offered a harsh choice: either 'double-cross' their German masters and begin work for MI5 or face trial and probable execution under the Treachery Act of 1940. It is no great surprise that most spies opted for the first course.

On the evening of 22 September, Haller arrived at Brady's accommodation and told him that he wasn't going. He was immediately placed under an armed guard and escorted to Oslo Military Prison for a short stay – he was told that Walsh was also there – before being moved via Denmark to the Lehrter Strasse Prison in Berlin. In October Brady was subjected to a lengthy interrogation by the Abwehr in Berlin. He was puzzled by his arrest and by the suspicions that the Germans had of him because the only person whom he had told of his supposed plan to 'double-cross' the Abwehr was Major McGrath at Friesack almost a year before, but in fact he was simply the victim of the entirely justifiable suspicions that the Germans harboured about the motivation of all their Irish volunteers. Even so he managed to allay suspicion of himself to the extent that he was given the opportunity, as an alternative to spying, of starting a career in radio propaganda.

Brady's radio career turned out to be a non-starter. He did so badly in the voice tests that Haller, still his controller, suggested instead that he try his hand at farm work in Pomerania, and in January 1943 he was moved to a farm at Kleinkesow, along with a small group of Irishmen who had also fallen foul of the Germans. There he met Frank Stringer again, who told him of his own training for a mission spying in Canada and the US which had also been cancelled.

Brady and his friends were so bored by their work that when an Abwehr officer named Fritz Richter arrived offering to find them jobs, they jumped at the chance despite their earlier harsh treatment by the organization. Shortly afterwards, Brady was taken via Berlin to a covert radio school in Lehnitz, where he once more went through an intensive course in radio work – this time in the company of two Dutchmen. But Brady's heart was no longer in spying; he did not get on well with Richter, his new controller, and a stay that they made in Berdiansk, on the Sea of Azov, exacerbated their mutual dislike. In September 1943 Brady was recalled to Berlin, where he was interviewed by Haller who told him that his reports were so bad that the Abwehr could no longer employ him; he offered Brady the choice of a return to the farm or service in the Armed Forces.

Brady's old companion Frank Stringer was also in Berlin at the time and the two had a long discussion about their future. In the end they opted for what they decided would be the more interesting life; they reported to an office on the Scheerstrasse where they were inducted into the Waffen-SS. They went straight from Scheerstrasse to the Waffen-SS European volunteers' training camp at Sennheim in Alsace. They were issued with uniforms, they had their blood groups tattooed on their left arms, and they went through a course of basic infantry training that lasted until March 1944. When they finished, Brady, Stringer and nearly thirty others were informed that they had been selected for training as part of a special unit. Shortly afterwards they were sent to a training camp at Friedenthal near Berlin.

The unit that Brady and Stringer joined had been set up as a direct result of Otto Skorzeny's successful rescue of Mussolini from a hotel in the Gran Sasso in Italy in September 1943. Apart from receiving a welter of medals from his grateful Führer, Skorzeny was initially authorized to set up a 'special forces' battalion, not entirely dissimilar to Britain's SAS, and later given control of all of Germany's 'special' units. The first of Skorzeny's units, SS-Jägerbataillon 502, was the one at Friedenthal to which Brady and Stringer were posted. The training course that they joined followed a curriculum that will be familiar to any soldier who has served in commando or special forces units. They received instruction in small-arms, map-reading, grenades, explosives and anti-tank warfare for more than three months before they were deemed ready to join an operational unit – in their case SS-Jagdverbände Mitte.

But the two young Irishmen – by now almost archetypal soldiers of fortune and trained as spies, saboteurs and commandos – swiftly became bored by their reversion to the role of simple infantrymen, no matter that it was with a special purpose unit, and both requested that they receive a posting in accordance with their virtually unique abilities. To this end they were sent back to Friedenthal from where they were despatched, with a group of about fifty others, to conduct a sort of mini scorched-earth operation in Rumania, destroying road and rail bridges in the face of the advancing Red Army. Their task lasted for a mere three weeks but by the end of it the unit had been reduced to twenty-two survivors, including Brady and Stringer who were able to return to Friedenthal for two weeks' rest.

Operation Panzerfaust, the last meaningful 'special operation' conducted by the Germans on the Eastern front, took place in Budapest in October 1944. Its background lay in the likelihood that Germany's erstwhile ally Hungary, under the dictator Admiral Horthy, seemed likely to sue for an armistice with the Russians. The operation was only in the reconnaissance stage when, on 30 August, Horthy dismissed his pro-German cabinet and replaced it with one deemed far more favourable to the Soviets, and little more than a month later a Hungarian Field Marshal had been sent to Moscow to make peace. Panzerfaust was a complex plan, requiring amongst other things the kidnapping of Horthy's son by SD officers, but the part played by Brady and Stringer, as members of 2 Company of Jagdverbände Mitte, was comparatively simple; they had to storm the citadel – the Burgberg – in central Budapest and arrest Horthy himself. To everyone's surprise this is precisely what they achieved, without even firing a shot. It was shortly after this success that Himmler confided to the German Finance Minister, Schwerin von Krosigk, that 'in the course of the last year, I have learned to believe in miracles again'.[13]

Following the success of Panzerfaust, 2 Company of Jagdverbände Mitte rested in Berlin, whilst their colleagues of 1 Company took part in Skorzeny's 'Trojan horse' operation during the Battle of the Bulge. But for both Brady and Stringer the end of the war was still a long way away.

Cushing, Walsh, O'Brien and Murphy, the four Irishmen who left Friesack with Brady, all eventually found themselves incarcerated in a special compound of Sachsenhausen concentration camp as German doubts about their essential loyalties grew. The Germans were right to be sceptical: none of the four had any real intention of working for the Nazis and all had taken McGrath's advice to heart; they finished the war with no stain on their characters.

The Germans made several further attempts to concentrate Irish prisoners at Friesack, and later at Stalag IIIa at Luckenwalde and the Buchenwald concentration camp.[14] None of these efforts bore much fruit. Major McGrath, the Friesack SBO, whose work with the potential renegades frustrated the German's plan to form an 'Irish brigade' – such a unit never existed – spent the last part of the war in segregation at Dachau concentration camp as a dangerous prisoner. In the midst of the collapse of Germany in 1945, he was taken with other prominent prisoners in the direction of the supposed Alpine Redoubt, but he was eventually released on the personal order of SS-Obergruppenführer Berger.

6

Our Flag Is
Going Forwards Too!

Surprising as it may seem, John Amery's abject failure as a recruiter did
not deter his German masters from persisting with their plan to establish
a unit of 'Englishmen' to fight against the Soviets. Indeed, in a directive
from the German Foreign Office in September 1943 the matter was
firmly placed in the court of the chief recruiter of the Waffen-SS, Obergruppenführer Gottlob Berger.[1] In his reply Berger expressed misgivings:
'I personally have no great belief in this unit,'[2] he wrote, but nevertheless
within three months the SS formally possessed a British unit.

To understand why there was any enthusiasm amongst the hierarchy
of the Third Reich for a British unit, and why it should have come under
the auspices of the Waffen-SS, it is necessary to look back to the period
before the outbreak of the Second World War when Heinrich Himmler
was struggling to establish the SS as an independent order within the
Nazi state. The origins of the SS lay in Hitler's need to have a force of
politically motivated strong-arm men that he himself could control during
the early days of his rise to power. In April 1925 he ordered his chauffeur,
Julius Schreck, to form a new 'Headquarters Guard' which, a fortnight
later, was christened the 'Schutzstaffel' ('Protection Squad'), shortened
to SS. At first, SS units were formed by area Nazi parties as an élite force
within the party organization and consisted of no more than an officer
and ten men in each locality. Members were ostensibly selected from

'the best and most reliable Party members to protect the movement and work selflessly and tirelessly within it',[3] but in fact the real purpose of the organization was always to act as a smaller and more loyal counter-weight to the larger and more independently inclined SA (Sturm-abteilung) or 'Brownshirts'.

Until 6 January 1929 the SS was just one Nazi party formation amongst many, but on that day Hitler placed at its head the man who was to transform the SS into probably the single most murderous organization that has ever existed: Heinrich Himmler. Born on 7 October 1900, the son of a Bavarian schoolmaster who had been tutor to members of the Bavarian Royal family, Himmler was just too young to see active service during the First World War, being commissioned into the 11 Bavarian Infantry Regiment in October 1918, but he took part in counter-revolutionary activities around Munich in 1919 as a member of a 'Free Corps' unit. Thereafter he allowed his military fervour to subside and he became a student of agriculture.

Himmler, the soldier who had never seen the disintegration of the German Army in the front line, was precisely the sort of person to believe the Nazi 'stab in the back' propaganda which sought to explain away defeat in the war by blaming Jews, communists, capitalists and any other convenient target. He was introduced to the Nazi party by Ernst Röhm, just prior to the Munich *putsch* in November 1923, during which the young Himmler carried the old imperial battle flag. Despite the failure of Hitler's Beer Hall *putsch*, Himmler stayed with the movement, where he earned a reputation as an energetic and efficient organizer and quickly became secretary to Gregor Strasser, whilst at the same time developing 'a schoolboyish adulation for his Führer'.[4] His devotion to the cause paid off: in 1925 he became the Deputy Gauleiter of Upper Bavaria and Swabia; in the same year Deputy Reich Propaganda Chief; and in 1927 Deputy Reichsführer SS.

Along with his hard work as a full-time Nazi Party Organizer, Himmler also did a great deal of thinking about the party's ideology. Probably more than any other high-ranking Nazi, Himmler swallowed the racial claptrap that was peddled by ideologues like Alfred Rosenberg and Walther Darré. He saw the 'Germanic' peoples as being involved in a titanic struggle for survival against the Slavic and Mongol hordes from the east; and against the 'alien' Jews within Germany itself. He came to conceive of the SS, which even before Himmler took charge was very selective, as a kind of racially 'pure', chivalric order of warrior-farmers who would eventually reoccupy the supposed ancestral lands of the east, farming the land but ready to drop their ploughs at a moment's notice to defend 'Germandom'. For this former agriculture student (he also ran a chicken farm as a sideline to his political activities) Germanic-ness was not a question of simple nationality but of blood. Once he had taken control of the SS, the recruiting criteria became extremely severe: potential members were placed in one of five categories: 'pure Nordic'; 'predominantly Nordic or Phalic'; 'harmonious bastard with "slight Alpine, Dinaric or Mediterranean characteristics" '; 'bastards of predominantly East-Baltic or Alpine origin'; and 'bastards of extra-European origin'.[5] Only applicants in the first three categories were allowed to join. From 1935 an even stricter test was applied. SS members were required to furnish a family tree showing that they were 'pure Aryans' back to 1750; in this, even some of the most senior members of the organization were found wanting and were forced quietly to retire.

In person, it is said, Himmler was diffident and schoolmasterly, and he certainly didn't look like the controller of the greatest mass-murder programme in history. But his decidedly mild appearance masked a personality that was both cunning and wildly ambitious. From the comparatively small beginnings of the SS when he took it over in 1929, he began to weld the organization into a large, effective and indispensable tool of totalitarian government. In the wake of the Nazi seizure of power, Himmler – together with Reinhard Heydrich, his *de facto* deputy – slowly took control of the German Police system. At the same time they began to build up an intelligence service – the SD (Sicherheitsdienst) – and instituted the notorious concentration camps initially as dumping grounds for political opponents.

Himmler ensured the long-term future of his organization within the Third Reich on 30 June 1934, when the SS took the leading role in exterminating the leaders of the SA and other potential opponents of the regime during the so-called 'night of the long knives'. The Army's leaders had become alarmed by the Brownshirts' Chief of Staff, Ernst Röhm, who felt that the traditional military should be replaced with his 'revolutionary' troops, and they looked to Hitler, who relied on the Army's support to retain power, to do something about it. For his part, Hitler turned to the SS – after all, it was what they had originally been founded to do – and Himmler and Heydrich were happy to oblige, even concocting false evidence of a *putsch* attempt by Röhm and his cronies. Thereafter Himmler's influence grew by leaps and bounds. What the Army's Generals didn't realize as they congratulated themselves after the massacre of the SA was that Himmler was just as intent on creating an alternative armed force as Röhm had ever been, but he was far more subtle in his methods.

In the early days of the SS, its membership was distinguished from the usual Nazi rabble by the uncharacteristic self-discipline and restraint that it was expected to show. Before going to political meetings, or out on the street making collections, SS leaders would search their men to ensure that they were not carrying illegal weapons or any other material that might obstruct the smooth, legal path of the Nazi rise to power. As soon as the Nazis had taken control, however, things changed very rapidly. After 30 January 1933, units of armed SS men began to spring up throughout Germany, usually styled as 'Headquarters Guards' to satisfy the *folie de grandeur* of local Nazi and SS satraps. Whenever possible the SS arranged for these units, officially called 'Sonderkommando', to be taken on to the strength of the local police as auxiliaries (in order that the police would have to pay them), and when they reached company strength or greater they were called 'Politische Bereitschaften' (political reaction squad) and began to receive full-time, if rudimentary, military training.

The significance of the Politsche Bereitschaften, which escaped most people at the time, was that they were actually an authorized armed force, parallel to the official armed forces of the state but not owing any allegiance to the state. Instead, these armed SS squads were explicitly pledged to the person of Adolf Hitler and were under no obligation whatsoever to accept the authority of any army or police commander who might try to assert it.

The most famous of the Politsche Bereitschaften was formed in Berlin by a bull-necked Bavarian ex-sergeant-major of the Reichswehr, Grup-penführer Josef 'Sepp' Dietrich. This was 'SS Headquarters Guard Berlin', renamed at the September 1933 Nuremberg Rally 'Leibstandarte Adolf Hitler' (Life Guard Regiment 'Adolf Hitler'). This unit actually received proper training from a regiment of the Reichswehr in Potsdam and it soon assumed responsibility for acting as Hitler's bodyguard and for providing sentries within the Reichs Chancellery and on ceremonial occasions.

Once Himmler had eliminated the SA leadership to his Führer's sat-isfaction, Hitler was prepared, to a limited degree, to fall in with his plans to expand the SS as a military force. With the grudging agreement of the Army, Himmler was to be allowed to raise three regiments of militarized SS troops, under the name 'SS-Verfügungstruppe' (SS-VT), tasked with the role of providing internal security for the Nazi regime. To command this new force, he assembled a motley collection of ex-Reichswehr officers and NCOs with sufficient know-how to weld what were, essentially, gangs of politically motivated thugs into a disciplined military organization. As things turned out, the SS-VT were to initiate an entirely new way of fighting wars.

The man who assumed responsibility for training the SS-VT was a retired Lieutenant-General of the Reichswehr, SS-Standartenführer Paul Hausser. Virtually his first act was to open a school for SS officer cadets at a castle near Braunschweig (Brunswick). Here SS men were drilled in the timeless training methods and regulations of the old German regular army, but at the same time Hausser and his instructors strove to inculcate a strong *élan* into their cadets: SS officers were to be stronger, harder and more ruthless than their Wehrmacht counterparts; field-training exercises were more realistic, often involving the limited use of live ammunition; the SS-VT developed and wore camouflaged clothing before it was commonplace; and relationships between officers and other ranks were much closer and were based on mutual respect for each other's skills rather than any notion of class. But above and beyond all that, it was hammered into the SS cadets, and into all SS-VT recruits, that they were, first and last, political soldiers and that National Socialism was their creed.

Shortly after Hausser launched the Braunschweig school, the SS-VT regiments themselves began to come into being. The 'Deutschland' Regiment was formed in Munich, followed by the 'Germania' Regiment in Hamburg, and finally the 'Der Führer' Regiment in Vienna after the Anschluss. Under Hausser the SS-VT units could easily have become a sort of politicized replica of the Reichswehr, but their training was taken in hand by a young ex-Army officer whose experiences on the Western Front in the latter part of the First World War had persuaded him that something different was needed to win a modern war. Felix Steiner was the man who moulded the SS-VT into what was later described as 'a force of military athletes';[6] he himself explained that he wanted 'a supple, adaptable type of soldier, athletic of bearing, capable of more than average endurance on the march and in combat',[7] and having achieved this he organized the SS-VT regiments into the small battle-groups, armed with automatic weapons that had had such an impact in the trenches in the last months of the First World War.

But despite the radical nature of the SS-VT, it wasn't until August 1938 that it had more than a tenuous grip on existence. Until that time, as the result of continuous pressure from the Reichswehr generals, Hitler had been forced to ban any further expansion by Himmler's troops: they could not be organized into a division; and they were forbidden from obtaining artillery. Hitler had even had to concede that, in the event of the outbreak of war, the SS-VT would either be placed under the control of the Army in formed units or even broken up and used for the reinforcement of Army units.

The situation for the SS-VT changed decisively as a result of events which took place in February 1938. In that month the anti-Nazi Commander-in-Chief of the Reichswehr, General von Fritsch, together with the Reich Minister of War, Field Marshal von Blomberg, were both ousted as the result of sex scandals (in which, it has to be said, the SS had taken a gleeful part). The Army was seriously weakened as a political force to the extent that Himmler could persuade Hitler to sign a decree stating that the SS-VT were recognized as a permanent force in both peace and war.

Even though the SS-VT had arrived on the scene as a 'permanent' force, the Army still had one powerful weapon up its sleeve in its campaign to prevent the emergence of a rival force: control of the conscription administration. The reintroduction of universal military service in Germany in 1935 was part of Hitler's repudiation of the terms of the Versailles Treaty, which had limited the strength of Germany's regular army to 100,000 men. Hitler correctly surmised that his plans for a strengthened and reunited Reich could not be carried through with such a small force, and by conscripting young men he was able to create a large pool of trained soldiers ready to take up the challenge of expansion within Europe. For the SS, however, this could have been something of a disaster: SS members outside the SS-VT were not, at that stage, considered part of the armed forces, and were as liable to be called up for duty as anyone else. Consequently SS men of military age almost all found themselves in the Wehrmacht. The man who solved this crisis for Himmler was, in 1938, the head of his recruiting office: SS-Brigadeführer Gottlob Berger.

Berger shared Himmler's dream of an armed SS force (Waffen-SS: the name began to be used at about this time) being created in parallel to the regular armed forces and as an eventual replacement for them. Beyond Himmler's wistful hopes, however, Berger had the cunning and administrative drive to do something concrete about it. Outside the SS-VT, Berger contrived to arrange that certain parts of the SS empire – namely the concentration camp guards and sections of the police – were exempted from military service on the grounds that they would be needed to reinforce the SS-VT in time of war. From this starting point, he was able to raise, on paper at least, two divisions of troops without infringing the Wermacht's recruiting restrictions: the SS-Totenkopf division and the SS-Polizei division.

The Waffen-SS units performed reasonably enough during the campaigns in Poland and France for the Wehrmacht grudgingly to accept them as part of the German order of battle, but the Army's leaders were still loath to allow Berger to take more than a minuscule percentage of the annual draft. To counteract this, Berger hit on the idea of tapping a source of potential soldiers that was totally closed to the Wehrmacht: foreigners. In fact individual foreigners had been allowed to enlist in the

SS since 1938. It was a policy that sprang from Himmler's belief in the value of 'Germanic' blood and his desire to unite 'Germans' from all over the world. Germans who happened to be nationals of other countries, like Thomas Cooper, were not to be barred from membership of Himmler's élite order simply because they held the wrong passport, and by May 1940 over a hundred foreigners (the largest contingent was forty-two Swiss; there were five Americans and one Englishman – Cooper) were serving in various parts of the SS empire.[8]

Berger's ambitions went much further than a gaggle of foreign Nazis, however. Throughout Central Europe and the Balkans there were hundreds of thousands of ethnic Germans (known to Nazi racial theorists as 'Volksdeutsche'), many of whom were intoxicated by Hitler's conquests. Berger planned to recruit as many of these as he could, with or without the consent of their governments, in order to expand his burgeoning army; with their strict recruiting quotas of 'real' Germans ('Reichsdeutsche') untouched, the Wehrmacht could only watch in impotence. Through these means, by the end of the war over 310,000 Volksdeutsche were serving in the Waffen-SS.[9]

The fall of Western Europe in the spring and summer of 1940 also had implications for SS recruiting. At first the Wehrmacht reduced its ground forces, the Waffen-SS losing three regiments of Totenkopf troops, but with Hitler's decision to begin planning for the invasion of the Soviet Union, a doubling in the number of Army panzer and motorized infantry divisions were envisaged. Despite Hitler's insistence that the Waffen-SS remained a political force whose primary duty was internal security tasks, he authorized Himmler to raise a further division (in addition to the SS-VT, Totenkopf and Polizei divisions, and the Leibstandarte which was of brigade strength), provided that its manpower was mainly foreign.

The main body of recruits for Himmler's new division, which was given the name 'Wiking', was found from Volksdeutsche volunteers but there was sufficient interest from young National Socialists in the occupied countries of North-West Europe for Berger to set up recruiting offices in the conquered capitals. The rationale behind this was that many of the western European ethnic groups were, in the eyes of Himmler and his racial theorists, essentially of Germanic or Nordic blood, and he was quite prepared to stretch a point, in the interests of expanding the Waffen-SS, to accept that Dutchmen, Flemings, Danes, Norwegians, Swedes and Swiss met the previously strict SS recruiting requirements. This was an important point; up to the end of 1940 the only foreigners accepted were those who were of strictly German ancestry; after this time, German-ness became a flexible concept, essentially applied by Himmler to any racial group who spoke a German-related language and who tended to be fair-skinned, tall and blond.

Foreign volunteers who came forward for service with the Waffen-SS during the autumn and winter of 1940 and spring 1941 were, by and large, incorporated into the 'Nordland' and 'Westland' regiments of the Wiking division (Nordland was intended for Danes and Norwegians, Westland for Dutchmen and Flemings), though they were not specifically segregated by nationality. However, the recruiters soon found that the early rush of volunteers dwindled to a trickle and it became apparent that those who had joined simply represented the combative fringe of the minority in Western Europe whose admiration for Germany and Nazism was great enough to overcome their natural loyalty to their defeated homelands. In fact by May 1941 the Wiking division contained a mere 1142 'Germanic' volunteers: 630 Dutchmen, 294 Norwegians, 216 Danes, one Swede and one Swiss.[10]

The situation was dramatically altered by the German invasion of the Soviet Union on 22 June 1941. Right-wing 'patriots' in countries occupied by the Germans, and anti-Communists in other neutral countries, were able to convince themselves (with the aid, of course, of German propaganda) that Hitler's action was the first step in a crusade against Bolshevism, and offers of help began to pour in to German diplomatic offices from individuals and organizations anxious to play their part. On 29 June Hitler gave his assent to the formation of 'Legions' of foreign volunteers to fight against the Russians.[11]

Foreign Legions have, of course, played a significant role in warfare for many hundreds of years. In the Middle Ages it was common for the rulers of states to employ units of foreign mercenaries and the tradition has persisted. George III deployed Hessian mercenaries during the American War of Independence, Napoleon maintained his Polish Lancers, the

Pope his Swiss Guards, and even today Britain maintains a brigade of Nepalese Gurkhas as an integral, and widely respected, part of the British Army. France, of course, still retains the services of its Foreign Legion, though there is a slight difference inasmuch as the *Légionnaires* are not segregated by nationality. The novelty of the German acquisition of foreign units for the war against Soviet Russia, however, was that the common cause of those who volunteered for them was not, usually, material advantage – they were, in the main, joined in fervid anti-Communism.

In order to co-ordinate and settle a policy for the use of foreign volunteers, the German Foreign Office called a conference on 30 June 1941, which was also attended by representatives of the Wehrmacht High Command (OKW), the Waffen-SS co-ordination office (SS-Führungshauptamt) and the Foreign Section of the Nazi party (Auslandsorganisation der NSDAP). It was decided that, if enough volunteers came forward, 'national' contingents would be recruited by the Waffen-SS and the Wehrmacht to fight in German uniform (though bearing distinctive badges), under the same pay and conditions as German soldiers, as part of the German armed forces though, where possible, directly commanded by officers of their own nationality. The Waffen-SS was given responsibility for 'Germanic' recruits and the Wehrmacht for all others, including Frenchmen, Walloons (French-speaking Belgians) and the Spanish division that was already being formed.

The Waffen-SS set to work organizing four separate national contingents for their volunteers to serve in: the 'Legion Niederlande', the 'Legion Flandern', the 'Legion Norwegen' and the 'Freikorps Danmark'. Recruits did not come forward in enormous numbers, but even so the Dutch Legion was eventually able to field a force of a little over 2000 men, whilst the others amounted to over 1000 men each. By contrast, the non-Germanic Légion des Volontaires Français within the Wehrmacht achieved a strength of nearly 6000 men, despite having turned down more than that number as unsuitable.

The recruitment of foreigners did not represent a particularly significant increase in combat power as far as the German armed forces as a whole were concerned, but for the Waffen-SS, still labouring under the strict recruiting ceilings imposed by the Wehrmacht, they were a considerable boon. At the same time, the notion of a 'European Crusade against Bolshevism' became one of the most significant themes of German propaganda, and the foreign legions represented tangible evidence of its accuracy. Recruiters for the legions swiftly realized that anti-Communism represented a train of thought sufficiently powerful to overcome dislike of Nazism and/or German occupation for many young, right-wing men in the conquered countries. They also offered anti-German propagandists pause for thought in their claims that Hitler was simply conducting a war of domination in Europe – after all, the legion recruiters could ask, if that was the case why were so many patriotic young Europeans joining the German armed forces?

Himmler and Berger both conceived an enthusiasm for using non-German troops that remained unabated until the end of the war. Berger himself stated: 'The Germanic volunteers in the Waffen-SS . . . will one day form the foundation upon which the Germanic empire will be built',[12] and within his SS-Hauptamt* he formed a new department, the 'Germanische Leitstelle' (GL [Germanic Administration]), to co-ordinate all matters relating to the Germanic recruits; also setting up out-stations in the Hague, Brussels, Oslo and Copenhagen.

The foundation of the GL and the search for foreign recruits was to have a strange effect upon the Waffen-SS. There were many members of the Nazi party and the SS for whom the more gross excesses of Nazi racial theory held no attraction. Even as, with the Russian campaign in full swing, SS and police units began the systematic elimination of the Jewish population of Eastern Europe, some Nazis began to doubt the truth of Nazi 'untermensch' propaganda. What the Waffen-SS had found in Russia was an enemy who fought hard, courageously and intelligently – certainly not the ape-like sub-humans that they had been led to expect – and they also saw that their non-German allies and legionaries could do

---

* The SS-Hauptamt (literally 'Head Office') was the administrative hub of the SS empire. Berger had taken it over in 1940, incorporating his recruiting department. As the war continued, its principle function became the provision of reinforcements to Waffen-SS divisions in the field and the formation of new Waffen-SS units. Although he had no command role, and was widely disliked amongst the hierarchy of the Waffen-SS, Berger was very much the 'father' of the Waffen-SS.

the same. The GL became a kind of rallying point for National Socialists who adopted a geo-political outlook: they agreed with the concept of German hegemony in western and central Europe, but they saw a need for a doctrine which accepted that the other races of Europe should have some form of outlet for their national aspirations. This was a train of thought fundamentally at odds with Hitler's concept of Europe as an entity completely subordinated to the needs and wishes of Germany, and it was one that the Führer was very keen to suppress. Nevertheless it became, to a limited extent, the orthodoxy within the hierarchy of the Waffen-SS and it was a principal cause of the breach between Hitler and his SS troops in the last days of the war.

The campaign in the Soviet Union in 1942 and the first half of 1943 proved to be a bloody baptism for the foreign legions. The small size of the units and the limited number of volunteers who came forward after the initial rush meant that the considerable numbers of casualties they suffered took a greater toll on their effectiveness than on comparable German formations. Nevertheless, the legions acquitted themselves well as fighting units and proved to be a valuable propaganda tool into the bargain by exciting a limited amount of enthusiasm in their homelands. Even so, it was clear in the spring of 1943 that the legions could not continue and they were withdrawn from combat on the Eastern Front for reorganization. The plan was simple: Himmler wanted to form a 'Germanic' Panzer Corps by combining the Wiking division with the legions, who would be formed into a new division, fully integrated into the Waffen-SS, called 'Nordland'. Despite the misgivings of some of the legionaries, who wanted to continue serving in purely national con-tingents, this scheme went ahead (legionaries who refused to serve on in the Nordland division were, by and large, allowed to return home).

From 1943 onwards, all 'foreign' units raised under the auspices of the GL were fully integrated into the Waffen-SS, a policy which left the racial exclusivity of the SS as a whole in ruins. Himmler had recognized that his ability to provide soldiers for the Eastern Front was a means by which he could increase his influence and favour with the Führer who, certainly after the fall of Stalingrad, had begun to see the writing on the wall. The strict racial criteria that had characterized the early Waffen-SS soldiers were simply brushed aside for the sake of expediency.

Even so, the first purely foreign division of the Waffen-SS represented an extraordinary change of policy. In February 1943 Hitler gave his permission for Himmler to raise a division recruited entirely from Bosnian Muslims. Even though they are of European rather than Arab extraction, they were a bizarre sight, dressed in a uniform that included a red fez with the SS eagle and skull insignia. The rationale behind the division was that the Bosnians were gripped by an ancestral loathing of the Christian Serbs who made up the bulk of Tito's partisans and showed a propensity to commit atrocities against them whenever possible; but many SS veterans found the thought of 'untermenschen' in SS uniform utterly abhorrent. Nevertheless, the formation of the Bosnian SS division allowed Himmler and Berger to drop their psychological inhibitions towards non-'Germanic' recruits in the SS, and during the next two years virtually every ethnic group within Europe and western Asia found representation within the Waffen-SS and the GL.

Thus the GL, under its first commander, SS-Obersturmbannführer Riedweg, a Swiss doctor, became the focus for nationalists from throughout Europe who were concerned by the prospect of a Soviet takeover of their countries, and it met them with the assurance that service in the Waffen-SS might form the most concrete means by which such an eventuality could be prevented. But in this the SS pan-Europeans were being disingenuous; they were fully aware that Hitler had utterly prohibited the fostering of nationalist sentiments amongst the conquered peoples of both east and west and was really only keen to use them as soldiers for his own, and Germany's, purposes. Hitler had no intention of granting self-government to any of the conquered nations, whatever the outcome of the war, and the increasing number of foreigners coming into the Waffen-SS were being recruited by fraud.

By the end of the war, of the little over 900,000 men in the Waffen-SS significantly more than half were born outside the borders of Germany. Aside from the Volksdeutsche and the 'Germanic' western Europeans, nationalities included Latvians, Lithuanians, Estonians, Spaniards, Frenchmen, Walloons, Italians, Byelorussians, Ruthenians, Azerbaijanis, Armenians, Bosnians, Albanians, Georgians, Crimeans, Turkomen,

Cossacks, Ukrainians, and even, perhaps most bizarrely of all, the 'Free Indian Legion', recruited from British Indian Army troops captured in North Africa (see Appendix 4, p. 212). Foreign units thus formed a very significant portion of the fighting power of the German armed forces as a whole and can be seen as one of the principal levers by which Himmler made himself one of the most powerful figures in the Third Reich.

This then is the context within which the Waffen-SS took responsibility for the attempt to found a British unit to fight in Russia. Amery's concept, essentially self-aggrandizing, was for a propaganda unit with himself playing the role of leader; and this might have been what attracted Hitler to the idea in the first instance. But by the time that Berger started the ball rolling in the autumn of 1943, German manpower needs on the Eastern Front were running out of control and only likely to increase. A British Regiment or Brigade on the Eastern Front would be a useful addition, with the extra impact of a propaganda value out of all proportion to its size. This was the attitude of the SS hierarchy to the 'Legion of St George'.

7

John Brown
and the
Genshagen Experiment

How do you raise a military formation from amongst the ranks of your enemies? That was the question troubling the German authorities in the summer of 1943. Notwithstanding the fact that there were undoubtedly British men and women who sympathized with the Nazi cause to some extent, the Germans knew full well that the vast majority of them were interned in the United Kingdom, kicking their heels pending the outcome of the war. Nevertheless it was reasonable to assume that there would be some sympathizers amongst the thousands of prisoners that they had captured during the first three years of the war; but how could they identify them?

John Amery's original recruiting scheme for the 'Legion of St George' presented to the German Foreign Office in October 1942 had envisaged a recruiting campaign amongst British prisoners of war only after an extensive propaganda campaign had taken place. As far as Amery himself was concerned, it was enough for him, representing himself as the delegate of 'a committee in England', to visit POW and civilian internment camps and make his pitch. But as we have seen, Amery only succeeded in collecting four volunteers at the St Denis camp and becoming the object of much derisive scorn. Dr Hesse and his England Committee were far more hard-headed; they realized that a more subtle form of indoctrination was necessary and they also believed that it was essential to isolate potential renegades from their comrades in the main Stalags. Their solution was ingenious: they decided to set up a holiday camp for prisoners.

Post-war books and films about life in POW camps in Germany have, by and large, succeeded in creating a very false impression of what conditions were actually like. *The Great Escape, The Wooden Horse* and their ilk have managed to foster the idea that prisoners enjoyed conditions that were not dissimilar to life in a British public school. It would be easy to gain the impression that life for the POWs consisted of an endless circuit of choir practice, amateur theatricals and escape attempts, fuelled by the tempting contents of parcels from home and from the Red Cross. In reality, it was very different.

There were several different types of POW camp, all of which came within the framework of the German attempts to subvert and recruit prisoners. The basic camp for other ranks, i.e. warrant officers and below, was the *Stammlager*, usually shortened to 'Stalag'. These were large compounds which often contained many thousands of prisoners who would be engaged on work in the local area, transit between working parties and the administration, from the prisoners' point of view, of dependent sub-camps. Normally commanded by a junior (in rank, at least) German officer, the leading prisoner, who would typically be a warrant officer, was known as the 'man of confidence'. Stalags were numbered according to a scheme that usually followed the number of the Wehrmacht Military District in which they were situated – so that, for example, Stalags in the Berlin area had the number III (e.g. Stalag IIIa at Luckenwalde, Stalag IIId at Steglitz). Each Stalag supported, in addition to the main camp, a group of satellite working parties or *Arbeitskommandos*, in which NCOs and private soldiers were put to work, often as agricultural labourers, miners, navvies and so on (privates were obliged to work for their captors but could not be used in work that was 'dangerous' or directly connected to the war effort; NCOs were supposed to supervise them). They were dependent on the Stalags for medical support, mail, Red Cross parcels and other administration, but generally members of the Arbeitskommandos were accommodated close to their workplace and they would elect their own man of confidence. As far as the Germans were concerned, it was usually sufficient to place an NCO in command of a handful of guards for security purposes.

The other main type of POW camp was the *Offizierlager* or Oflag. Usually much smaller than Stalags, they conformed much more to the fictional image of POW camps for the simple reason that officers were not under any obligation to work. Whilst this may not seem too disagreeable an existence, officer prisoners were generally kept on shorter rations than other ranks and had to fight continuously against the mind-numbing boredom of their inactivity; and the theatres that the Oflags possessed, as well as limited sporting facilities, were recognized by both sides as a way of alleviating the tedium and keeping the officers happy.

Then there were special camps for particular categories: Stalag Luft for airmen, the Ilag for civilian internees, and the unique Marlag/Milag camp at Westertimke near Bremen which was reserved for sailors of the naval and merchant fleets. Finally there were punishment camps: Straflager. These camps were reserved for POWs who had committed infractions against German military law, to which they were subject, and for persistent escapees. Probably the most famous was Oflag IV c, Colditz, but there were several others, normally situated as special compounds within larger camps where prisoners were subjected to harsher discipline and harder work for short periods. For particularly heinous crimes, the Germans also had the option of consigning POWs to German military prisons like Fort Zinna at Torgau and Graudenz; and ultimately there were the Concentration Camps.

Conditions varied between the camps, but virtually everywhere it became a struggle for survival. Most prisoners found themselves in unsanitary, overcrowded accommodation that was bitterly cold in winter and uncomfortably hot in summer. They were often inadequately clothed, having lost much of their equipment and spare gear on capture; and, of course, almost all had been subject to the severe physical and emotional trauma associated with combat, a large percentage having been wounded at the time they were taken prisoner. The Geneva Convention required that POWs be fed rations equivalent to those received by 'Depot Troops' but this was rarely the case. The food situation in Germany was such that, from the very start, most prisoners received just about enough food to keep them alive, although the parcels that were received from the Red Cross provided a welcome bonus.

Discipline amongst the prisoners could also be a problem. In the main Stalags it was often the responsibility of comparatively junior warrant officers who were faced with the task of administering thousands more men than they were accustomed to. This was, perhaps, not so difficult for the more experienced regular soldiers of the pre-war army, but as time passed and war-service conscripts achieved ranks that would normally be reserved for men with far longer service, discipline inevitably suffered and several camps became the preserve of violent razor-gangs formed by hard men from the ghettos of the big cities.

This then was the situation that the Germans hoped to exploit when they announced, in the summer of 1943, that they were to establish two holiday camps for prisoners who had spent long periods in captivity. They were unusual from the start in that, while they were administered and staffed by the POW directorate of the OKW, they were under formal command of the German Foreign Office's England Committee and their special representative, Arnold Hillen-Ziegfeld.

Hillen-Ziegfeld was a writer and cartographer who had spent the First World War as an internee on the Isle of Man. During the 1920s he became prominent amongst a group of conservative geopolitical theorists within the Weimar Republic, and as a result, after the Nazi seizure of power he was given a job within the literature section of the Propaganda Ministry. There he wrote two books, *England – The Hereditary Foe* and *Germany – Conscience of Europe*, which allowed him to achieve a certain reputation as an anti-British propagandist.' By 1943, however, Hillen-Ziegfeld's star was on the wane within the Propaganda Ministry, largely as the result of his haughty and arrogant manner, and he was foisted on to the England Committee because of his supposed expertise on British affairs. There he was employed in organizing the propaganda campaign amongst the British POWs.

The two holiday camps were both initially set up in the Berlin area as dependent camps of Stalag IIId: the officers' camp (Special Detachment 999) in a villa on the Kaunstrasse in Zehlendorf, the soldiers' camp (Special Detachment 517) in the suburb of Genshagen. Staff for both camps were selected from amongst German personnel with a thorough knowledge of the English language, and both were placed, for security purposes, under the Abwehr officer with responsibility for counter-intelligence work in POW camps, Major Heimpel. Heimpel's first task, particularly in relation to Genshagen, was to find a suitable NCO to act as the man of confidence in a camp that was, at this stage, specifically being established as a conduit for volunteers for the Legion of St George. Heimpel thought that he knew the ideal man. Battery Quartermaster Sergeant John Henry Owen Brown of the Royal Artillery.

For many British POWs John Brown was a very controversial figure. During his captivity, it appeared to almost all the British POWs that he came into contact with that, if he wasn't actively collaborating with the Germans, then he was certainly their dupe. In truth he was playing a very dangerous double game. Before the war John Brown was an office manager at Truman's Brewery in Surrey. A graduate of Oxford University, he had been a member of the BUF but also a convinced Christian; it was a combination of his cleverness, his Christianity and his Fascist credentials that would allow him to survive five years of German captivity more or less unscathed. He was captured by the Germans on 29 May 1940 as his regiment evacuated, helter-skelter, towards Dunkirk and safety. From Belgium he was marched, along with thousands of others, all the way to Trier on Germany's western border, from where he was loaded on to a cattle-truck and transported to Stalag VIIIb at Lamsdorff. From there he was moved to Arbeitskommando E/3 at Blechhammer, a site where the Germans used a total of 20,000 POWs and detainees of various nationalities to build a factory for artificial oil and rubber.

As a senior NCO, Brown was made foreman of a group of about thirty prisoners engaged on heavy construction tasks, and thus avoided too much manual labour himself. Nevertheless he sought, through the good offices of the camp interpreter, a Mancunian sergeant called Arthur Edge, to ingratiate himself as far as possible with the Germans. In his posthumously published autobiography,[2] he wrote that prior to his capture he had attended a special MI6 course designed to teach potential POWs how to communicate with home from their camps, and that he had started sending coded messages soon after he was caught; he claimed that his good relationship with the Germans was cultivated entirely in order to furnish himself with intelligence information to send home. However this claim was completely untrue. In a statement that he made in October 1945, Brown said that he started sending information back to Britain only from 'about the end of 1942'.[3]

In fact what Brown was doing was setting up a highly profitable black market racket. Using contacts amongst foreign workers on the building site and guards bribed with Red Cross luxuries, he was able to smuggle large amounts of contraband goods into the POW camp which he then distributed amongst the inmates. He obtained a radio set with which he was able to get BBC news bulletins, civilian clothing, extra food, tobacco and alcohol; all of which served to keep the prisoners on his side whilst, as an insurance policy, he was sycophantic enough to the Germans for them to believe that he was a genuine supporter of the Nazi cause.

He continued his successful black market operation until February 1942, when he was informed by the commandant at Blechhammer that he was being taken to Berlin for questioning. He travelled via Lamsdorff, where his reputation as a suspected collaborator had preceded him, to the headquarters of Stalag IIId at Steglitz in Berlin where he was met by Major Heimpel. From there he was sent to a house in a residential suburb of Berlin overlooking the Spree, where he found a small group of various nationalities.

The reason Brown had been sent to Berlin was to assess his suitability as a potential renegade. Whilst he was there he was interviewed by William Joyce, whom he had known by sight from before the war, and he was also present at a meeting where Joyce and others attempted to gain members for the 'Indian Legion' of the Wehrmacht which was then in the process of formation. He made a good enough impression to be allowed out for walks about town with a guard and he seems to have tried to continue with his comparatively luxurious life-style for as long as possible, but in August 1942 he was sent back to Blechhammer and the inevitable suspicions of his fellow prisoners.

Whilst in Berlin Brown had entrusted his black market operation to Gunner Newcomb who came from his own unit, and it had continued to be a big success, so much so that with the profits Brown was able to buy surgical equipment for the camp medical officer, a New Zealander called John Borrie, together with instruments for the camp band.

Towards the end of 1942 a new dental officer was sent to Blechhammer. Captain Julius Green was a Jewish Glaswegian who had successfully concealed his religion, enabling him to stay with the general POW population. According to Brown, ' "friend Julius" was just like a bull in a china shop; even the sergeant-majors seemed shocked at his behaviour.'[4] In fact Green was concealing a secret. He had been taught the codes which MI9 (not MI6 as Brown assumed) had developed for POWs to communicate home with, and recognizing that Brown was a canny operator he passed them on to him. It was at this time that Brown became a 'self-made spy' as he was later to describe himself.

Brown was keen to get himself back to Berlin and the comfortable existence at Stalag IIId, and now that he had a way of communicating intelligence to England he had an excellent excuse to do so. In consequence, he engineered an enormous row with his fellow senior NCOs at Blechhammer and then approached the Commandant, Rittmeister Prinz zu Höhenlöhe, with whom he was very friendly, and requested a transfer to Berlin. His request was granted, and on 12 June 1943 he was transferred back to Stalag IIId, and from there to a small hutted camp near the Gross Buren railway station: Genshagen.

The camp itself consisted of eighteen rooms, a wash-house and a concert hall, built around a field which would have been a good football pitch had it not been criss-crossed with air-raid trenches. The German in charge of the camp, Sonderführer Oskar Lange, was already known to Brown from Lamsdorff where he was called 'Canadian Joe' by the prisoners; actually Lange had been selected because of his high intelligence and fluent English, learned during his career as a longshoreman in New York. Brown was to be the British camp leader. By the time he arrived the Germans had already installed the handful of prisoners who were to become the nucleus of the British renegade legion. A few weeks later he also met a young man who, at this time, spoke only German and was going about in the company of Lange, wearing the uniform of an Unterscharführer in the Waffen-SS. He said that his name was Thomas Böttcher; as Brown soon realized, Böttcher is the German for 'Cooper'.

Despite the fact that he was very much in the minds of the England Committee and the SS-Hauptamt, Cooper's arrival at Genshagen was the result of a coincidence. After he had been wounded at Schablinov, he was evacuated back to the small town of Bad Muskau not far from Görlitz where he entered a military hospital. The presence in the town of an English NCO in the Waffen-SS became a 'nine-day wonder' in the local area, and on 1 June whilst he was drinking with some friends in a local bar, he encountered someone from the town who was very keen to make his acquaintance: Sonderführer Oskar Lange.

Cooper left Bad Muskau on 6 June to go to Berlin for fourteen days' leave but Lange was already at work, alerting Hillen-Ziegfeld to Cooper's presence and setting the gears in motion to engineer his transfer to Genshagen. Whilst he was on leave, Cooper was summoned to see Hesse at the England Committee's offices on the Von Der Heydt Strasse, where he was asked to write two pamphlets about National Socialism for distribution to British POWs. He did this and Hesse paid him 100 marks for his trouble. Cooper then finished his leave and travelled to Holland to join the convalescent company of his division in Nijmegen.

In Holland Cooper's wounds broke open and turned septic and he was returned to a hospital for a further five weeks, after which he was given another two weeks leave in Berlin. During this fortnight he was invited by Lange to visit the Genshagen camp, on condition that he didn't speak English to the inmates, and it was then that he met Brown for the first time. He went back two days later at Lange's request so that he could interview Francis Maton, a young commando NCO who had volunteered to join the Waffen-SS, and it was from this that he began to glean the purpose of the camp. As soon as his leave finished, he received a special order from the SS-Führungshauptamt, temporarily transferring him to the German Foreign Office for a 'special project' and he was given a briefing by Hesse outlining the purpose of Genshagen. He officially joined the staff on 1 September 1943.

John Brown had not been slow to realize that several of the prisoners in the camp had distinctly Fascist and pro-German attitudes, but he did not at first realize that the bulk of the first group of 'holidaymaking' prisoners that arrived had been specially selected by the German authorities because of their supposedly pro-Nazi outlook. As a 'self-made spy' at the centre of what was to become a matter of great concern to the military and intelligence authorities in Britain, he realized that he was in an ideal position both to hinder the German propaganda effort and to ensure that those prisoners who did arrive at Genshagen actually got a holiday from the harsh conditions in their base camps.

The group of prisoners who were at Genshagen when Brown arrived included several men who were subsequently to play an important role in the British volunteer unit which the Germans planned to form. Principal amongst them was a corporal from the New Zealand Expeditionary Force who had, in fact, been born in London: Roy Nicholas Courlander. Courlander was the illegitimate son of a young London woman who, in 1920, married a Jewish businessman of Lithuanian origin called Leonard Courlander who owned a copra plantation in the New Hebrides. He was adopted by Courlander after the marriage and sent to an English boarding school whilst his parents went to live on the plantation. In 1933 his parents divorced and Roy went to the New Hebrides to live with his adoptive father. On the outbreak of war he travelled to Auckland to enlist as a soldier and, after completing his training, served with the New Zealand division in the Western Desert and in Greece, where he was captured in April 1941.

For Courlander, imprisoned in Stalag XVIIId, the German attack on the Soviet Union in June 1941 provided an opportunity, as he saw it, to improve his conditions substantially and he took to posing as a white Russian émigré in the hope of obtaining his freedom. Despite an interview with a Gestapo official, to whom he volunteered to fight against the Soviets, he remained a POW, acting as the camp interpreter at Stalag XVIIIa from October 1941 onwards. Convinced of the inevitability of German victory, Courlander maintained his sycophantic mien towards the Germans throughout the next twenty months until, at the beginning of June 1943, he was selected to go to Genshagen. On his arrival in Berlin he was taken to meet John Amery, who explained the 'Legion of St George' scheme to him, and to Dr Hesse, who persuaded him that in the meantime he should make a few broadcasts for the Concordia Büro – a proposal to which he agreed with alacrity. He was given a pass and civilian clothes which allowed him to travel from Genshagen to the Rundfunkhaus in Berlin, and he continued to give broadcasts, whilst still notionally in a POW camp, for the next five months.

A man who was to become a close friend and collaborator of Courlander arrived at Genshagen at the same time and was part of the group that cleaned up the accommodation prior to the arrival of Brown. Francis Maton was a Territorial soldier in the Royal Artillery and a former member of the British Union. He was captured on Crete whilst serving as a corporal in 50 (Middle East) Commando after he was severely wounded in the legs. His pro-Fascist views brought him to the attention of the authorities at Stalag IVa, and in April 1943 he was moved to the interrogation centre at Luckenwalde where he was held for a month before being moved to a house in Berlin being used as a holding centre for potential broadcasters. At the house was a mixed group of men, including Walter Purdy, the naval officer broadcaster, Sergeant Arthur Chapple of the RASC, and Lieutenant-Colonel Stevenson of the South African army, all of whom were more or less in sympathy with the Germans (Stevenson had just been taken to see the site of the Soviet executions of Polish prisoners in the Katyn Woods). Maton went with Chapple to Genshagen at the beginning of June.

The last of the pro-Nazi British POWs to join the Genshagen 'staff' before Brown's arrival were William Charles Britten, a lance-corporal of the Royal Warwickshire Regiment who was serving in 4 Commando at the time of his capture in Suda Bay, Crete, in June 1941, and Frederick Lewis, an ex-BUF member who had been interned as a merchant seaman at Milag. Britten had held the job of camp tailor at his Arbeitskommando in Silesia and suffered from frequent bouts of malaria and jaundice which he had contracted in North Africa.

Having determined to interfere with the Germans' plan to propagandize POWs, and aware that he could not possibly trust the prisoners that he found in the camp on his arrival, Brown decided that he needed to assemble his own team of helpers at Genshagen to assist his efforts. His apparently pro-German outlook over several years had placed him in a very good standing with Hesse and Hillen-Ziegfeld of the England Committee, even if Major Heimpel, the counter-intelligence officer, entertained doubts, and Brown's requests to have specific prisoners sent to assist him were largely granted. Thus he obtained the services of Bombardier Blewitt, Driver Newcomb and several others from his former camp at Blechhammer, as well as Lance-Corporal Gordon Bowler, a medical orderly who was believed by the Germans to be sympathetic to their cause.

The first group of 200 prisoners arrived for their holiday in August, to be greeted by a strange situation. Most were intensely suspicious of the purpose of the camp, believing that they were being forced to take part in some form of propaganda stunt, and they found that the staff who greeted them were behaving extremely oddly. On the one hand, Brown and his confederates were organizing activities, sports and trips for them, doing their best to ensure that the prisoners received good food and had the opportunity to exchange old clothing and so forth; whilst on the other, Lange, Cooper, Courlander and the other pro-Germans were passing amongst them, seeking out former members of the BUF and other Fascist groups and apparently sounding them out about their views on the Soviet Union and Communism. The atmosphere rapidly became so sour that individual 'holidaymakers' began to ask to be returned to their base camps. Ziegfeld and Hesse realized that they had a problem on their hands and came up with an ingenious solution: through the OKW, they requested that the senior British POW, Major-General Fortune, who had been captured with his 51st Highland Division at St Valery-en-Caux in 1940, send a personal representative to inspect the Genshagen camp to see that nothing untoward was being done.

General Fortune's selected delegate was Brigadier Leonard Parrington, late of the Royal Artillery. Born in 1890, Parrington became an officer in the regular army just before the outbreak of the First World War. He was captured in Greece in April 1941 along with some 8,000 other troops abandoned on the evacuation beach at Kalamata. He visited Genshagen in August 1943 and spoke to all the prisoners, permanent and 'holidaymaking', at a parade after he had looked at the facilities. In the course of his speech Parrington remarked that he 'knew the purpose of the camp' and that the inmates were not to worry; he also gave them permission to go on 'parole' walks around Berlin with German guards.

In fact Parrington did not know the purpose of the camp and had taken it at face value as a rest centre. In the atmosphere of mistrust and hostility that prevailed, Brown had not confided his suspicions to Parrington and the brigadier remained oblivious to the Germans' intentions; nevertheless his remark was sufficient to convince Courlander and several of his fantasist cronies that Parrington knew of, and approved, their activities.

Parrington's visit cleared the air at Genshagen and most of the inmates were able to enjoy their break from the hard work of the Arbeitskommandos, yet Lange, Cooper and Courlander continued their efforts as assiduously as before. By the time that the first group of prisoners were ready to leave, they had succeeded in persuading one definite defector to join them and planted seeds in the minds of several others. The first recruit was a merchant seaman from Surrey, Alfred Vivian Minchin, who had been taken prisoner by a German destroyer after his ship, the SS *Empire Ranger*, was sunk by German bombers off Norway as part of a Murmansk convoy. Interned at Milag, he was persuaded to go to Genshagen by Frederick Lewis, the ex-BUF member, along with five other prisoners. He volunteered to join the renegade legion after a long talk with Cooper and Lange, during the course of which he was shown a number of colour posters and pamphlets and told that 'there were quite a few men'[5] in the unit already and that they would have a 'marvellous time'.[6] Minchin later said: 'Cooper did not tell me what the aims of the Legion were and they were never laid down at any time. I thought it was just a propaganda unit in order to bring Germany and England together. I decided to join to find out what Germany was really like.'[7]

One of Minchin's companions from Milag, Douglas Maylin, also decided to join, but for some reason fell foul of Cooper, who used his influence with Major Heimpel to prevent him from enlisting in the embryonic legion. Lance-Corporal William How of the Military Police listened to the recruiter but he did not decide to join until the spring of 1944.

The full implications of the recruiting project were finally leaked to Brown towards the end of September 1943. Carl Britten, to whom Brown had given the job of camp librarian, fell ill with a recurrence of his malaria and was not expected to live. In fact he did survive, nursed back to health by Brown and 'Don' Bowler, the medical orderly, but while he was convalescing Brown felt that he had established a close enough bond with the renegade to pump him for information. Britten told him everything, but when Brown tried to talk him out of joining, claimed that he was being forced into it by Courlander and Cooper. Even though he had failed to dissuade Britten, Brown was now in a position to make a startling report by coded letter to MI9. For their part, MI9 passed the information to MI5 who began monitoring the fledgling legion.

Shortly after the first draft of prisoners left Genshagen, and as Brown and his circle were preparing the camp for the next batch, an air raid on Berlin destroyed a large section of the camp. This immediately threw the Germans' plans into confusion; there was clearly going to be a con-siderable delay before the propaganda work could continue, and they decided, for security reasons, to move the first group of renegades away from the camp as soon as possible.

In the meantime, two more volunteers arrived to join the 'Legion of St George'. The first was Francis George MacLardy, a pharmacist from Liverpool. Born in Waterloo, Liverpool, in 1915, he had left school at the age of eighteen and gone on to continue his studies at the Liverpool Technical College whilst being articled to a Formby chemist as a trainee pharmacist. He joined the Liverpool branch of the BUF in April 1934, eventually becoming the district secretary, although he ceased to be an active member of the party in September 1938. He qualified as a phar-macist in July 1939 and was called up for military service in the Royal Army Medical Corps in March 1940. Because of his technical quali-fications, MacLardy only did three weeks of basic training before being promoted to sergeant and sent to a unit in Kent. Shortly afterwards, on 9 May, they were sent across the channel to France.

On 31 May he was separated from his unit and captured by the Germans at Wormhoudt in Belgium. (Wormhoudt had been the scene, just three days before, of a massacre in which members of the 'Lieb-standarte' Waffen-SS regiment had summarily executed some eighty British POWs. MacLardy was lucky.) From there he was transferred to Stalag XXa at Thorn and then to XXId at Schildberg where he remained the pharmacist in the camp hospital until September 1943. In the summer of 1943 he suffered a series of illnesses and, it appears, became convinced that he would not survive 'another winter in Poland'.[8] His solution was to follow the example of a number of Dutch officers from his camp: he applied to join the Waffen-SS.

MacLardy arrived at Genshagen on 1 October, at much the same time as another volunteer, Edwin Barnard Martin, a Canadian from Riverside, Ontario. Martin was a private in the Canadian army's Essex Scottish Regiment who had been captured during the controversial raid on Dieppe in August 1942. He had started to collaborate with the Germans soon after his capture, and came to Genshagen from the nearby camp at Luckenwalde where he had been working on a related project.

The renegades were removed from Genshagen on 2 November and taken to a requisitioned café in the Pankow district of Berlin in the care of Wilhelm 'Bob' Rössler, a Wehrmacht interpreter. With him went Courlander, Lewis, Britten, MacLardy, Martin and Minchin; and they were joined, shortly afterwards, by Kenneth Berry, the one surviving recruit from Amery's trip to St Denis. Maton and Chapple had both declined for the time being to join the legion, and went instead to the Concordia Büro where they wrote and broadcast as 'Manxman' and 'Lang' on Radio National.

Genshagen camp continued to provide holidays for British POWs, and a comparatively soft life for Brown and his friends, until December 1944, but the clumsy handling by the Germans during the first few months forced them to discontinue their attempts to recruit prisoners for the renegade legion. As soon as the first batch of traitors had left, Brown was able to question Hillen-Ziegfeld, Cooper and Lange openly about its purpose and obtain an undertaking that the recruiting would stop. He did this by arguing that the recruiters were fostering suspicion and distrust of the purpose of the camp, which was counter-productive to the idea of persuading prisoners to adopt a more pro-German point of view. Incredibly, Hillen-Ziegfeld believed him. Cooper, however, remained at Genshagen until the end of December 1943, serving out his attachment to the Foreign Office and getting closer and closer to Brown. As he became more relaxed in Brown's company he confided to him that he had taken part in anti-Jewish atrocities and shot Russian POWs; and he also outlined his plans should Germany win the war: his intention was to become a Gauleiter and get his revenge on the people who had made him work for next to nothing before the war. As Brown later described him: 'He was just an immature boy trying to behave like a grown-up: but what a dangerous bugger to have around a camp like Genshagen!'[9]

Taken in isolation, the Genshagen scheme was a clever idea that might have netted a great many POWs for the renegade legion had it been handled more circumspectly. The greatest flaw in the project was the Germans' selection of personnel; had they been able to attract a renegade with Brown's intelligence but who was a wholehearted Fascist or National Socialist, Genshagen would have been a far more dangerous place for British POWs to visit. As it was, 'their' man was a calculating racketeer, certainly interested in his own comfort but loyal enough to take the considerable risks that his activities as an intelligence source exposed him to. In the year after the renegades left Genshagen, he was able to take advantage of his trusty status and roam Berlin virtually at will, acquiring a girlfriend and socializing with Cooper, and even John Amery when he was in town. The work that he did on behalf of Allied intelligence was later recognized by the award of the Distinguished Conduct Medal, part of the citation for which read:

Realizing the Germans intended to use Genshagen Holiday Camp for their own ends, Battery Quartermaster Sergeant John Henry Owen Brown determined to thwart them. Despite the very real danger involved, he pretended to be working for the Germans, whilst at the same time he was really using the comparative freedom accorded to him to further the cause of the Allies . . .

Acting as he did on his own initiative, he fully realized that in all probability he might be suspected of betraying his own country. This did in fact happen, but it has now been established that he did acquire and transmit to this country valuable information.

Through his continuous efforts, the British Free Corps, which the Germans hoped to expand from the men sent to Genshagen, gained few recruits and eventually the project became a complete failure.[10]

8

Luckenwalde: The Intimidators

The recruiting hiatus caused by the bombing of Genshagen on 1 September did not last for long. Oskar Lange, the NCO in charge of the camp, saw in the Legion of St George the opportunity to enhance his own prestige and authority considerably by becoming the central figure in the recruiting of British traitors, and he hit upon an idea that would greatly increase the strength of the unit. Lange's scheme centred upon Stalag IIIa at Luckenwalde, a short distance away from Genshagen, where the Army High Command (OKH) maintained a special facility for the interrogation of newly-captured prisoners.

The Luckenwalde camp was quite similar to the Luftwaffe's interrogation centre at Dulag Luft in Oberursel near Frankfurt. At both camps the Germans maintained small, highly secret teams of traitors who were used to extract information from newly-captured, and hopefully (as far as the Germans were concerned) confused, prisoners. The special compound at Luckenwalde was presided over by Hauptmann Hellmerich, an Abwehr officer on the staff of OKH who had previously been based at Lamsdorff, assisted by his chief interrogator, Feldwebel Scharper.

Scharper controlled a team of renegades at Luckenwalde whose actions must place them, morally, as amongst the worst traitors of the war. The group initially comprised Edwin Martin of the Essex Scottish Regiment; John Gordon Galaher, a Canadian of the same regiment who was also captured at Dieppe; Private John Welch of the Durham Light Infantry; and Stoker Henry Herbert Rose of the Royal Navy. Rose became a captive of the Germans in March 1943 when his MT8 was sunk off the Dutch coast and he was imprisoned in Marlag Nord. In May he was approached by an American named Williams who was planning to escape in the company of another American called Scharper, and Rose agreed to exchange identities with him. Unfortunately both were provocateurs, and shortly afterwards Rose was taken from the camp and subjected to an extremely harsh interrogation. Unable to stand up to the threats of death and violence that he was subjected to, he eventually agreed to work for Scharper.

Welch was also the victim of an entrapment by Scharper. After his capture in Belgium in 1940 he worked as a carpenter on an Arbeits-kommando attached to Lamsdorff until, one day in 1943, whilst he was working alone in a sawmill, a young woman came in and inveigled him into having sex with her. Shortly afterwards he was arrested and brought in front of Scharper, who threatened him with execution unless he agreed to collaborate. Welch duly did so. Interestingly, Scharper continued to use sex as a psychological weapon against Welch: shortly after he was removed from Lamsdorff, he went with Scharper and Galaher to stay in a house near Luckenwalde where he was to be given further indoc-trination and training. At the house he discovered that he was to share a room with Scharper, a large ugly man who had to wear elastic bandages to relieve the pain of extensive varicose veins. During the first night, the girl who had entrapped Welch at the sawmill reappeared and tried to get into bed with him. Welch refused her advances and so she clambered into bed with Scharper and had sex with him instead.

The next day Welch, Scharper and the girl were in the garden of the house when another girl appeared and started to talk to them. With little preamble the second girl removed her clothes and made love with Scharper on the lawn in front of Welch and the first girl, to Welch's awestruck disgust. It is difficult to determine Scharper's precise motiv-ation for these bizarre acts; it is possible that he was trying to show Welch what a good time he could have as an informer, or alternatively it might have been an act to demonstrate Scharper's great power and machismo. Whatever the reason, for the informer team prostitutes and sexual oppor-tunity were reputedly to form a much larger part of their lives than for any other group of traitors.

Scharper's informer team was established around June 1943, and whilst they mostly worked at Luckenwalde, they were occasionally moved around for special operations; but the use that Lange envisaged and which he discussed with Hellmerich and Scharper in September 1943, meant that they could stay at their permanent base. It seemed to Lange that the POWs he was attempting to subvert at Genshagen were too settled and stable to convert easily. Most of the prisoners who arrived at the 'holiday camp' had been in captivity for three years or more; they were largely aware of the rules and regulations prescribed by the Geneva Convention, and they had a good idea how the Germans were likely to react to any given situation. Lange felt that it might be considerably easier to convert newly-captured prisoners by the simple expedient of frightening them half out of their wits and then offering them the opportunity of enlisting in the Legion of St George as an escape route. Lange, who was acting on his own initiative, gained the agreement of Major Heimpel, the Abwehr officer in charge of counter-espionage in the POW camps, and Hellmerich and Scharper agreed to give it a try; although Hillen-Ziegfeld and Cooper, employees of the Foreign Office, were kept out of the picture.

One of the central tenets of the interrogation and indoctrination of prisoners of war is that the process of conditioning should start as soon as possible after they are taken; nowadays this is explicitly described as 'maintaining the shock of capture'. The reasons for this are obvious: soldiers maintain a measure of psychological equilibrium in combat through a number of ways, but one of the most important derives from the security that they feel as a member of a team. They gain confidence from having comrades with them who are going through a similar experience, and together they are able to buoy each other up at moments of great stress; and they are particularly reliant through these periods on their leaders, whether officers, NCOs or other private soldiers of strong character. Capture by an enemy is a moment of extreme stress and uncertainty, and it is very often at this time that a soldier finds himself alone, separated from his friends and leaders, sometimes because he has been left behind by his unit, sometimes because he is one of few survivors of an action. Very frequently shock sets in. Whether the prisoner is able to recover his equilibrium after capture then largely depends on how he is treated by his captors. The Geneva Conventions prescribe that prisoners of war should be treated fairly, allowed to retain personal effects and protective equipment, be given access to medical care and be removed from danger; and generally speaking, bearing in mind the differing circumstances in which prisoners were taken, this is what happened to the majority of POWs on both sides on the western fronts.

If a prisoner is treated kindly, allowed to mix with other prisoners and told what will happen to him (i.e. that he is being taken to a POW cage and being treated in accordance with the Geneva Convention, etc.), then more often than not he will recover from the shock of capture fairly quickly; if, alternatively, he is harshly treated, perhaps not spoken to and kept in isolation, then in many cases the state of extreme anxiety and uncertainty will remain with the prisoner. This is the state in which Lange was looking to find his potential recruits.

The subjects for the Luckenwalde recruiting experiment came from the Allied operations being carried out in the Dodecanese and Southern Italy in September and October 1943. Trooper John Eric Wilson of No. 3 Commando landed at Bova Marina with a small party under the command of Lt J. F. Nixon on the night of 27 August, with a mission to capture a German or Italian prisoner, check to see if one bridge was prepared for demolition, blow another, and conduct a beach reconnaissance for further operations. Unfortunately for Wilson, the group was compromised on 28 August and he was captured. Wilson was only twenty-one at the time; he had been born in October 1921, the son of a Lancashire chemist, and attended his local school until he was sixteen. He then worked for his father as an assistant but the company went bust, and in April 1939 John Wilson enlisted in the Military Police. He served in France from October 1939 until 20 June 1940 as a member of the 1st Armoured Division Provost Company, and was one of the comparatively few to be evacuated via St-Malo on the Brittany coast. After his experience in France, Wilson applied for aircrew training and, after appearing in front of a board, was selected. Whilst he was waiting to start his training, he was posted to the depot staff of the RASC at Halifax, but then his orders were cancelled and he found himself sent as a driver to an RASC transport company. In June 1942 the company received orders posting them overseas and they left soon afterwards, travelling via South Africa to Suez. There they were attached to 7th Armoured Division, and as a truck driver Wilson took part in the great battles that followed Montgomery's assumption of command of the 8th Army.

Despite being promoted to lance-corporal, life in the RASC was too dull for Wilson, and in February 1943 he volunteered for the Commandos. Perhaps a little surprisingly for a trucker, he did well during his training and as a result was able to take part in some of the original raids on Sicily and mainland Italy after the fall of Tunis. In only his second operation as a member of 3 Commando he was captured at Catania, but through his courage, resourcefulness and good fortune, he succeeded in escaping after two days and returned to his unit where he resumed his career as a private soldier until the fateful raid on Bova Marina.

Within hours of being captured in Italy, Wilson was on a train to Berlin, being escorted by a German sergeant and two guards. Less than forty-eight hours after falling into German hands he arrived at the special compound at Luckenwalde. As a commando Wilson would have been regarded as 'prone to capture' and should, as part of his training, have received a lecture from a representative of MI9 about conduct after capture. His mind was certainly working along the right lines because he had surreptitiously destroyed his Army paybook during the journey. Nevertheless, the treatment that he was given by the Germans was a classic example of POW subversion and Wilson fell for it entirely.

Shortly after his arrival at Luckenwalde, Wilson was given a detailed strip-search, and was forced to watch whilst the Germans shredded his uniform in front of him before giving him a blanket to wear. The purpose of the search was threefold: first to discover if Wilson actually was carrying any escape material or other incriminating items; secondly to humiliate him and condition him to respond to orders; thirdly, and most importantly, to assess his character and ability to resist. After the search he was left, clad only in a blanket, for two days. His food consisted of 250 grammes of bread and a pint of cabbage soup every day; and he was only allowed out of his cell to empty his lavatory bucket. On the third day he was dragged in front of a man who was introduced as 'Captain Williams'. In fact it was Feldwebel Scharper of the Abwehr using his

John Amery and companion, shortly after his capture by Italian partisans in April 1945. Amery's last act of the war was to don Fascist uniform to show his support for Mussolini.

Left Walter Purdy, a Merchant Navy officer who informed on his POW camp comrades and broadcast for the Nazis.

Right Thomas Cooper (Waffen-SS and British Free Corps).

Left John Leister, recruited to the BFC from the Marlag/Milag camp.

Right Eric Pleasants (British Free Corps) in German uniform.

Below left 'Bob' Rössler, Wehrmacht interpreter to the British Free Corps.

Below right Francis MacLardy, an RAMC sergeant who joined the British Free Corps.

William Joyce (Lord Haw-Haw), broadcasting in the BUF's 'uniform'.

Alfred Minchin, a former merchant seaman, in BFC uniform.

Alfred Minchin (second right) and Kenneth Berry (second left) in BFC uniform (note the Union Jack flash and armband on the lower left sleeve).

Railton Freeman, the renegade RAF officer who broadcast for the Nazis after his capture in 1942.

American persona. Scharper asked Wilson the usual questions – name, rank and number, and date of birth – before returning him to the cells. (Wilson used this opportunity to tell Scharper that he was a staff-sergeant, a falsehood that later led to him becoming the senior NCO of the renegade legion.)

Some time later, the door to Wilson's cell opened and an Englishman entered, wearing the uniform of a sergeant in the Durham Light Infantry. He introduced himself as 'Johnnie' and gave Wilson a cigarette as well as promising to get him a cup of tea later; he then furtively left as if he were dodging the guards. A few hours later 'Johnnie' returned, bearing the promised mug of tea and another cigarette which were both gratefully received. He sat down and they started to chat. Johnnie opened the conversation by remarking that since he was captured at Dunkirk the British Army had certainly improved its weaponry, and they began to talk in a friendly way about the PIAT, a British hand-held anti-tank weapon that used a shaped-charge warhead. After a short while a German guard entered the cell and started shouting at Johnnie, who responded, to Wilson's considerable surprise, by shouting back and pushing the German from the cell. Wilson immediately became suspicious and refused to talk any further so Johnnie left.

With hindsight, it seems obvious that Wilson was being pumped for information. Yet it must be remembered that he had been isolated from any friendly company immediately after he was captured. 'Johnnie', who was of course John Welch, the informer, was clearly English, and as far as Wilson was concerned should have been in a position to reassure him about his predicament – he had certainly been the only person to show him any kindness since his capture. It is only natural, in these circumstances, to cling to any lifeline that appears.

After Welch's departure, Wilson was left to stew for another three days, naked in a cell containing a mattress, a blanket, a lavatory bucket and some propaganda pamphlets. Then he was dragged back in front of Scharper who confronted him about the commandos, the raid that Wilson was on, and other details of his career. He presented Wilson with a stark choice: either join the Legion of St George or face the rest of the war in solitary confinement. Wilson demurred and was taken back to his cell.

The next day he was offered the same choice; this time Scharper expanded a little on the Legion, claiming that it was 30,000 strong and commanded by Brigadier Parrington, but again Wilson refused. Finally, on the third day after the confrontation, Wilson agreed that he would join the Legion. He was put back in his cell, given a British uniform and a meal, and two days later went to join the other renegades via a brief stopover in Genshagen.

Wilson was the first renegade to be coerced into joining the Legion (it is impossible to say if he was the first on whom the coercion technique was tried) and the result of the success was to persuade Lange and Scharper that they had hit upon a sound method of swelling numbers for the project. Thereafter, they agreed to attempt coercion on a much wider scale, on the basis, as Cooper later described it, of 'men at any price'.[1]

Henry Alfred Symonds was just nineteen when he was captured in Italy on 4 October 1943. Born in Willesden in 1924, he had originally joined the East Surreys at the age of seventeen, and then volunteered to become a paratrooper but had lost his nerve after his third jump and been transferred into Princess Louise's Kensington Regiment. He went through much the same reception at Luckenwalde as Wilson had done, though it was Galaher who was planted in his cell rather than Welch, and he broke after five days' solitary in the belief that he would be joining a legion of two divisions under Parrington's command and with the tacit approval of the British government. He was followed through Luckenwalde by a Private Chapman, Arthur James Crydermann, a soldier in the Saskatchewan Light Infantry from Manitoba, Robert Reginald Heighes of the Hampshire Regiment, Robert Henry Lane and Norman Rose of the East Surreys, John Wilson and Cyril Haines of the Durham Light Infantry, Gunners Clifford Dowden, 'Nobby' Clarke and Tom Kipling of the Royal Artillery, Alfred Browning of the Argyll and Sutherland Highlanders, Sergeant Harry Blackman of the Essex Regiment, Private Leigh of the Lancashire Fusiliers, and Private Van Heerden of the Long Range Desert Group.

This group of pressed men trickled into the Legion's accommodation on the Schönholtzerstrasse in Pankow during October and November of 1943. They were bewildered and frightened, weakened both physically and psychologically by their treatment at the hands of Scharper and his renegade stool-pigeons, and yet still expecting to join a force consisting of several thousand men under the command of Brigadier Parrington. When they arrived at the run-down former beerhouse-cum-café, they were incensed to find that Scharper's two divisions consisted, in reality, of a handful of Fascists and opportunists.

The entire Luckenwalde group immediately began to protest at the deception that had been practised on them, but the only man who seemed to have any authority at Pankow, Courlander, was totally uninterested, telling them that if they tried to leave they would be sent to an SS punishment camp. Surprisingly, Edwin Martin, the ex-informer from Luckenwalde, rallied to their cause, making contact with those men he thought might help him to sabotage the unit but they did very little that was concrete. It may well be that Martin felt guilty about his activities as a stool-pigeon for he later claimed that he only joined the Legion in order to 'get a kick back at Jerry',' and several members, including Cooper, later reported that Martin did everything in his power to sabotage the formation of the unit by sowing disorder amongst the Luckenwalde men.

The plight of the Luckenwalde group came to the attention of Cooper and Hillen-Ziegfeld, who were effectively in charge of the nascent Legion, via a circuitous route. Two of the men, Wilson of the DLI and Van Heerden of the LRDG, managed to break out of the Schönholtzerstrasse café and gain entrance to Genshagen, where they got in contact with John Brown and his discipline sergeant, Trinder. Before they were recaptured and sent back to Pankow they managed to brief Brown on what had happened to them, and Brown felt strongly enough to complain directly to Cooper.

Neither Hillen-Ziegfeld nor Cooper had had any inkling about Lange's new recruitment method, although it had been sanctioned by Major Heimpel, and both realized that a unit composed largely of very disgruntled pressed men was hardly likely to succeed. Cooper paid a visit to the Pankow billet on his own in the middle of December and spoke privately to all of the Luckenwalde group, sounding them out to see if they were interested in remaining with the unit. Finding that most of them weren't, he returned just before Christmas in company with Hillen-

Ziegfeld, Hauptmann Bentmann of the OKH and a very reluctant Oskar Lange. After Ziegfeld and Bentmann had spoken to the men they agreed that Dowden, Kipling, Clark, Haines, Wilson (of the DLI), Heighes, Lane, Rose, Van Heerden, Chapman, Leigh, Cryderman, Blackman and Browning should be allowed to leave; Harry Symonds and John Wilson of the Commandos decided, after some initial hesitation, to stay on. Frederick Lewis, the Fascist merchant seaman, also left at this point; he found the stress of the frequent British bombing raids on Berlin too much to bear and he was allowed to return to Milag on the basis that he would continue to recruit for the legion.

The return of the Luckenwalde group presented the Germans with a security problem. Obviously, with recruiting expected to be stepped up, it would be unwise to have, in the general POW population, men who knew the truth about the size and composition of the renegade legion, and the Luckenwalde recusants were therefore temporarily isolated at a barracks in Lichtefelde while the OKW tried to obtain more suitable accommodation. Eventually they were given a permanent camp on a farm in the Mecklenburg village of Drönnewitz, where they spent the rest of the war on agricultural work, their numbers gradually swelling with other rejects from the legion.

As a method of recruiting volunteers for a fighting force, which was always the German intention in forming the renegade legion, coercion and intimidation in the Luckenwalde special compound was a abject failure. Lange lost his job at Genshagen, returning to Lamsdorff, and he was replaced by another Sonderführer, Max Meier, whose remit did not include trawling for recruits. Scharper continued with his team of informers, sending them into POW camps to penetrate escape organisations until shortly before the end of the war, when they were dispersed, in fear of their lives, amongst stalags where it was hoped that they would not be recognized.

The Luckenwalde intimidation scheme, however, did raise the strength of the proto-legion (it should be noted that it did not become a military unit until 1 January 1944 under the name 'The British Free Corps'; the 'Legion of St George' never existed in any formal sense) to twenty-two during November 1943 when it was little more than an experimental scheme. Taken as a snapshot by one of the interested parties – the OKW, the German Foreign Office or the Waffen-SS – this must have appeared most encouraging; particularly so when it was recognized that Genshagen camp was only ever supposed to create a nucleus for the unit. It is likely that this inflated recruitment figure went some way to persuading the Germans that the scheme to recruit British renegades for a fighting unit could, contrary to the fears of the principals, actually succeed. Even so, the end of December saw the renegade legion with a strength of just eight men when it was entering one of the crucial stages of its existence – embodiment as a unit of the Waffen-SS.

9

Fellow Countrymen: The British Free Corps of the Waffen-SS

The year 1943 had been bad for Germany: at the end of January Field Marshall von Paulus had surrendered the surviving German forces in Stalingrad to the Russians; in May the remnants of the German and Italian forces in North Africa had capitulated to the British and Americans; and in September Italy had signed an armistice with the Western Allies. Apart from a few tactical successes in the cauldron of the Eastern Front, the strategic picture was decidedly gloomy. Operation Zitadelle at Kursk, an attempt to return to the grand style of German blitzkrieg victories, had been decisively defeated by the Russians during the summer, and as the year drew to a close there was nothing to cheer Hitler and his High Command.

On a much smaller scale there appeared to be little hope for the latest element in the Third Reich's propaganda campaign against Britain, because as the winter of 1943 drew on it was very apparent to the German authorities that their project to recruit a British unit for service on the Eastern Front was in danger of being stillborn. From the many thousands of British POWs in their hands, only a dozen or so had come forward to take part in the project, and of these, one was an inarticulate 18-year-old and several more were the scared remnants of the Luckenwalde group. Nevertheless, orders being orders, there was no question of not persisting with the scheme and the unit began to shape up.

The first move was the appointment, by the SS-Hauptamt, of a suitable commander. For an operation as sensitive as the British SS unit – its existence remained officially secret throughout the war – Obergruppenführer Berger took pains to select an officer of the highest quality. The criteria for selection, beyond the normal purely military and administrative skills, were high intelligence and fluent English. The officer selected was already serving on the staff of the SS-Hauptamt; he was SS-Hauptsturmführer Hans Werner Roepke.

Roepke was born on 14 May 1916 in the Charlottenburg district of Central Berlin. His father, Dr Fitz Roepke, a university official, and his mother Ilse were also both Berliners. He was educated at the Richard-Wagner-Reform-Realgymnasium in Berlin before, in October 1934, enlisting for a year as a volunteer in the Reichswehr. He finished his first stint of soldiering in November 1935 with the rank of Gefreiter (approximately a lance-corporal) and immediately began a course in law at Berlin University. His use as a potential commander for the British SS unit came from the year he spent in the USA as an exchange student where he acquired an easy fluency in spoken and written English. The outbreak of war had found him having just completed his first set of national law examinations, a Wachtmeister of the army reserve and a member of the Allgemeine-SS. He was not called up for service immediately, but instead went to work at SS-Headquarters in Berlin with the rank of Untersturmführer. His turn for combat duty came following eight months with the SS artillery training regiment (SS-Art. E. Regt) from March to November 1941; he was posted as an anti-aircraft officer with the SS-Wiking division – a unit largely composed of non-Germans – where he remained until March 1943, when he was posted back to work under Berger in the SS-Hauptamt with the rank of Hauptsturmführer. It was then that he came to the attention of the hierarchy as a potential leader of the proposed British unit. The appointment was made – officially he became the 'liaison officer' – in November 1943.

Under the prompting of the Waffen-SS and the Foreign Office, shortly after he assumed his new appointment Roepke convened a series of meetings at an office on the Potsdamer Strasse to thrash out the aims and principles of the British unit. The participants were the 'senior', and apparently more committed, volunteers, Arnold Hillen-Ziegfeld, the Foreign Office representative, Rössler as interpreter and Roepke himself. The British group – Cooper, MacLardy, Courlander, Martin, Minchin and Wilson – later became known among the renegades as the 'Big Six', although this was a notional élite whose membership shifted periodically as members fell into and out of favour.

The first question that was resolved was the name. Amery's original suggestion of 'The Legion of St George' found little favour amongst the volunteers, who felt that it was too specifically English and conveyed inappropriate religious overtones. From the German side it was proposed that the unit be known simply as the 'British Legion' – a proposal in line with the existing policy which the SS had adopted for other foreign units – but it was quickly pointed out that this term was already in use as the name of the British First World War veterans group. In the end they settled on 'British Free Corps' (BFC) at the suggestion of Alfred Minchin who had read an article in the English edition of *Signal* magazine about the 'Freikorps Danmark'. Interestingly, while the BFC was often referred to in correspondence as the 'Britisches Freikorps', or even the 'Britisches Frei-Corps', its official name was the English language version.

The next question to settle was the purpose of the unit. All the volunteers were adamant that they wanted the BFC to be a fighting unit and not simply a propaganda tool. As far as the 'Big Six' were concerned, they were the spearhead of Britain's contribution to the war against Bolshevism and they wanted to take a full part. Or at least, that is what they said – later events were to demonstrate a certain reluctance on the part of several of the 'Big Six' to do much more than enjoy their comparatively free and easy life. In principle the Germans were happy with this concept; by the end of 1943 they had suffered enough reverses in the Soviet Union to realize that they had probably bitten off more than they could chew, their manpower situation was becoming critical to their ability to continue the campaign in the East, and they knew that they needed all the help that they could get. However, for practical purposes, if the BFC was going to take the field as a separate national contingent in its own right, both the Waffen-SS and the Foreign Office were adamant that it should, at the very least, attain the strength of an infantry platoon – thirty men. This condition was accepted by the volunteers. Finally, in deciding the purpose of the unit it was agreed that under no circumstances would its members take part in operations against British or Commonwealth forces or be used for intelligence-gathering purposes.

From the principles of the BFC, the meeting ranged on to practicalities. Courlander, particularly, was keen to be made an officer, but the Waffen-SS were less sure. Roepke explained that the Waffen-SS position was that, until a suitable British officer presented himself, the BFC would remain under his temporary command as the liaison officer. There were practical reasons for this: the BFC was unlikely to attract officers and NCOs if they knew that they would find themselves under the orders of ex-lance-corporals. Nevertheless, still under the mistaken impression that Brigadier Parrington was a potential volunteer, it was unanimously agreed to approach him to act at least as the titular commander of the BFC.

Finally they looked at some minor questions. The meeting agreed that BFC volunteers would not have to swear an oath to Hitler (they had, they agreed, already sworn an oath to the British Crown which they felt they could not break), and they would not have their blood groups tattooed under their arms (which was the normal practice with SS members), nor would they be subject to German military law. They would receive the normal pay of German soldiers appropriate to the rank that they held, and they would wear the normal field-grey German uniform, though with appropriate unit insignia (Amery had wanted the 'Legion of St George' to go to the front in British battledress but the BFC members were adamantly opposed to this – they could clearly foresee the complications that it would have caused). Before the meeting broke up, MacLardy was asked by Hillen-Ziegfeld to write some recruiting leaflets, and Martin offered to design a banner for the unit (it was never made).

Roepke and Hillen-Ziegfeld spent the next few days setting the organization in train to place the BFC on a more formal footing. Roepke arranged accommodation for the unit at the St Michaeli Kloster in Hildesheim, a small town near Hannover, and ordered 800 sets of special insignia from the SS clothing department; and the volunteers began to plan their recruiting effort.

The British Free Corps of the Waffen-SS officially came into being on 1 January 1944, an event announced by a slightly drunk Cooper at a party held in John Brown's room at Genshagen. MacLardy had written three recruiting pamphlets by then, two of which were to achieve wide circulation amongst British POWs. Considering the lavatorial use to which many of them were put, they were conveniently printed on cheap, flimsy paper. The first, and most widely seen, read:

Fellow Countrymen!
We of the British Free Corps are fighting for YOU!
We are fighting with the best of Europe's youth to preserve our European civilisation and our common cultural heritage from the menace of Jewish Communism.
MAKE NO MISTAKE ABOUT IT! Europe includes England. Should Soviet Russia ever overcome Germany and the other European countries fighting with her, nothing on this earth would save the Continent from Communism, and our own country would inevitably sooner or later succumb.
We are British. We love England and all it stands for. Most of us have fought on the battlefields of France, of Lybia [*sic*], Greece, or Italy, and many of our best comrades are lying there – sacrificed in this war of Jewish revenge. We felt then that we were being lied to and betrayed. Now we know it for certain. This conflict between England and Germany is racial SUICIDE. We must UNITE and take up arms against the common enemy. We ask you to join with us in our struggle. We ask you to come into our ranks and fight shoulder to shoulder with us for Europe and for England.
Published by the British Free Corps.

For the five weeks following the Corps' official embodiment its handful of members remained at their shabby billet in Pankow. Cooper was still fully employed at Genshagen, scouting amongst the inmates for potential recruits, whilst Courlander continued to broadcast occasionally for Radio National and the 'Empire Senders'. For the rest of the volunteers time passed slowly. Only those who were able to speak German were allowed to go out unescorted, and they had yet to be issued with uniforms and identity documents; the only money that they had came from Courlander's Concordia pay (which he generously shared out amongst his friends), so even under 'Bob' Rössler's supervision there was not much entertainment to be had.

Eventually, in the first week of February 1944, Roepke ordered the BFC to move to Hildesheim. The St Michaeli Kloster was a former monastery which had been converted, during the 1930s, into an 'SS Nordic Study Centre' and a barracks for foreign workers assisting the SS, and renamed the 'Haus Germanien'. When the BFC moved there, the unit consisted of a grand total of eight members, not including the Germans: MacLardy, Courlander, Minchin, Britten, Martin, Symonds, Wilson and Berry; Cooper was still at Genshagen. Nevertheless, despite the pathetically small number who had joined, it seems that initially there was an atmosphere of enthusiasm and excitement amongst the renegades. The Fascist element had the satisfaction of being part of the great crusade against Bolshevism whilst the others regained their freedom after, for some, years in POW camps. By 1944 one in every four workers in Germany was foreign and the BFC men, now allowed out to sample the nightlife of Hildesheim, did not attract any particular attention; they were able to walk about freely, to drink in bars and cafés, and form relationships with women without fear of punishment.

Following the move to Hildesheim the priority became recruiting. The first trickle came from the group which had received the brainwashing treatment at Luckenwalde. They had returned to Luckenwalde whilst plans were made to send them to an isolation camp to keep them away from the general Stalag population; rumour had it that this was to be under SS guard and this caused several to rethink their attitude to BFC membership. Welcomed back into the fold were Robert Heighes, a Petersfield butcher who had been an acting CSM in the Royal Hampshire Regiment, Robert Lane of the East Surreys and Norman Rose, a long-serving regular army lance-corporal.

The first recruits to arrive without previous experience of Genshagen or Luckenwalde were a Corporal Wood of the Australian Army and his friend Thomas Freeman, a private in 7 Commando of Layforce, who were recruited by Courlander from Stalag XVIIIa in Austria in February 1944. Wood only stayed with the BFC for three weeks before demanding to be returned to camp but Freeman, a big man in all senses of the word, stayed on for several months; his case is particularly interesting in that he was the only member of the BFC to be unequivocally cleared of any guilt for his involvement after the war. MI 5 later noted: 'Private Freeman was a member of the British Free Corps but has been cleared of suspicion as it is now abundantly clear that he joined with the object of escaping and of sabotaging the movement.' He succeeded in at least one of these aims.

It was at the time of the arrival of Freeman and Wood that Roepke ordered BFC members to adopt aliases for official purposes,* although several declined to do so; they also received the first issue of military clothing: plain field-grey working uniforms, temporarily without badges; ankle boots and gaiters; a greatcoat and a field cap; and an SS-pattern leather waistbelt bearing the motto 'Meine Ehre heisst Treue' ('My honour is loyalty').

With the unit beginning to take shape, individuals received specific tasks, and almost inevitably factions began to form. Administratively the heaviest load fell upon Roepke, who drafted MacLardy and Rössler to assist him in the 'orderly room'; the experienced Rose was given the job of storeman and also placed in charge of the distribution of the Red Cross parcels that the volunteers, technically still POWs, continued to receive, and Britten became the Corps' tailor, in charge of the clothing store and responsible for making their shapeless uniforms wearable. Cooper, an Unterscharführer in the Waffen-SS proper, was still only making irregular visits but during one of these he taught his charges the rudiments of German drill and how to give the Nazi-style salute with enough conviction for them to be allowed out of the barracks occasionally. Courlander, who had compiled a list of about 300 men whom he thought might be suitable BFC members, was placed in charge of recruiting. Apart from PT lessons conducted by Wilson, who was a fit and physically impressive man, the rest passed their time in comparative idleness, cleaning their rooms and attending to minor personal chores.

This period of aimlessness between February and April 1944 created a situation in the BFC that Freeman, intent on wrecking the unit, was

* In the interest of clarity I have used the real names of the renegades throughout this book. The use of pseudonyms caused confusion amongst the traitors themselves, particularly so in the BFC which had a constantly shifting membership.

able to exploit. The main impetus amongst the British volunteers had been provided, during the early days of the project, by the committed Fascists like Courlander and MacLardy. They had been able to sweep weaker-willed characters along in the tide of their enthusiasm so that, even when they realized that the BFC only amounted to a tiny handful of men rather than the thousands that they had been promised, they could see themselves as the nucleus of something big to come. But with the 'Big Six' diverted by administration and recruiting, Freeman took the opportunity to start making his own propaganda with the remainder. The result was a division of the BFC into what was called the 'Kohlenklau'* led by Freeman whose principal lieutenant was Symonds and the Nazi party led by Courlander and MacLardy. It was an unequal struggle. Courlander was often away from Hildesheim during the first few months visiting POW camps and working parties, whilst MacLardy was a solitary, intense and deeply unpopular figure; consequently the majority of BFC members fell directly into Freeman's orbit. To everybody's surprise, one of the earliest adherents to Freeman's group was the sinister Edwin Martin, the Canadian who had already spent time as a Stalag informer. Even before Freeman's arrival he had earned the distrust of the 'Nazi Party' and he had spoken to Cooper, expressing his regret for his involvement.[2] In March 1944, Martin voluntarily left BFC for the isolation camp, by then situated near Schwerin in Mecklenburg.

Freeman was able to hide his antipathy to the German cause well enough to be allowed to go on a recruiting trip with Wilson in early April, and also for Roepke to select him as the future senior NCO. Freeman's recruiting effort was very much intended to further his own aims; Wilson later recalled: '[Freeman] told me that we could make a real jumble up of the Free Corps and having been in a Stalag he knew the right sort of bloke to make a real mess . . .'[3] The trip back to XVIIIa at Spittal gained Freeman and Wilson three volunteers, Charlie Chipchase and Albert Stokes of the Australian Army, and Sergeant Theo Ellsmore, a Belgian masquerading as a South African. In fact Chipchase only stayed

* The Kohlenklau (Coal-snaffler) was a figure of German home propaganda who closely resembled the British 'Squanderbug'. The Kohlenklau was characterized as the non-patriotic German who took every opportunity to waste or hoard food and deal on the black market at the expense of loyal Germans.

for a couple of days before going to the isolation camp, but both of the other two were to play a significant part in the BFC.

The first watershed in the BFC's short existence was reached on 20 April 1944, Adolf Hitler's fifty-fifth and penultimate birthday. A few days before, Britten, the Corps' tailor, had taken delivery of a consignment of special insignia. These consisted of a black lozenge-shaped patch to be worn on the right collar, showing three lions 'passant guardant' as on the British Royal standard, a union-jack patch in the shape of a shield to be worn on the lower left sleeve, and an armband worn a few inches above the left cuff, bearing the title 'British Free Corps' embroidered in English in a gothic-type script. Britten, assisted by Symonds, spent all day and much of the evening of 19 April sewing these badges on to the renegades' uniforms in preparation for a parade to be held the next day.

At 8 a.m. on 20 April, Freeman reported the British Free Corps as being 'all present and correct' to Cooper who then informed Roepke. Standing the parade 'at ease', Roepke made a short speech during which he informed the BFC that their preparation phase was now over and that, with the issue of uniforms, side-arms and German soldiers' paybooks, they were now able to mount a full-scale recruiting drive. Thereupon he announced the following promotions: Thomas Cooper was promoted to Oberscharführer and sent to man a transit camp for new recruits at a villa in the Grunewald district of Berlin; Freeman was also promoted Oberscharführer but with responsibility as discipline NCO ('Spiess' in German military parlance) at Hildesheim; Wilson, Courlander and MacLardy were promoted Unterscharführer; Symonds, Britten and Rose became Rottenführers; Minchin, Heighes and Ellsmore became Sturm-männer; Berry, Lane and Stokes were privates.

The days following the 20 April parade saw most members of the BFC departing from Hildesheim to the many Stalags, Oflags and working parties throughout Germany and Austria, in search, ostensibly at least, of new recruits. Courlander's scheme was to send his recruiters, where possible, to the area in which they had been held prisoner themselves, in the hope that they would be able to exploit personal contacts and friend-ships. As it turned out, this idea probably had a negative effect.

The first BFC member to attract a new recruit was Carl Britten. In

April 1944 he was briefly visiting Stalag VIIIb at Lamsdorff when he met an acquaintance called William How, a lance-corporal in the Military Police from Rochester in Kent. How was intrigued by Britten's apparent freedom (Britten was wearing a British uniform), and in conversation discovered that he had 'a soft job looking after a major'[4] in Berlin. Britten offered his friend the chance to join him, though without specifying what he was doing, and How jumped at the chance. Shortly afterwards he was removed to Stalag IIId in Berlin where, by chance, he met Tom Freeman, was interviewed by Major Heimpel and saw Minchin. A few days later Freeman took him to Hildesheim.

The next to join was Ernest Nicholls, a private soldier in the Royal Army Service Corps. Nicholls was born in Chiswick, West London, in 1916; his father had died on the Western Front when he was two and his mother died when he was four, leaving him in the care of his grandmother and an aunt. He drifted around West London for several years before joining the army, and at the age of twenty-three found himself in France as a petrol storeman with the British Expeditionary Force. On 20 May 1940 he was captured during the retreat towards Dunkirk and thereafter spent four years as a labourer, latterly making coffins at a work party in Riesenburg. Returning to his accommodation at the end of April 1944, he and his comrades discovered that it was littered with BFC pamphlets. Dim-witted, bored with his work (he was, as he put it, 'browned off'[5]), and without the imagination to understand the consequence of his actions, Nicholls applied to join.

One of the more successful recruiting teams consisted of the merchant seamen Alfred Minchin and Kenneth Berry. They made two trips to Marlag/Milag Nord, the special camp for sailors near Bremen, at the beginning of May and in June 1944. Their first visit succeeded in netting Herbert Rowlands and Ronald Barker, both members of the merchant navy. Rowlands was a Londoner who, bizarrely enough, had fought in, and deserted from, the International Brigade during the Spanish Civil War; by all accounts he exhibited great resentment towards any kind of authority and by joining the BFC he seems to have been making a gesture of defiance at the prisoner leadership in Milag. Barker, on the other hand, seems to have been entirely seduced by the prospect of more food, alcohol, tobacco and, above all, the opportunity to associate with women. Described by Cooper as 'a man of very inferior intelligence,'[6] he was an Australian, from Goulburn, New South Wales, and was captured on his ship, the MV *British Advocate*, by the German pocket battleship *Admiral von Scheer* in the Indian Ocean in 1941.[7]

Whilst Minchin was successfully inveigling Barker and Rowlands into the BFC, Kenneth Berry, who was still only eighteen despite having been in captivity for nearly four years, was making his first desperate attempts to leave the Corps. His visit to Marlag/Milag put him, for the first time since he had been recruited by John Amery in April 1943, in the company of loyal Britons. Whilst he was waiting for Minchin in the German part of the camp, Berry spoke to Captain Robert Notman, the camp leader. He explained to Notman, and to some other officers, that he wanted to leave the BFC and that he was very unhappy with what he was doing. Unsure about how to advise the young renegade, Notman suggested that he visit the Swiss embassy in Berlin, (a course of action that the immature but trusting Berry followed, with no result, a month later). When Minchin reappeared a little later, with Rowlands in tow, they briefly paused outside for some photographs before returning to Hildesheim.

Minchin and Berry's second visit to Marlag/Milag, in June, netted two of the more prominent characters in the BFC – John Leister and Eric Pleasants. Pleasants was born in 1911 in Norfolk, where his father was a gamekeeper on a large estate; at a young age he became interested in physical fitness, body-building and sport, earning a local reputation as an amateur boxer and wrestler. With the patronage of the Bowes-Lyon family he was able to attend Loughborough College, where he obtained a diploma in physical education and physiotherapy, and he made his living as a PE instructor and a professional wrestler (using the name 'Panther Pleasants'). In the mid-1930s he was invited by the Norwich branch of the BUF to become a member of their protection squad, acting as a bouncer at meetings; but in reality doctrinaire politics was losing its appeal for him (he had briefly flirted with Communism as a teenager)[8] and he didn't stay long. With the war looming, Pleasants – who espoused, surprisingly enough, a pacifist view – decided that he wanted no part of it and, whilst he was considering registering as a conscientious objector, he was offered the opportunity to go to Jersey to work as an agricultural labourer, which he did in May 1940. It was in Jersey that he met John Leister.

Leister, born in 1922, was the son of a reasonably prosperous north London baker of German descent. Following the separation of his parents when he was eight, he lived with his German-born grandmother in Tufnell Park and visited Germany with her every year on holiday. In 1935 and 1936 he actually lived with his great-aunt in Germany, attending school and learning to speak the language fluently. Thus, not surprisingly, the outbreak of war in 1939 presented him with a certain conflict of loyalties and he too became involved in the Peace Pledge Union Scheme providing agricultural labourers for the Channel Islands.

When the Germans took control of the Channel Islands in July 1940, the situation appeared bleak for Pleasants and Leister but, undaunted, they both did what they could to scratch a living. Leister became an interpreter for the German authorities whilst Pleasants, teaming up with the safe-breaker Eddie Chapman (later to be known as the British double agent ZigZag), spent some time looting abandoned properties. Late in 1940, along with another young Englishman called Keith Barnes, they located a motor boat and, attempting to steal petrol to take it to England, were caught by the Germans. At a military trial Pleasants and Leister, who exonerated Barnes of any blame, received six-month jail sentences and were sent to serve them in Dijon. With their sentences served both men, being of military age, were packed off to the civilian internment camp at Kreuzberg. After an abortive escape attempt in December 1942, Leister spent a further six months in a Gestapo prison near Breslau, but on his return again teamed up with Pleasants. Now both were claiming to be merchant seamen and demanding transfer to a POW camp (they had been told that the rations were better). Finally, in March 1944, their transfer came through and they were sent to Marlag/Milag.

When Minchin and Berry first visited the camp, Leister and Pleasants discussed the matter at length and decided that, if the opportunity arose again, they would join. Their reasons were simple: they did not like living on short rations (Pleasants was well versed in the requirements for a healthy diet and knew he wasn't getting one); they did not like being separated from female company; they did not like the discipline of camp life (although Milag – the Merchant Navy section of the camp – was notably riotous), and above all they did not like having their freedom curtailed because of a war which both of them opposed. Both felt that life in the BFC was likely to be considerably more comfortable and neither had any intention whatsoever of doing any fighting against anyone. When Pleasants was interviewed by Berry and Minchin, he told them to their faces that they were 'stupid bastards' if they thought they would persuade anyone to join by trotting out the line about a crusade against Bolshevism; he was in it to have a good time.[9]

As with all volunteers, Leister and Pleasants arrived at Hildesheim having travelled via the villa in Berlin supervised by Tom Cooper. It was there that they underwent a very limited process to weed out any outright undesirables, signed the recruiting forms which set out the terms and conditions of service, and were issued with civilian clothes. Cooper's job had given him the freedom to continue with his enthusiasm for oriental languages (which had earned him the nickname of 'The Mikado' from Freeman), and also allowed him to continue to associate with John Brown who regularly pumped him for information about the Corps. Cooper's relationship with the new recruits was problematic; whilst he was sensitive and perceptive to some extent, his military experience was entirely with the Waffen-SS, an organization with a somewhat harsher attitude towards its junior members than was normal in the British army, from which most of his charges were drawn. The result was that the renegades deeply resented any attempt by Cooper to discipline them, and they certainly did not care for the SS-style methods that he used. Reflecting later, Pleasants was to describe him as 'intelligent – but a stupid bastard as well', remembering occasions when he witnessed Cooper, in all seriousness, practising his goose-step marching in the BFC billet.[10] Recognizing this, the Germans only ever used him as a liaison officer between Roepke and the 'British' senior NCOs (firstly Freeman, later Wilson).

Volunteers from the first recruiting drive did not begin to trickle into Hildesheim until early June, and for the enthusiastic Courlander they represented a considerable disappointment. Apart from Nicholls, How and the four from Marlag/Milag, they included Harry Dean Batchelor, a sapper in the Royal Engineers from Kent who was captured by the Germans in Crete and recruited from Stalag in Austria; Hugh Cowie, a private from the Gordon Highlanders who, after being captured in France in 1940, had made several escape attempts and joined the BFC to avoid court-martial for having a clandestine radio at his Upper Silesian work party; Roy Futcher, a private in the DCLI who was being threatened with court-martial for associating with German women; Frank Maton, the Commando corporal who had already broadcast for Radio National; and Tom Perkins, a lance-corporal in the Military Police. Of these, only Maton with his pronounced Fascist sympathies appeared to be good BFC material and several proved ideal recruits for Freeman's Kohlenklau faction.

Nevertheless, the BFC was undoubtedly expanding – which caused Freeman a certain amount of worry. In June the strength had crept up to twenty-three, not far short of the total which would allow Berger to incorporate the unit into the 'Wiking' division and send it into action. He decided to act before this could happen. His method was crude and direct: assisted by Ellsmore, he drew up a letter requesting that he be returned to a Stalag, and he, Ellsmore and fourteen others (including all the new recruits except Maton) signed it. The result was to throw the recruiting effort into turmoil and to destroy any atmosphere of trust that had built up between the renegade soldiers and their German leaders. Tom Cooper was in Berlin at the time, but the 'Nazi Party' exerted all their influence directly with Roepke to have Freeman and Ellsmore removed. The pair were charged with mutiny on 20 June and sent to Stutthof concentration camp near Danzig. As Freeman remembered: 'The charge of mutiny included allegations that I was trying to obstruct the efficient working of the Corps, encouraging insubordination, etc.'[11] Freeman succeeded in escaping from Stutthof in November 1944 and managed to reach Russian lines; he was repatriated in March 1945.

In fact Freeman's 'mutiny' simply brought to a head the tension between the 'Nazi Party' and the Kohlenklau that had been simmering for some time. Ellsmore in particular had been a tormentor of MacLardy, known as 'Teeny Weeny' to the Kohlenklau, and frequently resorted to physical violence against him. Arguments between the groups were long-lasting and fierce, and could be sparked off by the slightest difference of opinion; on one occasion Britten, at the instigation of MacLardy, hung a swastika flag in his barrack room only for Perkins to tear it down. When the Bürgermeister of Hildesheim complained about the rowdy behaviour of some BFC members in a local café, MacLardy suggested that the Corps be confined to barracks, only to be twice beaten up by Ellsmore in the showers in retaliation. But the tension should be kept in proportion: most post-war accounts have suggested that the BFC was simply a gaggle of rowdy drunks,[12] but the truth was that their behaviour was neither better nor worse than one would expect from any similarly heterogeneous group of men in those circumstances. Some drank too much, some resorted to prostitutes, but as Roepke later stated: 'Their general behaviour was absolutely correct and disciplined . . . and I feel they should be given credit for acting in good faith even when faced with a total lack of comprehension on the part of the German authorities.'[13]

With Freeman gone, Wilson was appointed senior NCO in charge of Corps discipline on the basis of his claimed rank of staff-sergeant in the Commandos. This was a bad mistake as far as the Germans were concerned – Wilson had certainly been a commando but he never got beyond the rank of private. In fact he had a very ambivalent attitude towards the BFC: on the one hand he fully realized that he had committed a gross breach of loyalty by joining and then remaining with the unit, but on the other he knew that he would be unable to find any outlet for his considerable libido inside a Stalag – in the view of several members of the unit, Wilson was sexually obsessed.[14]

Three of the four men who joined the BFC in August were not recruited by the renegades but joined as the result of blackmail by the German military authorities. Frederick Croft, a bombardier in the Royal Artillery from Finchley, had escaped a total of five times from his working party, until in July 1944 he was put in solitary confinement for a five-week stretch; he was given the opportunity to join the BFC several times before he caved in and was escorted to Hildesheim by Maton. Edward Jackson, a private in the King's Own Royal Regiment, was also often absent from his working party, but in his case the reason was different:

he had acquired a girlfriend in the local area; this came to the attention of the Gestapo in Dresden who arrested him and made him an offer that he felt he couldn't refuse. Charlie Munns, a Scotsman in the Durham Light Infantry, found himself in a similar situation in his POW camp near Danzig, though in his case his girlfriend was pregnant, an offence technically punishable by death.

The fourth man to join the BFC in August was Lieutenant William Shearer, the only British officer to accept the blandishments of Courlander. But he represented a special case: at the time he 'volunteered' he was confined in a mental hospital being treated for schizophrenia. Courlander's aim in bringing Shearer to Hildesheim was simply to have an officer as a front man – he didn't expect him to have to do anything – and Shearer wasn't even up to the limited role that Courlander envisaged: he rarely left his room and wouldn't put on his BFC uniform, and after a few weeks he was quietly returned to the Ausbach mental asylum to await repatriation on medical grounds.

Unsurprisingly, press-ganging men into the BFC had a very negative effect on morale within the unit. Members continued to make recruiting forays around Germany but their efforts were half-hearted at best, and when they were at the Hans Germanien, they still lacked anything to occupy their time beyond German lessons, conducted by Cooper and MacLardy, and PT sessions run by Pleasants. Wilson proved to be unequal to the task of maintaining discipline and petty niggles continued to sour the atmosphere between the increasingly isolated Fascist element and the rest. One storm in a teacup concerned the wearing of the Union-Jack badge in a position below the German eagle on the volunteers' left arms; at this time (July 1944) most foreign volunteers in the German armed forces wore their national symbols on the right shoulder, and a few of the BFC men felt that Britain was being slighted. This situation was only resolved with the intervention of Heinrich Himmler, the Reichsführer-SS, who gave his permission for the uniforms to be altered.

Another contributory factor to the decline in morale was, of course, the successful D-Day landings on 6 June. Isolated from the Stalags, which usually had covert access to BBC news, most BFC men didn't fully appreciate the significance of these events but there were some who did.

In a conversation with John Brown, who was by now maintaining a flat in Berlin, Cooper told him that he realized he had been a 'bloody fool',[15] that England was bound to win the war, and that he wanted to do something to secure his position in case he was captured; Brown promised to look into the matter for him. Courlander and Maton had come to the same conclusion as Cooper – they were both anxious to get back to Britain before news of their treachery reached home.

Two incidents which took place in August contributed to a major change in policy on the part of the SS-Hauptamt towards the British Free Corps. The first took place when, during a party held in their accommodation, Tom Perkins stole a pistol from an office in the same building and sold it to a foreign worker. Perkins claimed to have been a prison officer before the war, but according to Cooper 'his general character and behaviour led me to believe that his knowledge of prisons was very probably from the inside rather than the outside of a cell'.[16] When Cooper found out about the theft, he, MacLardy and Britten immediately arrested Perkins and, after he had spent a couple of days in close confinement, sent him away to the isolation camp. This incident caused considerable resentment – Perkins was popular with the Kohlenklau element – and provoked an outbreak of mulishness amongst the others which came to the boil when they were ordered to assist other inhabitants of the Haus Germanien in laying out a football pitch. Led by Pleasants, who felt that Cooper and the 'Nazis' were picking on him, eight of the renegades refused to take part and demanded to be returned to their camps. After being interviewed by Roepke, who by now was becoming impatient with the antics of several of the soldiers, they were stripped of their uniforms and summarily despatched to an SS punishment camp near Schwerin. Pleasants, Leister, How, Rose, Futcher, Rowlands and Croft found themselves working in a road-making gang, whilst Lane was returned to a Stalag.

Apart from cutting the strength of the BFC by a third, this incident caused the SS-Hauptamt to take a long look at what was happening to their British unit. A conference had been held in Berlin as early as 13 June to analyse why the BFC were failing to recruit significant numbers of volunteers, and whilst it came to no particular conclusions, it decided at the instigation of an SS-Sturmbannführer named Vivian Stranders to use specially selected German recruiters to supplement the efforts of the BFC men. The new recruiters did not commence operations until the autumn but in the meantime, with the strength of the unit at under twenty, it was clearly becoming more trouble than it was worth. The solution, it appeared to Obergruppenführer Berger, was simply to get as many volunteers together as possible, give them a course of military refresher training, and integrate them into a unit for service on the Eastern Front as soon as possible. Whilst plans were being made to do this, Stranders, who was working within Section D of the 'Germanische Leitstelle',* was intriguing against the leadership of the BFC – Roepke and Cooper – whose performance he felt was so bad that they could be described as having sabotaged the Corps. Stranders was largely motivated by self-interest – he liked the idea of monopolizing the recruitment of Britons for the unit and perhaps commanding it – but he was held in high esteem by Berger who was a long-standing acquaintance and his views were taken seriously. Stranders had been for some time cultivating the Fascist element within the Corps and was fully aware of the many difficulties at Hildesheim.

Stranders himself was an interesting character. He was born in London in 1881, the son of a professor at the Guildhall School of Music. After studying at King Edward's Grammar School in Birmingham and London University, where he took a degree in classical philology, he moved to Germany in 1903 to work as a language teacher whilst continuing his studies as an external student to gain a Master's qualification. After a year in Germany he returned to London and for the next ten years worked as a teacher and volunteer in the Territorial Army, in which he had risen to the rank of Lieutenant by 1913. Bearing in mind his later career, it is possible that Stranders was recruited as a German agent as early as 1903 although there is no concrete evidence. He certainly fought on the British side during the First World War, serving at first as an ammunition officer on the Western Front until 1916 and subsequently as an equipment officer

---

* The Germanische Leitselle (Germanic Administration) was the section of the SS Hauptamt responsible for recruiting and other matters involving the Nordic or Germanic countries. Section D was the branch which sponsored, amongst others, the BFC.

for the Royal Flying Corps and the Royal Air Force, where he rose to the rank of Captain. At the end of the war he was appointed military interpreter to the Reparations Commission in the Kiel and Hamburg area, and then to the 'Inter Allied Aeronautical Commission of Control' in Berlin, from which he was demobilized in 1921. In the same year he set himself up as an importer of English motorcycles in Düsseldorf (as a result of Allied restrictions, most German aircraft being produced then ran on motorcycle engines) and began to travel in western Europe using his business as a cover, for he was by then undoubtedly a German agent, using his contacts to further Germany's secret rearmament.

Stranders' spying career came to an end in 1927 when he received a two-year sentence from a French court for espionage. Released in 1928, he then embarked on a career as a journalist and polemicist, decrying the effects of the Treaty of Versailles on the German nation. In 1932 he joined the Nazi party, receiving, he often claimed, a membership card signed personally by Hitler, and in 1933 he was naturalized as a German citizen. Thereafter he applied himself to academic work, gaining a doctorate and lectureships at several universities, culminating in his appointment as a professor at Halle in 1943. His appointment in the Waffen-SS as their expert in British affairs, which was a result of his friendship with the chief of the Germanische Leitstelle, came in 1944.

For their part, at the beginning of September the 'Nazi Party' decided that they had had enough. MacLardy, without doubt the most blindly fanatical of the group, volunteered to join the Waffen-SS medical service and was sent to the medical supplies depot at Lichtenberg. As he later said, 'I had little to do with the BFC men and no friends in town'[17] – he wasn't missed by his former comrades. Maton and Courlander, more calculatingly, had realized that a German defeat was now inevitable and were keen to escape. Their solution, which caused a near riot amongst the BFC, was to volunteer for service with the 'Kurt Eggers' propaganda regiment on the Western Front. In truth their cynical intention was to defect as soon as they got anywhere near the front. Britten, who decided to stay with the Corps, removed the compromising BFC insignia from their uniform and replaced them with standard Waffen-SS badges and they left Berlin by train on 2 September, en route for Brussels in the company of a Flemish Waffen-SS battalion. Arriving on the 3rd they immediately made themselves scarce, hiding in a house near the Palace of Justice. The next day they moved to another house – where Maton accidentally shot his hostess in the leg with his pistol – before handing themselves over to a British officer. They were the first BFC men to make it home.

In Hildesheim, the Corps continued to tick over. Two new recruits arrived towards the end of September. William Alexander, a Glaswegian private in the Highland Light Infantry, and Harry Nightingale, a private in the Royal Artillery from Burnley, were both the victims of compulsion because of their sexual liaisons with German girls. Meanwhile, with Rose in the punishment camp, Heighes had taken control of the unit's stores and had discovered that he could considerably increase his wealth by selling their contents to other occupants of the barracks. Wilson, out of his depth as senior NCO, had enlisted the help of Cowie and Symonds to help him maintain order and attempt some form of training, but they were able to achieve little. Exasperated, the German barracks commander made representations to Roepke about moving the Corps somewhere else; he was relieved to be told that a decision had been made and that the BFC was to transfer from Hildesheim to the Waffen-SS Pioneer school in Dresden, to start military training for service on the Eastern Front.

10

Other Traitors:
Other Treasons

The radio propaganda broadcasters and the members of the British Free Corps formed the two largest group of renegades, but there were of course others. Two of the most singular characters of the war trod the path of treason outside the mainstream renegade activities. Both were, in their own ways, grotesque caricatures of a certain type: one the irascible, blimpish, reactionary Fascist of the British upper class; the other a vicious, dishonest, womanizing, petty crook.

Benson Railton Metcalf Freeman entered the world in Newbury, Berkshire, on 6 October 1903, the son of Commander Fletcher Freeman of the Royal Navy and his wife Olive, née Metcalf. His father was based at Portsmouth, where the family lived until he was eighteen though he was sent to school at St Helens College in Southsea, and later to Newton College in Devon. In 1922 he entered the Royal Military College at Sandhurst as a gentleman cadet, and in August 1924 he was commissioned into the King's Own Royal Regiment as a second lieutenant, joining his battalion at Shorncliffe in Kent. During the first two years of his military career Freeman developed an interest in flying, and in September 1926 he was promoted to the rank of lieutenant and posted to an RAF flying school near Chester for training as a pilot.

By the time his course finished a year later, Freeman had shown sufficient aptitude to qualify as a fighter pilot and be formally transferred into the RAF as a flying officer, and thereafter he was posted to 16 Squadron near Salisbury as an operational flier, he also took the opportunity to marry his fiancée, a widow named Muriel Treharne who came from Kent. His career in the RAF continued until 1931. He qualified as an instructor, allowed to fly all types of aircraft, and took part in trials of special high-speed aircraft during 1930, but decided the next year to retire from military service, buy an estate in Gloucestershire and settle down to life as a farmer.[1]

As a rural landowner Freeman had time to develop his political views, but they turned into a strange collection of morbid fears. As he later stated:

I have been bitterly opposed to the appalling menace of Soviet Communism for a long time. I have studied Moscow propaganda . . . and its hideous exploitation by World Jewry and I am more than dismayed by the fearful fate that awaits this country and western Europe, and eventually the whole world, when this menace overpowers them. I came to these conclusions long before I ever heard of Mosley or Hitler, therefore it is inaccurate to describe my views or actions as Nazi . . . National Socialism merely provided the one apparently solid barrier in the path of this asiatic doctrine from which opposition could be made.[2]

But despite his claim of ideological independence, he joined the BUF in 1937 and remained a member until the war.

Freeman was almost unable to believe it when war broke out in September 1939. He described himself as 'stunned by the shock'[3] and he was also extremely irritated to receive a letter from the Air Ministry suggesting that if he didn't volunteer for service, he might be called up 'without officer rank'.[4] Even though he was very agitated by the conflict of loyalties that the war had created, he returned to the RAF as a non-combatant (so he assumed) flying instructor, posted to No. 24 Squadron. His duties at this time consisted of instructing newly arrived pilots in the use of various transport aircraft, which he didn't enjoy flying, but he found that his performance was suffering anyway because of the enormous anxiety that he was feeling about the war. He was literally becoming, in his own words, 'sick with worry',[5] and this was manifested by his falling asleep at the controls. In the end he was grounded for safety reason whilst the RAF tried to decide what to do with him.

The nature of Freeman's future employment by the Air Force was taken out of their hands by the German invasion of western Europe. The situation was so bad that on 22 May 1940 Freeman was ordered to fly with his squadron from Croydon to Merville. Almost as soon as they had landed the squadron was in trouble; a flight of German Messerschmitt 109s strafed it on the ground, destroying several aircraft and leaving only a few flyable. Freeman and several others got aboard a DC3 with a Belgian pilot, but only minutes after it had taken off they were hit by ground fire and forced down; as the plane crash-landed in a field it was surrounded by German infantry and Freeman and the other survivors were captured.

Freeman was initially taken to Stalag IIa in Neu-Brandenburg, but his outspoken views came to the attention of the Germans very quickly and he was moved, after ten days, to the Luftwaffe interrogation and transit centre at Dulag Luft in Oberursel near Frankfurt. Dulag Luft was a special camp opened early in the war where the Luftwaffe hoped to obtain intelligence on RAF (and later USAAF) technical advances from newly-captured aircrew. There they pioneered the techniques, later used by Hellmerich and Scharper at Luckenwalde, of introducing stool-pigeons to lull anxious prisoners into a false state of security and worm information out of them. But this was all in the future, and Freeman was taken there simply because he appeared to be profoundly sympathetic to the Nazi cause.

Whilst it was obvious to the Commandant of Dulag, Major Rumpel, that Freeman was pro-Nazi, he was also sensitive enough to realize that he would not be able to sway him from his loyalty to 'King and Country' by a direct approach. Instead, he took the trouble to cultivate Freeman through a series of long discussions about politics, the war and the Bolshevik threat to Europe. Freeman became a permanent inmate at the camp, assisting in the administration of the British side, but more and more closely involved with the Luftwaffe intelligence who ran the place. For all his Fascist views, however, he still held to his personal concept of honour as an officer. Amongst the other prisoners in Dulag was Squadron Leader Roger Bushell, an Australian-born barrister who was to become famous after being shot by the Gestapo for organizing the 'Great Escape',[6] but who was already deeply involved in escape plans and tunnel-digging. Freeman and Bushell strongly disliked each other, but the close nature of their confinement inevitably meant that Freeman and the handful of other officers who were Fascist sympathizers (none were as extreme as Freeman, and none followed his renegade path) knew of his escape plans. As far as Freeman was concerned, 'I did not actually assist in this affair, was not asked to, and frankly I was not interested';[7] even so, and more importantly, he did not tell the Germans about it and almost certainly would not have done so had they pressed him. At one stage he even succeeded in creating a diversion to allow a tunnel entrance to be concealed during a snap German raid on the British quarters.

Freeman's resistance to working constructively for the Germans finally ceased after Rumpel inveigled him into a conversation about William Joyce and the effect of the 'Haw-Haw' broadcasts on British public opinion. To Freeman, Joyce was 'a howling disaster and a hate maker of the worst possible kind'; Rumpel was quick to assure him that many Germans felt the same way but that, as Joyce had been given a free hand by Goebbels, there was little they could do about it. He gave Freeman a copy of Joyce's *Twilight Over England* and suggested that he should write to the author. Freeman discussed this idea with one of his few British friends, Flight Lieutenant G. L. D. Byrne, and eventually agreed that he would write a flattering letter, even though, as he put it, 'I detested the book and the author, but it seemed little enough to do, so I wrote to Joyce.'[8]

Freeman sent his letter to Joyce in the spring of 1942. By then his position in the camp was becoming very difficult; he was enraged to discover, for example, that he was being mentioned in briefings given by MI9 to aircrew as 'a German informer at Dulag Luft', which he most certainly wasn't. In any case: 'Owing to the political outlook of most people in the RAF, their insane propagandist hatred of the Germans and pro-Soviet attitude, I seldom, if ever, sought the company of newcomers.'[9] Eventually, after a series of rows with other inmates, Freeman and a few of the longer-term prisoners were asked to sign a document requesting their removal from the camp. Freeman reluctantly agreed.

His first staging-post after leaving Dulag was a farm ostensibly owned by one of the Luftwaffe intelligence officers, Leutnant Eberhard, where he stayed for three months. From there he was eventually taken to Berlin for a meeting with Hesse. There is no doubt that the Germans realized that they had recruited a strange man: at his first meeting with Hesse, Freeman took pains to explain that he had become 'convinced that Germany had completely failed against the Soviets; and would eventually collapse',[10] yet this was only June 1942 and the Wehrmacht were still sweeping across the plains of southern Russia towards Stalingrad. Despite this, Hesse asked Freeman if he was prepared to help in the 'promotion of peace and the frustration of Bolshevist plans',[11] and Freeman allowed that he was.

Freeman does not seem to have considered how he would be helping in the promotion of peace and the frustration of Bolshevism and he was irritated to find, after being introduced to Hetzler at the Reichssportfeld and made to sign a pledge of secrecy, that he was at the NBBS: 'I was extremely dismayed at this news because this was in no way what I wanted',[12] he said. He refused to play any part in the G-Senders and, after a couple of days of panicky indecision between Hesse and Hetzler, was taken away from the Concordia Büro to work at the Foreign Office. Freeman was pleased at the move as he felt that 'this NBBS had the finest collection of poor-type Englishmen',[13] but his next employment was little better. He was given an office at a Foreign Office building at 60 Saarlandstrasse where he found that he was sharing with Norman Baillie-Stewart who, he decided, 'had all the outward characteristics of an English Officer and gentleman but was just about the weakest moral specimen I ever met'.[14] Nevertheless, he was put to work writing cross-talk and wise cracks with Baillie-Stewart, for transmission on the overt 'Germany Calling' service.

Even though the Germans had taken a great deal of trouble to cultivate Freeman and persuade him to work for them, his prickly character and obsessional forebodings about the outcome of the war made him pretty much useless to them. He was in constant disagreement with his controllers about the nature of the programmes that they were broadcasting, believing that their content could not help to avert the coming defeat, and he virtually refused to take part in any propaganda work from November 1943 onwards, after a particularly fierce row with Hesse. In the course of the argument Freeman had told Hesse that he 'could visualize Berlin being occupied by Soviet hordes all the time [he] walked through it',[15] but he was, in turn, enraged to be told by Hesse that he had 'an obsession over the Soviet danger'.[16] After this argument Freeman rarely went to his office, spending fine days paddling about the Wannsee lake in a canoe that he had bought, and the rest of the time staying on a farm owned by a Foreign Office colleague where Hesse hoped to keep him out of the way.

He continued this idle existence, to his great chagrin, for almost a year. But in September 1944 he at last came into contact with an organization which he felt was doing something concrete about the Soviet menace: the Waffen-SS. By chance Freeman met the chief Waffen-SS propaganda expert, SS-Standartenführer Gunther D'Alquen, at a social function in Berlin. D'Alquen commanded the 'Kurt Eggers' Regiment which was responsible for providing Waffen-SS war correspondents and also for the implementation of tactical psychological operations in the front line, including the 'Skorpion Ost' and 'Skorpion West' plans. D'Alquen was also one of the leading sceptics within the Waffen-SS of the Nazi state's ludicrous racial theories – he was, for example, a champion of the anti-Communist Russian General Vlasov's 'Russian National Liberation Army' – but he took a liking to Freeman and shared his views on the likelihood of Germany's imminent defeat in the east. The result of the meeting was that D'Alquen offered Freeman a commission in the 'Kurt Eggers' Regiment.

Freeman joined the Waffen-SS in October 1944 after making a declaration that he was 'an Englishman of Aryan descent and have never, neither now or previously, been a member of a Freemasons Lodge nor any other secret society'.[17] His duties were not too onerous; he was not required to command troops but simply to vet propaganda material being prepared for use in Skorpion West against the allies, and he fulfilled this role dutifully. He had found his ideological niche as an SS Officer; he later stated: 'The comradeship was terrific, the relationship between Officer and man the most democratic I have known, yet the discipline was solid as a rock',[18] but it did not last for long. Towards the end of April 1945 D'Alquen decided that the time had come to evacuate his remaining staff from Berlin, and he went with his deputy,

Sturmbannführer Anton Kriegbaum, an American SS-Haupsturmführer called Ackerman and Freeman, to an airfield at Potsdam where they commandeered three 'Storch' aircraft to fly them to the south-east.

During a stopover that the group made in Lenggries in south-western Germany they tried to persuade Freeman to take some civilian clothes and fly one of the aircraft to Switzerland, but he was not about to abandon his new-found loyalty. 'I thanked him very much but said I would stay with them until the last day and then I wished to return to England. What I had done was for the best and if certain people thought I was a traitor, I had much the same opinion of these people and that was that.'[19] Freeman surrendered himself to US forces in the Lenggries area on 9 May.

The smallest group of traitors was also, in terms of the material effect that they had on the course of the war, probably the most damaging, though at the same time the most obscure: the British citizens who worked for the German intelligence services.

The first of the spies to be captured was Duncan Alexander Croall Scott-Ford, a Scottish merchant seaman. He had joined the Royal Navy as a 'writer' (a naval clerk) in March 1937; after serving on HMS *Gloucester*, HMS *Medway* and HMS *Nile*, he was court-martialled at Alexandria in March 1941 on seven counts of forgery and embezzlement, to which he pleaded guilty and was dismissed from the service and sent back to Britain to serve a short term of imprisonment. Released in July 1941, he found employment two months later in the merchant navy as a seaman on board the SS *Finland*.

In June 1942 the *Finland* made the first of two voyages to Lisbon, in neutral Portugal, with Scott-Ford on board. Throughout the Second World War Lisbon was a hotbed of espionage activity for both the Axis and the Allies, as one of the few places on the continent of Europe where their agents could operate in comparative safety. As a result, all mail going to and coming from Portugal (and, indeed, Spain) was routinely checked by British censorship who also made tests for secret writing; and any personnel who visited Lisbon, including merchant seamen who took shore leave there, were screened by MI5 port security officers on their return. Whilst Scott-Ford was ashore in Lisbon, he was approached by two agents from the local Abwehr station who asked him to provide them with information about the movements and composition of the convoy that he was in: he agreed to do so in return for a payment of 1000 escudos (about £10). Unfortunately for him, the Lisbon Abwehr reported their successful contact with him back to Berlin by radio, using an ISOS cypher that had been cracked by Britain's signals intelligence service (GC & CS – the forerunner of GCHQ), and MI5 were quickly informed.

When Scott-Ford's ship reached Liverpool towards the end of June, he and several other seamen were taken aside by the port security officials and asked if they had had any contact with the German secret service. Scott-Ford immediately admitted that he had but claimed that he had rebuffed them without giving any information. Whilst MI5 remained suspicious, they did not have conclusive proof at this stage of his treachery and he was allowed to remain at large, sailing for Lisbon again in July. He was again contacted by the Abwehr soon after he went ashore. His handler was most unhappy with the quality of information that Scott-Ford gave him and issued an ultimatum: either he provide full details of his next convoy and other information about shipbuilding in Britain, or the Abwehr would denounce him to the British Consul. Scott-Ford agreed to co-operate and the German gave him a further 600 escudos on account.

Once again MI5 learnt of Scott-Ford's activities through radio intercepts, and on his return he was subjected to a far more searching interrogation. On the first day of questioning he gave a description of an individual who had tried to pump him about Communism in Britain but denied further contact with the Germans; on the second day, however, his resistance collapsed and he made a full confession. Essentially a humane organization, even in time of war, MI5 normally made every effort to 'play back' captured enemy agents as 'doubles' rather than allow them to be tried and executed, but in Scott-Ford's case there was no practical way of doing so without exposing a thoroughly untrustworthy character to the Abwehr. Reluctantly, MI5 allowed him to be prosecuted under the Treachery Act of 1940 and he was hanged by Albert Pierrepoint in November 1942. He had profited to the tune of £16 by his treachery.[20]

The man who, by a simple body count, was the most damaging British traitor might, in slightly altered circumstances, have ended the war a hero. Harold Cole was born in London in 1906 into a working-class East End family; his father died on the Western Front when he was ten, and his mother remarried the following year to a carman named Mason. Harold Cole grew up in the criminal milieu of the East End and soon proved to be a reasonably adept, if not very successful, con man. He served his first term of imprisonment in 1923, at the age of seventeen, and was again incarcerated in 1928, on both occasions for small-time swindles. At some stage during the 1930s, when he wasn't in prison, he is believed to have served in the British Army in the Far East under an assumed name, but by 1938 he was again in prison, serving a short term for petty fraud.

In September 1939, with war declared and just released from prison, Cole enlisted in the Royal Engineers as a private. He falsely claimed to have served for fifteen years in the King's African Rifles, but certainly showed sufficient knowledge of basic military skills to be promoted to lance-corporal within a week of enlisting. On 24 September his unit, the 18th Field Park Company, Royal Engineers, was sent to France with the British Expeditionary Force. They were billeted in a village north of Lille, La Madeleine-lès-Lille, whilst they were constructing fortifications on the Franco-Belgian frontier. In February Cole was promoted to lance-sergeant (equivalent to the rank of corporal but carrying with it the privilege of membership of the sergeants' mess) in recognition of his evident abilities, but only the next month a strong-box was stolen from the company office containing the NCOs' mess funds and the evidence began to point to Cole as the culprit. Although Cole made every effort to avoid the blame, Military Police surveillance eventually led to a flat in Lille where he had hidden the loot and maintained a couple of prostitutes. He was arrested and charged with the theft. Although the hierarchy of his unit were shocked and dismayed, for the sappers serving under him it came as no surprise; those who had met him were of the opinion that he was 'fresh out of one of His Majesty's penal institutions'.[21]

Cole managed to escape from military custody four times during the next two months, but on each occasion he was recaptured. He was finally jailed in the Citadelle at Lille, an old fortress, but in June, with the German army approaching, his British guard let him go with the words:

'I don't give a bugger what you do, we're off!' In the wake of Dunkirk he was just one of the hundreds of British soldiers roaming Belgium and northern France trying to evade capture by the Wehrmacht. If they managed to stay out of the clutches of the Germans, most of these men were eventually taken in hand by sympathetic locals, and gradually, in the months after the armistice, groups of people willing to risk their lives attempting to get British evaders home began to spring up. In the Lille area a mysterious British officer, claiming to be a representative of the British Secret Service, started to organize and co-ordinate the activities of several of the groups; in fact it was none other than Harold Cole.

It is difficult to understand why Cole took upon himself the role of evasion co-ordinator. His past record as a petty thief and fraudster showed no evidence whatsoever of his having an altruistic cell in his body, yet he did the job and did it well. It is possible that he saw an opportunity to make a profit from his activities, inasmuch as he genuinely needed to use large sums of money to get his evaders into the unnoccupied zone safely, and he was certainly able to obtain sexual favours from women who admired his courage and daring. But these considerations are unlikely to have outweighed in his mind the enormous risks that he was taking every second of every day. It is possible that he had a yearning, for once, to be a real hero, genuinely to do something of which he could be proud. Whatever his motives, for the first ten months of his operation Cole behaved impeccably.

The escape organization for which Cole worked was controlled in France by a group of people in Marseille, at that time in the unoccupied Vichy zone. The first leader was Ian Garrow, a captain in the Seaforth Highlanders, who had headed south with four soldiers after the surrender of the 51st Highland Division at St Valery-en-Caux. When he arrived in Marseille, he found the town full of disorientated British servicemen and decided that it was his duty to try and get them back to Britain and into active service again. In Marseille Garrow built up a network of helpers from amongst those of the local community who felt strongly enough about France's defeat by Germany to want to risk their lives doing something about it. He organized safe-houses for evaders and guides to get them over the Pyrenees into neutral Spain; he also made contact with

London, from where he was able to obtain money and guidance from MI6 and the fledgling escape and evasion organization, MI9.

Cole first showed up in Marseille in November 1940, bringing with him a party of evaders from Lille – a considerable achievement as his French was very poor – and thereafter he was frequently in the town to be paid and briefed by Garrow who trusted and admired him. During this period there is little doubt that Cole was genuinely working in the British interest, but even so several members of the escape line had their doubts about him. Principal amongst these was a Belgian doctor who had become Garrow's deputy, Albert-Marie Guérisse, better known under his *nom de guerre* 'Pat O'Leary'. O'Leary later said: 'I heard the way this man spoke to Ian: and the way he presented his case. To me from the first moment I set eyes on him . . . he was a nobody. No good at all. And most certainly not the sort of person for us to be in harness with';[22] whilst Jimmy Langley, who was later to be in charge of liaison between MI6 and MI9, 'found him a rather colourless character with a faintly subservient manner which I dislike. Physically tough, he had a weak face with close-set eyes and was in no way my idea of a man capable of ruthless action, ingenuity and cunning. My judgement could not have been more wrong.'[23]

Garrow eventually attempted to check Cole through London and it was there that this record as a minor East End con man was discovered; more worryingly, Scotland Yard were keen to arrest him for manslaughter. It was decided by MI9 that the best thing to do with Cole was to pull him out of France and give him a medal, as it was too dangerous to let him stay with the escape line. By mid-1941 it was becoming clear that Cole was reverting to his old ways: he frequently obtained funds from the richer members of the organization which he squandered in restaurants and night-clubs, and he had taken to depriving RAF evaders of the cash that they carried in their escape kits. At the same time, it was observed by his assistants that he was becoming dangerously reckless in his dealings with the authorities when escorting evaders and it was felt that it was only a matter of time before he was arrested.

In the first week of October 1941 Garrow sent O'Leary from Marseille to Lille to check over Cole's end of the organization discreetly. What he discovered deeply troubled him: cash which had been provided for Cole and which he claimed to have lodged with his local 'banker' was not there at all; in fact the banker told O'Leary that Cole had borrowed large sums from him as well. Altogether, Cole appeared to have embezzled over 300,000 francs. He was absent at this time, conducting a group of evaders towards the Vichy zone, and O'Leary decided to take the banker, François Duprez, to Marseille so that Cole could be confronted when he arrived there. However, by the time O'Leary reached Marseille with his vital information, Garrow had been arrested by the Vichy police and could not be contacted. It appears that Garrow had already decided, on his own account, that Cole was so dangerous that he would have to be executed, but he had not told O'Leary of his decision. Trying to take over the escape line after Garrow's arrest, O'Leary was concerned that if he killed Cole it would cause trouble with London. Thus, when Cole was eventually confronted at a safe-house in the Vieux Port area of Marseille on 1 November and duly confessed to the thefts, O'Leary did not immediately shoot him (he did, however, punch him in the face so hard that he fractured one of his own knuckles). Cole was locked in a bathroom whilst O'Leary discussed what to do with him with his assistants, but alerted by a noise they found that he had escaped.

Cole fled back to northern France in the hope of escaping the wrath of the escape organization, but in Lille he was also a target for the Abwehr counter-intelligence branch who had been after him for some time. On the morning of 6 December 1941 he was arrested by the Geheime Feldpolizei – the Wehrmacht's security police. Under interrogation, with the threat of execution hanging over him, he confessed immediately, naming almost everybody in the northern part of the organization. The arrests began, with Cole taking part in many of them, on 8 December.

Cole's betrayal of the 'PAT' escape line to the Germans certainly resulted in the deaths of fifty French and Belgian patriots, and possibly as many as 150; it also effectively closed the line down as a conduit by which Allied soldier and airmen could return to action. But his collaboration with the Nazis did not stop at informing. During the spring and early summer of 1942, Cole was an active *provocateur* for the Abwehr against evasion and resistance groups throughout northern France.

The first phase of Cole's treason came to an abrupt halt in June 1942 when he was arrested by the Vichy police in Lyon. Despite the co-operation between the Vichy government and the Germans, many officials in the French security organizations were inclined to be sympathetic to the British and even the resistance; and large numbers of German agents were arrested for operating in the unoccupied zone. Cole was picked up in Lyon as, it appears, he was trying to escape from France. He had with him a young Frenchwoman with whom he had gone through a form of marriage (before robbing the homes of several of her relations). Cole made the mistake of approaching several people who knew, from O'Leary, that he had turned traitor. The first was the US Vice-Consul in Lyon, George Whittinghill, who lent him some money but phoned O'Leary as soon as Cole had left him; the second was a government official named Jean Biche who also lent him money, but called the police to tell them that 'a notorious German agent was in town'.[24] Alerted by Whittinghill, O'Leary hurried to Lyon with a pistol in order to shoot the traitor, but he found that he was too late; Cole had already been picked up by the police.

Under interrogation Cole broke again, eventually giving details of his traitorous activities on behalf of the Germans, though claiming at the same time to be a British double agent. The French security officials and policemen found him a disgusting creature; they discovered that he had set up his wife, who was pregnant by him, to be arrested by the Germans, presumably as a way of ridding himself of excess baggage, and when he was tried for espionage in July they pressed for the toughest sentence. In the event, Cole was condemned to death, civic degradation and confiscation of all his property.

His future appeared to brighten in November 1942 when the Germans seized control of the unoccupied zone in France in the wake of the Allied landings in North Africa, and his sentence was duly commuted to life imprisonment in July 1943. Shortly after this he was moved by the Germans to Compiègne prison whilst they sorted out what to do with him.

In the second phase of his career as a traitor Cole found himself working for the SD, the SS intelligence service, who at first used him as a stool-pigeon in Compiègne prison and as a *provocateur* against escape and intelligence networks in Belgium and northern France. As their confidence in him grew, he became an interrogator, working under the control of SS-Sturmbannführer Hans Kieffer – a senior member of the SD in France – who used him against agents of the SOE and MI6, exploiting his knowledge of intelligence practices and tradecraft. Following the liberation Cole followed his new master to Germany and managed to drop out of sight, temporarily at least, as the Third Reich collapsed around them.

Of the other British citizens who worked for German intelligence, the three most significant were Theodor Schürch, 'Sergeant' Styles and Mariette Smart. The case of Schürch remains shrouded in mystery. He was born in London, of Swiss parents, in 1918 and in 1934 joined the BUF because he was bullied at school. He claimed that he joined the army in 1936 on instructions from the BUF, and when he was captured in North Africa by the Italians, he lost little time in volunteering to work for them. His early work as a collaborator was as a stool-pigeon in North African POW cages, but by 1944 he was operating on behalf of the Abwehr in southern France, northern Italy and Switzerland, controlled by Graf von Thun.

Mariette Smart, born in 1900, was a British expatriate living in Cannes at the end of 1942 with her German mother. She seems to have conformed to the stereotype of the spiteful, shrewish spinster for, with the arrival of the Germans, she seems to have taken great delight in denouncing neighbours and people who she felt had wronged her to the occupation authorities. Before the war she had been an overseas member of the BUF, and she certainly knew, and was friendly with, John Amery when he was resident on the Riviera. During the course of 1943 she became more closely involved with the Germans, acting as an interpreter for them during interrogations and accompanying Gestapo squads during raids on Jewish-owned property. Eventually she was recruited as an agent by the Abwehr and undertook missions for them in Italy and Switzerland, where on one occasion she met Schürch. Her work for the Abwehr was of no crucial importance but her activities in Cannes earned her a death sentence from the French authorities when she was captured in 1945.

Richard Styles was a private in the Gloucestershire Regiment who made a minor impact in the press when he 'escaped' from Germany to Sweden in 1944. His account of his escape aroused so much suspicion that an MI5 officer, Reginald Spooner, was despatched to Stockholm to check him out. In the course of the few weeks that he was in the Swedish capital, Styles was observed visiting a known Abwehr cover address, and it eventually emerged that he had bought his freedom by agreeing to penetrate an escape line for the Germans. The line was closed down but Styles, who had told the British press that he was a sergeant and had been awarded the DCM, was tried in February 1945 and given a seven-year sentence for aiding the enemy.

11

The British Free Corps in Dresden: The Inferno Approaches

On 12 February 1945 the city of Dresden had been little touched by the physical effects of the war. With its population increased to more than one million because of refugees from Silesia and Pomerania, the old town of historic medieval and renaissance buildings was, if anything, more animated and cosmopolitan than ever as the inhabitants attempted to put a brave face on Germany's inexorable decline by attending the cinemas, dance halls and circuses which continued to flourish despite the bleak war situation. But at ten o'clock that night the desperate laughter stopped. Pathfinders of the RAF illuminated the city with enormous flares, and less than a quarter of an hour later, the first bombs began to fall, igniting the town centre. Over the next three days the Allied air forces continued to attack and, aided by a strong north-westerly wind, a firestorm of terrifying ferocity developed, feeding on air sucked at hundreds of miles an hour into the heart of the blaze. It was not to be extinguished for seven days. By then the charred wreckage of the city that had been described as the 'Florence of the Elbe' contained the bodies of not less than 40,000 victims – most of them civilian refugees – and probably many more, blown apart, burnt or suffocated by the high explosives and incendiaries that had rained upon them. It was a scene that even the amoral renegades of the British Free Corps would remember with horror for the rest of their lives.

The BFC had arrived in Dresden to start training on 11 October 1944. It wasn't a moment too soon: the purge of Pleasants, Leister and friends; the obvious success of the Allied landings in France and the Soviets in the East, and the feeble recruiting figures, had combined to crush the morale of the renegade unit. In Hildesheim the volunteers had spent much of their time on trivial tasks and idleness, but in Dresden they were promised the opportunity to train as part of an élite within the German land forces – they were to be fashioned into assault pioneers.

The traditional image of pioneers within the British Army is of soldiers employed on heavy construction tasks and manual labour, but in the German Army and Waffen-SS 'pioniere' more closely resemble combat engineers. The SS pioneer school at the Wildermann Kaserne in Dresden was designed to train soldiers in the techniques needed to breach field defences, clear minefields, use explosives and operate support weapons at the very cutting edge of assaulting troops. To the commander of the pioneer school, SS-Obersturmbannführer Hugo Eichhorn, the small British unit which jumped down from its vehicle to parade in front of him on 11 October must have appeared a sorry sight. Apart from the permanent staff, Roepke, Rössler and Cooper, who were also now supplemented by a friend of Cooper's, 'Fred' Stürmer, a US-educated medical orderly he had known in the Polizei Division, the unit on parade consisted of Wilson, Minchin, Heighes, Symonds, Berry, Stokes, Batchelor, Nicholls, Cowie, Barker, Munns, Nightingale and Alexander – hardly a force to shake the Soviets. Nevertheless Eichhorn made a short speech of welcome and introduced them to the two officers who were to be responsible for their training, Hauptsturmführers Jeep and Marzinger.

In the first week or so at Dresden the BFC managed to contrive a semblance of purposefulness. They were issued with rifles, steel helmets, gas masks and camouflaged SS field uniforms, and they began to ease back into a routine of military training. They received lectures in the use of German weapons, including machine-guns, flame-throwers and explosives, and they restarted their physical training programmes, which had languished since Pleasants' expulsion, with a series of route marches and runs. They also took their turn on guard duty at the barracks. But the brief flurry of military activity towards the end of October proved to be a charade which, in reality, simply heralded yet another demoralizing interlude in the British Free Corps' short history. On 1 November Roepke was summoned back to the SS-Hauptamt, where he was informed that he was being relieved of his appointment with effect from 5 November and was being replaced by another officer from the Germanic Administration, SS-Obersturmführer Dr Walther Kühlich. He returned on the 3rd to pack his bags and tell Cooper; in fact he was not sorry to be leaving.

Kühlich was an ex-officer of the 'Das Reich' division of the Waffen-SS whose severe wounds, sustained on the Eastern Front, had left him unfit for active combat duty. Thereafter he had, in 1943, been given a post within the Germanische Leitstelle as an assistant to the chief of the 'Hauptabteilung Nord', Hauptsturmführer Dr Rabius, whose department included sections dealing with recruitment from Norway, Denmark, Sweden, Finland and Memel, together with the 'England' section under Stranders. Kühlich's wounds made travel difficult, and as a result he was rarely able to visit the BFC throughout his tenure as 'liaison' officer.

Roepke's dismissal was the direct result of Stranders' intrigues within the Germanic Administration. Kühlich was then one of his protégés although they subsequently fell out, but it was symptomatic of the tinkering and muddle-headedness that ensured that the BFC was to remain an abject failure. The reason that the BFC didn't get 'past first base', as Roepke described it, was not simply because of the way that it was commanded; in reality the whole project had been deeply flawed from the first. In his strange way Railton Freeman put his finger on the root cause of the BFC's failure when he described it as being made up of 'camp stool-pigeons and poor types that formed a nucleus that prevented any decent soldier from associating with them'.[1] Freeman later described how he had, in January 1945, looked through a file containing over 1100 applications from British prisoners of war to fight against the Soviets. Even allowing for exaggeration – and Freeman's recollections were remarkably candid – this represents a considerable total. What kept them out of the BFC was the deeply unsavoury reputation that it acquired from the very start.

The gossip grapevine amongst POWs in Germany was strong and

effective from an early stage of the war, even before intelligence bulletins from MI9 became commonplace. The consequence of this was that any rumours of POW defections spread rapidly through the Stalags and working parties, although they were often wildly inaccurate. Few prisoners were under any illusions about the nature of the Nazi regime and they were normally wise to German efforts to propagandize them – particularly because of the crass nature of early issues of *The Camp* and similar efforts. The average British POW, particularly when being led by hard-headed long-service NCOs, was thus, not surprisingly, deeply suspicious of the Genshagen holiday camp, supervised by the apparent collaborator John Brown, and even more so of the British Free Corps whose most visible members, at the start, included the notorious opportunist, Roy Courlander and the outspoken Fascist, Frank MacLardy.

It almost goes without saying that most POWs would have welcomed the dramatic improvement in living conditions that went with collaboration – as mentioned Stalag food was just about enough to stay alive on – but their experience of German propaganda and their knowledge of the characters involved was enough to persuade the overwhelming majority of them that the BFC could not be taken at face value, even assuming that they accepted the requirement to fight the Soviets. This was the main factor that the German authorities – the Foreign Office, the Wehrmacht and the Waffen-SS – failed to realize; they could see that service in the BFC wasn't exactly a popular choice amongst POWs, even though they were well aware that many British soldiers were strongly anti-Communist, but they never really worked out why.

Kühlich took over at the Wildermann Kaserne on 4 November and Roepke left the same day. Cooper, resigned to the fact that Germany had lost the war and desperate to retrieve his position, decided that the time had come to bow out of the BFC. He made plans to meet Wilson, who claimed to be of the same opinion, in Berlin on the 7th, when the pair aimed to go to the SS-Hauptamt and request a move to a Stalag. But the scheme was thwarted: Wilson's real purpose for going to Berlin was to see his numerous girlfriends; he never met Cooper – and when Cooper arrived alone at the Hedemannstrasse office of the Germanic Administration, he was immediately put in close arrest on a charge of sabotaging the BFC.

Cooper was confronted at Hedemannstrasse by Stranders and Kühlich. Before he was able to make his request to leave the BFC, Stranders got in first, informing him that he was dismissed from the Corps. Taking his cue from Stranders, Kühlich then showed Cooper signed statements from Maton, MacLardy, Rose and Rössler alleging various heinous anti-Nazi crimes on his part, informed him that, pending disciplinary proceedings, he was to be posted to another Waffen-SS unit, and returned him to the guardroom under arrest. Sitting in his cell, Cooper was surprised to receive a visit from Wilson, who was dressed in civilian clothes. Wilson told him that he had been barred from leaving the BFC, placed in charge of recruiting, and was to return to Dresden 'in charge of the Corps on the English side'.[2]

The next day Cooper was escorted in front of an SS prosecutor and formally charged. He was taken to the depot of the 'Panzer-Grenadier' training battalion of the élite 'Leibstandarte Adolf Hitler' division of the SS (Stammkompanie SS-Panzer-Grenadier-Ausbildungs-und-Ersatz Bataillon 1), where he spent the next six months working as a military policeman.

At Dresden the priority became, once again, recruiting. As far as the Germans were concerned thirty remained the magic number of volunteers that would allow them to send the unit into combat, and by hook or by crook they were still determined to do it. Wilson had no intention of exerting himself over the new recruiting ideas put to him by Kühlich and Stranders; instead, his first move on taking control of recruiting was to engineer the return of Pleasants and his fellow mutineers, from the SS punishment camp at Bandekow near Schwerin. They had languished there for over three months and were thoroughly miserable; they had been forced to do back-breaking work, food was sparse, and they were guarded by dangerously trigger-happy SS auxiliaries of Eastern European origin. The group, minus Perkins who was sent to the isolation camp and Rowlands who had escaped and was hiding out with Herbert Smallwood, an elderly English ex-soldier, in the Berlin suburb of Spandau, arrived in Dresden in mid-November.

The returning prodigals were also joined by a new recruit, one of a small influx which was to make the winter of 1944-5 the peak period of BFC membership. He was a South African, Pieter Andries Hendrik Labuschagne (he was always called Smith by BFC members, most of whom were unable to pronounce his real surname), who succumbed to one of Stranders' German recruiters, Unterscharführer Hans Kauss, whilst working on a road gang.

As their numbers began to swell, the BFC settled into their new routine. Pleasants was once again responsible for PT, Cowie took drill parades (Wilson – in reality only a private in the Royal Army Service Corps despite his commando training and claimed rank – did not know how to), and the German staff of the school instructed in weapons and tactics. Despite this the BFC was the object of much derision amongst the tough Waffen-SS men at the pioneer barracks because of their comparatively easy life. Wilson, by now the unfortunate victim of considerable discomfort due to chronic gonorrhoea,[3] responded to the taunts with a pathetic display of bombast, styling himself 'RSM Montgomery MM' on all correspondence as well as the BFC's routine orders, and goading the BFC men to 'put up a good show'[4] in front of the Germans. (Wilson used the alias 'Montgomery' during recruiting forays and was variously represented as the British Field Marshal's nephew, son and brother.)

Diversions for the troops came in the form of evenings out in the city, where many acquired girlfriends, recruiting tours around the local area, and in sport. Pleasants and Alexander, a tough Glaswegian, were both selected to box for the SS pioneers against the SS police in Prague and spent much of November and early December in training with their German comrades (Pleasants won his bout, Alexander lost).[5] At the same time Pleasants met and began to pursue a relationship with Kühlich's secretary, a young German woman called Annaliese Nietschner, which led to marriage in February 1945.

Even as the BFC was being slowly moulded into the semblance of a fighting unit, their masters in the Germanische Leitstelle were considering a way in which the unit could be used as part of a last, desperate propaganda campaign. The Germanische Leitstelle was largely staffed by a group of young Nazi intellectuals who were realistic enough to realize that Germany had no prospect of turning the tide of the war unaided, and they foresaw, and greatly feared, that their country would be more or less entirely overrun by the Soviet Union. Their solution was to attempt to drive a wedge between Churchill and Roosevelt on one side, and Stalin on the other – although in fact desultory but highly secret negotiations had been taking place in a number of central European capitals between representatives of Nazi Germany and the Soviet Union from 1942 right up until the beginning of 1945.

The main plank of their effort, codenamed 'Operation Königgrätz', involved the formation of the 'European – British Peace League' as a desperate attempt to propagandize British POWs who were, in early 1945, being marched from POW camps in Poland and eastern Germany towards the centre of the Reich to avoid the advancing Soviets. Columns of prisoners were approached by Waffen-SS NCOs handing out leaflets which read:

Take Your Choice!
Soviet Dictatorship [or] European-British Peace
If Germany collapses, she will go Bolshevist – of that there is not the slightest doubt. The other countries of Europe are well on their way to becoming Soviet Republics.
What does this mean to you?
Stop for a moment and think what the position of Britain would be in such a case. Even though theoretically on the winning side, Britain would be isolated in face of a Soviet-Europe and Asia stretching from the Atlantic to the Pacific.
The inevitable result would be the end of her wealth, her trade, her civilisation and her Empire!
What is the alternative?
A union of all the nations of the Continent and their collaboration with Britain and the British Empire.
By this means Europe would be safeguarded against aggression from the East, the continued existence of the Empire would be guaranteed and permanent peace would be assured for Europe after a long period of bloody fratricidal wars.
Then the present conflict would mark the end of European warfare and strife.
The European–British Peace League

No takers came forward as a result of this initiative, but for the men behind the operation it was important enough for Alexander Dolezalek, who was Head of the Planning Department of the Germanische Leitstelle (now renamed the 'Europa Amt' or European Office), to go to see the Reichs Propaganda Minister, Goebbels, to discuss how to exploit the forthcoming appearance of the BFC on the Eastern Front within the framework of 'Königgrätz'.

Dolezalek was also involved in a more subtle strand of the operation for which Vivian Stranders was the unwitting linchpin. Dolezalek and several colleagues were absolutely convinced that Stranders was a British spy and in communication with MI6 in London, a suspicion heightened after the war by their discovery of his Jewish background, and they would deliberately leave information concerning the German–Soviet talks for him to read, in the hope that it would be transmitted back to his supposed spymasters.[6] In truth Stranders does not appear to have been anything of the sort – he had been a member of the Nazi Party since 1932 after all – and their hopes were forlorn. Dolezalek's last efforts, discussion with Dr Ernst Kaltenbrunner, the Chief of the Reich Security Head Office (RSHA) and controller of the Gestapo, with a view to staging fake Communist actions within Germany, also came to nothing.[7] As with so many schemes in Germany at this time, it was too little too late.

The BFC volunteers had no knowledge of the background to their activities in Dresden, and in any case military training and more convivial pursuits could not disguise from them the fact that they had made a very serious mistake by joining the unit. Under Wilson's dissolute leadership and with Kühlich absent in Berlin most of the time, their morale was approaching rock bottom and the Corps had lost all sense of cohesion. Despite this, volunteers continued to trickle in during December 1944 and January 1945. This group included William Miller, a gunner from the Royal Artillery captured at Tobruk in 1943, who was persuaded to join the BFC in preference to serving a four-month sentence at the military prison in Graudenz, and Lourens Viljoen, a South African corporal, who joined through the good offices of a friendly SS NCO in charge of his working party.

Three other soldiers who joined around Christmas 1944 deserve special mention. Douglas Cecil Mardon, the third of the trio of South Africans who joined the Corps at Dresden, possessed very rigid views on the threat to the free world of Soviet success on the Eastern Front. As a POW he had seen Russian prisoners and had come to distinctly racist conclusions about them – perhaps not surprisingly, considering where he was brought up – which, when he read BFC recruiting literature, caused him to volunteer with alacrity. George Croft and John Sommerville, who had both been in captivity since 1940, also held strong views about Communism, but in the working party where their long familiarity with the language had led to their employment as interpreters, they were also under physical threat from unruly gangs which had grown up amongst the other prisoners. After some discussion, the pair decided that their best option was to join the Waffen-SS, preferably in the 'Totenkopf' division which they had read about in the English version of *Signal* magazine. As soon as they made their views known they were hustled to Berlin for an interview with Kühlich, who persuaded them to join the BFC instead.

So it was that in the first week of January 1945 the BFC reached its peak strength of twenty-seven members, not including attached German personnel. This may have caused some quiet satisfaction at the SS-Haupt-tamt but it is unlikely; it was clear now that the war was all but over and the project to recruit British soldiers to fight the Soviets had failed miserably. Within the BFC, some astute members had reached the same conclusion and were beginning to make plans to get out.

The chief instigator was Hugh Cowie, the Gordon Highlander from Aberdeen. Following Wilson's rise to prominence he had become the British second-in-command but he had little enthusiasm for the job beyond exerting enough discipline to keep the renegades in order. Whilst at Dresden he had dealt with an incident during which Barker, the worse for wear after an evening's drinking, had attacked and disarmed a sentry at the barracks gate, and had also had cause to jail Jackson on several occasions for repeated absences without leave (Jackson spent as much time as he could with his girlfriend). He was also instrumental in having six Maoris, recruited by Hans Kauss, returned to their work party on the basis that the BFC was a 'whites only' unit. But during the second week of January he decided that he had had enough. Wilson was temporarily absent in Berlin, leaving Cowie in charge, and during a conversation with Futcher he remarked that it would be easy to get away as he had access to all of the travel documentation. Futcher replied that 'there's no time like the present'[8] and Cowie started filling out the necessary paperwork. Along with Alexander, Miller, Nightingale, Symonds and Batchelor, they planned to use official documentation to get themselves as close to the Soviet lines as possible, and then lie up, waiting to be overrun.

Oddly enough, on the day that they planned to leave, under the pretext of a recruiting trip, the BFC's penultimate recruit arrived. Alexander MacKinnon was a lance-corporal in the Cameron Highlanders who was pressured into joining the Corps to avoid punishment for 'sabotaging' agricultural produce.[9] He had barely been introduced to the acting senior NCO before Cowie and his five cohorts (the vacillating Symonds had failed to show up at their rendezvous) set off for the Sudetenland.[10] The group caught a train from Dresden to Prague where they changed for Teschen. During the journey Futcher managed to steal a pistol from a policeman on the train, and they also removed the Union-Jack badges and 'British Free Corps' cuff-titles from their sleeves. Instead of going to Teschen, they decided to leave the train at Olmutz at the instigation of Alexander who claimed to know the area well from his time as a prisoner there. At this point things began to go wrong.

Looking for shelter for the night they approached an innkeeper who agreed to put them up; he also reported their presence to the local police. They were woken the next morning by a military policeman who escorted them to Hohenstadt where they were interviewed by an officer. He was inclined to accept their story and documentation at face value and allowed them to stay the night in a local drill hall, but by the next morning the Gestapo had been alerted to their absence from Dresden and they were rounded up. For the next five days they occupied a cell in the local Gestapo prison. They were retrieved from there by an armed escort comprising Barker, Obersturmführer Tormulde (an officer from the Wildermann Kaserne) and two German NCOs. During the journey Barker, the Australian sybarite, tied their hands together and issued threats of beatings. As they reached Dresden station Alexander rounded on Barker, calling him a 'dirty German'. His response was immediate: 'I know I'm a German, I'm going to volunteer for the front.'

Cowie's deserters failed to maintain their façade of unity for long. After threats from Kühlich, Batchelor, Miller and Nightingale all agreed to stay with the Corps; only Cowie, Futcher and Alexander were sent to the isolation camp at Drönnewitz. Strangely enough Charlie Munns, the Scotsman from the Durham Light Infantry, was allowed to leave the BFC at the same time in order to return to his fiancée in Danzig – it is not clear how he was employed there.

Cowie's desertion was a serious blow to the British Free Corps but the real collapse came some three weeks later. On the evening of Monday 12 February, with the day's routine over, the BFC and their comrades from the pioneer school dispersed to their usual nocturnal haunts. At approximately half-past ten that evening, the first bombs of what was to become one of the most notorious raids of the war began to fall on a city that was overcrowded with refugees and virtually undefended. More raids during the next two days helped to create the firestorm in which at least 40,000 people perished.

Eric Pleasants was spending the evening with his wife and her parents in their house in the hills a few miles from the city. Alerted by the drone of bombers flying overhead and the sound of explosions, they stood in the garden and watched the destruction of Dresden. As the evening passed and the wind began to build up, they noticed a steady rain of black cinders falling around them; debris of the city and its inhabitants, sucked into the sky by the firestorm.[11] In the days following the raids, the entire city of Dresden was in a state of utter chaos. From the first morning, those inhabitants of the pioneer barracks who could be found were sent out into the streets, digging for survivors and bodies in the rubble of the ruined city; a few shocked members of the BFC took their turn at this, as well as helping to burn with flame-throwers the piles of unburied, decomposing corpses that appeared to be everywhere. As he travelled through the wreckage the day after the raid, Pleasants was dumbfounded: 'I couldn't understand how one human being could inflict this on another,' he later said.[12]

But the BFC's days in Dresden were numbered. Britten, the former

'Nazi', had long since lost his enthusiasm for the unit and was planning an escape. During a conversation with his girlfriend, a Norwegian nurse, he boasted of his plans and also claimed that he had foreknowledge of the bombing raids. Shocked by this, she denounced him almost immediately to the Gestapo and the BFC were arrested *en masse*.

By incredible good fortune, the only member of the BFC to be injured during the Dresden raids was Viljoen, the South African, who was hospitalized with burns. But in the confusion after the bombing Heighes and How both successfully deserted from the unit and joined a column of POWs being evacuated west; they were never to return to the ranks of the renegades.

12

The End Game

The mass arrest of the British Free Corps in Dresden after the bombing raid was the final straw for the unit. Kühlich sent Wilson and Mardon from Berlin, where they had been visiting, to spring their comrades from the local jail and escort them back to the capital. The decision had now been made; even though the unit numbered much less than thirty men, they were finally going to have to fight. As Kühlich told Wilson: 'The British Free Corps has had a damn good run, now they must prove they are sincere.'[1]

If any of the BFC men hadn't realized the state that Germany had been reduced to, the journey from Dresden to Berlin on 24 February put them straight. Rössler recalled: 'It took us eight or ten hours to get to Berlin and normally you could do it in about three.'[2] In fact Marshal Konev's 1st Ukrainian Front was, by now, little more than 100 kilometres to the east of Dresden, halted while Stalin and his advisers pondered whether to concentrate their main effort against the German capital. And to the west, the 1st and 9th US Armies were already fighting on German soil east of Aachen.

On their arrival in Berlin, Wilson conducted the BFC to a requisitioned school on the Schönhauser Allee where they were to wait whilst arrangements were made to send them into action. Incredible as it may seem, it was at this point that the last volunteer came forward. Frank Axon, from Crewe, had been taken prisoner in Greece in April 1941 where he was serving as a lance-corporal in the RASC. Since then he had been employed as an agricultural labourer in detachments centred around Stalag XVIIIa at Wolfsberg in Austria, where in February 1945 he was accused of striking a cow, causing it to calve early. Threatened with punishment for this he was offered the alternative of joining the BFC which, unbelievable as it may seem, he accepted.

For the next two weeks, the BFC hung around the devastated capital and faced the prospect of going into battle against the Russians. There were still a few bars and cafés operating amidst the ruins, but for some these did not offer sufficient compensation for the likelihood of combat against the Red Army. In the opinion of Symonds, 'It was useless to go on like this,'³ and he made representations, along with Rose and Nightingale, to go to the isolation camp at Drönnewitz. Fortunately for the trio, their pleas were heard by Alexander Dolezalek, the sympathetic officer behind the 'European – British Peace Movement', who was able to provide them with British POW battledress and send them away. Although he was one of the sponsors of the project in its later stages he had realized that there was nothing to be gained by committing the minuscule force to combat.

Pleasants and Leister, typically, sought a more circuitous route to evade the fighting. Leister, through his girlfriend Lena Jürgens, managed to engineer a transfer to the 'Kurt Eggers' Regiment, for whom she worked as a secretary, and Pleasants got himself attached to Stranders' embryonic 'Peace Camp' – in reality he spent his time giving exhibition bouts against Max Schmeling in German officers' messes.

For the rest, decision time arrived on 8 March. On that day the remnants of the BFC were taken to the Hedemannstrasse office, where each was interviewed by Kühlich. They were given a simple choice: incarceration in the isolation camp at Drönnewitz or service against the Soviets. Perhaps because they had become used to a life of comparative comfort, none of the BFC men took the first option outright – although Wilson refused to go to the front and engineered for himself the role of liaison between the Corps and the Berlin office. The outcome was that Douglas Mardon received promotion to Unterscharführer and was given command of a section consisting of Axon, Barker, Batchelor, Berry, Frederick Croft, George Croft, MacKinnon, Nicholls, Sommerville and Stokes, together with the ever present 'Bob' Rössler as interpreter. Labuschagne and Miller were both deemed to be so useless by Mardon that he refused to take them, and Minchin was being treated for scabies in the SS hospital at Lichtefelde-West.

It is difficult now to pin down the motives of these volunteers. Mardon was undoubtedly sincere in his wish to fight against the advance of Communism, but several of the others were long-standing members of the 'anti-German' faction of the Corps. Albert Stokes, the quiet Australian, had actually joined at the same time as his friend Tom Freeman with the specific intention of sabotaging the unit. Batchelor later suggested, 'They didn't want the Jerries to think they were frightened so they just went'[4] which is perhaps the best explanation. In any case, before they could be deployed at the front it was deemed wise to give them an intensive refresher training course.

Mardon's first task as the senior BFC NCO was to get his small unit to an emergency close-combat training camp in the village of Niemeck, a few miles to the north-west of Berlin. For four days the Corps received intensive instruction in the latest techniques for tank destruction, using 'Panzerfaust' rocket-launchers and improvised mines and explosives; and they were issued with the revolutionary MP44 assault-rifle (the weapon on which the Soviet AK47 was later based). Finally realizing that the British Free Corps was really going to have to fight, Barker suddenly lost all of his former enthusiasm for anti-Communism and made himself ill by smoking aspirins; he was sent back to Berlin by a gullible medical officer. He was followed, the next day, by the rest of the Corps, who had been granted two days of leave before going into action.

For the BFC, their last two days in Berlin were spent in the time-honoured manner of soldiers about to go into battle. The atmosphere in Berlin at this time was frantic – as the Russians neared, tension amongst the population was becoming unbearable – and the renegades sought solace in alcohol and female company. Nevertheless, at the appointed time on 15 March the British Free Corps finally boarded the truck that was to take them to the Eastern Front, as the British Commonwealth's own pathetic contribution to the 'Crusade against Bolshevism'. After several hours of travelling, during which most members removed the tell-tale BFC insignia from their uniforms, Mardon and Rössler reported with their men to the headquarters of III. (Germanisches) SS-Panzer-

Korps in a suburb of Stettin. The 'Germanic' Panzer Corps was formed in April 1943 and was intended as the showpiece formation in which the Western European SS units would be concentrated. For much of its existence it was based around the 'Nordland' division — which was partly made up of Danes and Norwegians — and the mainly Dutch 'Nederland' brigade, but in practice, despite the intentions of Himmler and his Pan-Germanic colleagues, the majority of troops were Germans or Volksdeutsche.[5]

Despite the cosmopolitan composition of their formation, the staff at the headquarters of the Panzer Corps were taken aback to receive a group of British reinforcements and their reaction was to billet the BFC in a private house on the western edge of Stettin whilst they decided how to employ them. The BFC waited for a week, under sporadic artillery and mortar fire, before they received their orders, and while they waited lost yet another man to sickness. This was George Croft, who suddenly found himself stricken with gonorrhoea serious enough for him to be sent to a military hospital in Neubrandenburg; he had caught it from his girlfriend in Berlin, who had, she claimed in a letter to him, been raped by Wilson in the BFC billet in the Schönhauser Allee.[6]

The BFC's orders came through on 22 March detailing them to move to the headquarters of the Nordland division at Angermünde, a little way to the south. From there they were sent to join the divisional armoured reconnaissance battalion (11. SS-Panzer-Aufklärungs-Abteilung) located in Grüssow. The battalion commander was Sturmbannführer Rudolf Saalbach, who had been a member of the SS since 1932 and had won the Knight's Cross (the highest German bravery decoration) the year before. Whatever he thought of having Britons in his unit, he was desperate for reinforcements and gave the BFC a friendly speech of welcome before allocating them to the 3rd Company, under the command of the Swedish Obersturmführer Hano-Goesta Perrson. Perrson gave the BFC an armoured personnel carrier and an amphibious 'Schwimmwagen' jeep and detailed them to construct dug-outs within the company perimeter.

The battalion that the BFC had joined was probably one of the most cosmopolitan in the German armed forces, consisting when the Britons arrived, of Germans, Dutchmen, Danes, Norwegians, Flemings, Swedes,

Swiss and Volksdeutsche from throughout Europe; nevertheless the Union Jack patches still on the right shoulders of a few of the renegades caused a flurry of interest amongst the SS veterans. They made their new British comrades welcome – MacKinnon remembers them as 'a good bunch of lads'[7] – and together they awaited events.

When the BFC joined the battalion, the whole division was being held as a reserve, with as many troops as possible being rested for the inevitable Russian assault over the river Oder that was expected any day. In consequence, the BFC was not required to do any fighting although they could quite clearly see the Russians from their position. But despite the fact that they weren't in combat, rations and ammunition were in desperately short supply, and Mardon, Berry and Nicholls were forced to barter some of their cigarettes for a few bullets so that they could shoot a deer in the nearby forest to eat.

Even though, during the four weeks that they spent with the armoured reconnaissance battalion, the BFC was in imminent danger of actually having to fight the Red Army, their predicament still failed to unite the renegades. Mardon remained keen to 'have a go' at the Russians, but Batchelor, Stokes, Croft, Nicholls and Axon were so unenthusiastic that it prompted Mardon to start calling them 'Yellow bastards'.[8] In the end, though, even he bowed to the pressure being exerted by his companions and made representations to their company commander to get them pulled out.

Even as Mardon was attempting to get the BFC withdrawn from the front line, the man who was actually to save them was about to return to the fold. Thomas Cooper had spent a quiet six months in the Leibstandarte Adolf Hitler as a military policeman, checking the papers of soldiers passing through Spreenhagen railway station. But on 6 April he received orders posting him to the headquarters of the Germanic Panzer Corps with effect from the 9th. Realizing that he was going back into action, and with an eye on a possible escape attempt, he burned most of his SS papers and packed a brown civilian suit into his kit-bag. He arrived at the Corps headquarters, now situated in Steinhöffl on the Oder, on 11 April. As he climbed down from his truck dressed to all intents and purposes like any other member of the Waffen-SS, he was very taken aback to be asked by an officer if he was Oberscharführer 'Montgomery' (i.e. Wilson). He replied that, no, he was Cooper, but asked if there were any other Englishmen about; to his amazement he learned that there were 'ten somewhere near the front'.[9] Shortly afterwards he met Sturmbannführer Schonfelde, the Corps adjutant, who told him that Obergruppenführer Steiner, the Corps Commander, required his presence at dinner that evening; nonplussed, he headed off to find a billet.

Later the same afternoon Cooper was called to return to the Corps headquarters, where he was met by Obersturmbannführer Riedweg, whom he recognized as the former chief of the 'Germanische Leitstelle' in the SS-Hauptamt. When Cooper asked why he had been given 'such a glorious reception' Riedweg explained that the BFC had been sent to the front but nobody knew what to do with them. Later, at dinner, Obergruppenführer Steiner ordered Cooper to travel with him to visit the BFC the next morning, as he had decided to inspect the unit.

Steiner and Cooper made an early start the next day and reached the BFC's position later in the morning. During the drive Cooper briefed the general about the background to the BFC, emphasizing that he did not think it wise to use the unit in a combat role. Steiner agreed, although he was also somewhat perturbed about the post-war legal implications for himself if he committed the BFC against the Russians. When they arrived at Grüssow, Cooper found the BFC in 'a pretty desperate state of mind'[10] but he paraded the unit for the General. Steiner shook each member by the hand and made a short speech, telling them that it was a great shame that young Englishmen and Germans were spilling each other's blood on the Western Front, that both peoples were of the same race, and that he was sure that one day England and Germany would unite and conquer the world. He then told them that he had decided to use them as medical orderlies and left.

With Steiner gone, Cooper was finally able to talk to the renegades and catch up on their news. He found that they were laying the blame squarely on Wilson and Mardon for their troubles, and that Stokes, Axon and Batchelor were planning to desert. Fortunately for them, Cooper managed to talk them out of this course of action. He knew full well that behind the front line squads of military police were rounding up and executing any soldier who could not account for his presence as suspected deserters. Instead, on the afternoon of 13 April Cooper took Mardon to the HQ of the Nordland division to discuss the BFC with the commander, Brigadeführer Ziegler. Cooper briefed Ziegler on the background to the BFC, emphasizing that most of its members had been press-ganged into joining and that they could only be a very uncertain factor in combat. Ziegler agreed and sent the two to get Steiner's formal consent to withdraw the BFC from the front line.

Mardon and Cooper arrived the same afternoon but Steiner remained unavailable until the next day. When they finally got to see him, Cooper repeated the briefing that he had given to Ziegler but added that he thought the BFC could be safely employed as truck drivers behind the front line. Steiner accepted this and issued the necessary orders; Mardon and Cooper returned to Grüssow. The next day orders arrived at the armoured recce battalion for the BFC to move back to Corps HQ. When they got there they were given travel orders and rations to get them to Templin, where they were to join the transport company of Steiner's HQ staff (Kraftfahrstaffel StabSteiner). They arrived on 16 April and were billeted in a requisitioned college.

One of the principal gripes of the BFC when they were at the front was that they no longer had access to Red Cross food parcels. Wilson's ostensible job as liaison officer had been to keep the flow of parcels moving to the front, but all he had done, together with Barker, was steal a few before deserting Berlin on 9 April. Consequently Cooper took a truck and four men back into Berlin on the 17th to see if they could get their hands on a supply. They returned to Templin on the 19th to find a surprise in store. Talking expansively to Mardon was a muscularly-built, blond-haired Englishman of medium height, dressed in a black SS tank uniform bearing the insignia of a Hauptsturmführer in the British Free Corps! Mardon introduced them and Cooper discovered that he was talking to Haupsturmführer Douglas Berneville-Claye, who had, he explained, come to lead the BFC into battle.

It remains obscure how Berneville-Claye came to join the SS, but the known facts of his case are as follows: he was born Douglas Berneville Webster Claye in the London suburb of Plumstead in 1917, the son of a staff-sergeant in the RASC. In 1932 he was sent to the Army Apprentices College at Chepstow, where he remained until 1935 when he left the Army to try to find a civilian job. After spending time helping his father, now retired from the army, run a pub in Harrogate, he became an instructor at a riding school in Thames Ditton, where he also married in October 1936. He split with his pregnant wife the next year but did not seek a divorce, and then spent the period up to the outbreak of war scratching a living as a freelance journalist in Leeds.

At the start of the war Claye volunteered for, and was accepted by, the RAF as an aircrew trainee, but in April 1940 discovered that his girlfriend was pregnant. His reaction was to go absent without leave and bigamously marry her; the RAF, unaware of his bigamy, discharged him nevertheless. Claye then worked for a while in an aircraft factory and joined the Home Guard in Leeds. It was there that he exhibited the first symptoms of the fantasy world in which he lived: instead of wearing the normal Home Guard battledress, he bought an officer's service-dress uniform to which he added pilot's wings. Dressed in this outfit he was involved in a car crash, and after treatment in a local hospital was sent to an officers' convalescent home. Here he stole a number of cheques from a Scottish major and fraudulently obtained £5.10s before being caught as a result of police investigations.

Claye was fined £7 by magistrates for representing himself to be a member of the forces and committed for trial at the local quarter sessions for theft of the cheques and fraud. By paying back the money that was stolen, he contrived to be only bound over for two years when his trial came up, and shortly afterwards, in January 1941, he disappeared into the Army, enlisting as a private soldier in the West Yorkshire Regiment under the name Douglas Webster Berneville-Claye.

Despite his record, or perhaps because he succeeded in concealing it, Berneville-Claye was commissioned as a second lieutenant in October 1941 and sent with his battalion to the Middle East. At some point during the latter half of 1942 he volunteered for training with the Special Air Service and was accepted, joining the regiment's 'B' Squadron in October as a trained parachutist and behind-the-lines commando. It must be remembered that 1 SAS in 1942 was a very different organization to the

SAS Regiment of today; despite the presence of legendary soldiers such as David Stirling and 'Paddy' Mayne, the early SAS was often forced to make use of men who only became available because their own units didn't want them. Berneville-Claye, who by now was calling himself 'Lord Charlesworth', was even so a notably undistinguished SAS officer, accounted so 'useless' and dangerous by veterans of that period that many refused to go on operations with him.[11]

In December 1942, whilst operating with a patrol of 'B' Squadron deep behind enemy lines, Berneville-Claye was captured by an Afrika Korps unit and transported across the Mediterranean to a POW camp in Italy. He was later to boast that he had broken out of Italian POW camps four times before being taken to Oflag 79 in Brunswick, but whatever the truth, by the time he got to the Oflag he was working as an informer for the Germans. His activities became known to the other British officers in the camp, and shortly after Christmas 1944 he was removed by the Germans for his own safety. No information is to be found regarding his activities between the time that he left Oflag 79 and turned up at Templin on 19 March 1945. He told Cooper that he had only been in the SS for two months but did not say what he had been doing.

After chatting to Cooper for a few minutes, Berneville-Claye then asked to speak to 'the Englishmen'[12] and Cooper led him over to where they were gathered. To everybody's surprise Berneville-Claye launched into a speech, announcing that he was the son of an earl, a captain in the Coldstream Guards and was going to collect two armoured cars and lead them against the Russians. He also guaranteed that the BFC men would be in no trouble with the British authorities, telling them that Britain would be a war with the Russians within a few days.

Cooper was incensed. 'You've come to drop them back in the shit after I just got them out of it!' he shouted,[13] and he finally met with the approval of all of his men. 'For once he had spoken like a true Englishman,' according to Batchelor.[14] Berneville Claye continued to bluster for a few minutes but he realized his bluff had been called. Turning to Mardon, he ordered him to keep an eye on Cooper but he left for good a few minutes later, taking MacKinnon with him as his driver.[15] They made their way, over the next few days, to Bad Kleinen, a small town on the north shore of the Schweriner See, where Berneville-Claye changed into a British uniform, including a camouflaged jacket with SAS markings,[16] and Mac-Kinnon borrowed a farmer's jacket. Thereupon they split up and, separately, handed themselves over to the advancing Allies during the next few days.[17]

As the only recorded traitor in the history of the SAS was bowing out of the Waffen-SS, the BFC's erstwhile colleagues in the Nordland division were moving into Berlin to take part in the battle for the capital of the Third Reich. With them went 'Bob' Rössler, the BFC's phlegmatic, one-eyed interpreter. After the return of Cooper he had decided that there was no further need to stay with the traitors and he felt duty-bound to take part in the last stand against the Soviets. In the days that followed the Nordland division fought to a standstill amidst the ruins of the city, alongside elderly Volkssturm men, young Hitler Youths, and a strange collection of foreign volunteers who included a French SS brigade, a Spanish SS battalion and even James Brady and Frank Stringer, the two young Irishmen. Only a handful survived.

Although the BFC had been withdrawn from a combat role they still had a job to do, and surprisingly enough they stuck with it. After Berneville-Claye's departure the transport company followed Steiner's Headquarter's to Neustrelitz and the BFC went with it. There Cooper and his unit were witnesses to one of the final dramas of the Third Reich. On 21 April Hitler, now effectively trapped in his bunker in Berlin, raised the status of Steiner's command to that of an 'Army Detachment' (Armeeabteilung) and ordered him to launch an attack to restore the front to the north and east of Berlin. If Hitler thought that the increase in the prestige of Steiner's command would embolden him he was wrong. Steiner doggedly refused to launch an operation which he knew to be doomed to failure and which would certainly cost the lives of many of his men. Despite frantic telephone calls and messages from the Führer's entourage, and even a physical assault by Field Marshal Keitel, Steiner refused to budge, effectively sealing the fate of Hitler and his high-ranking Nazi cronies still stuck in Berlin.

The BFC continued with their work, driving trucks, directing traffic and helping with the evacuation of civilian refugees in the Neustrelitz and

Reinershagen area up until the day before Hitler's suicide. On 29 April Steiner summoned his staff and told them of his decision to break contact with the Russians and order his forces to head west into Anglo-American captivity. Cooper, the senior NCO in the transport company, was placed in command of a group of around thirty soldiers, including all the BFC men, and a few vehicles. He was told to taken them to a position just outside the town of Schwerin in Mecklenburg, and then to await orders. He set off fairly quickly, leaving behind Ken Berry who could not be found, and during the evening laagered his men into a camp in a wood on the Criwitz-Schwerin road, eight kilometres outside Schwerin. During the night a military police (Feldgendarmerie) squad stumbled across them and, discovering that Cooper's convoy didn't have the correct papers, threatened to arrest them. Cooper was only able to extract his men from the clutches of the Feldgendarmerie by taking some of them to the rump of Steiner's headquarters, in a farmhouse called 'Gut-Neuhof*, about forty kilometres to their north. There Obersturmbannführer von Bülow was able to issue the necessary authorizations to allow Cooper to continue on his way. For safety's sake Cooper decided to leave his second-in-command, Douglas Mardon, with the HQ for liaison purposes.

Cooper returned to the camp in the woods in the early hours of the morning of 2 May. By then he had not slept for three days and so, when he got into his tent, he fell into a deep slumber. He was woken at noon by one of the German drivers who told him that the US Army had arrived in Schwerin and were only six kilometres from their position. Cooper got up immediately, trying to decide what to do. Shortly afterwards he resolved to change into his civilian suit and, while he was doing this, he instructed the Germans in his party to change out of uniform as far as possible and to disperse. Then he collected together the remains of the BFC who were lurking deeper in the woods, shouting at the reluctant Nicholls, 'Come on out you silly bastard, the war is over'.[18] At this point

---

* Batchelor believed that the military police were suspicious of Waffen-SS soldiers speaking English — he was probably right — but, bizarre as it may seem considering the state of chaos in Germany on 1 May 1945, in the first instance Cooper was questioned because he didn't have the necessary permits to be on that particular road.

he found that Batchelor and Stokes had already gone, but he collected together Nicholls, Sommerville, Croft and Axon, and between them they decided to try to get some food and then make contact with the Americans.

As the German forces laid down their arms, there were a large number of Allied POWs roaming around the countryside, attempting to make contact with the advancing British and American forces. Cooper spoke to a number of these, trying to find a British officer to report to, but all he succeeded in obtaining was a pair of US Army trousers and a British battledress jacket, with which he hoped to be able to blend in as an ex-POW. As he left one large group, which had just taken 160 casualties from an Allied air attack, Nicholls and Sommerville drew up on motor-cycles and Cooper told them to stick with the ex-prisoners.

The only member of the BFC still with Cooper was Fred Croft, the London-born gunner, and together they decided to try to find a British officer in Schwerin. After an altercation with an American Military Policeman they eventually made it into the town, where they came across the headquarters of 121st Infantry Regiment, the lead element of 8 US Division. Cooper spoke to a group of American NCOs, telling them that he was a British secret agent and that he knew the whereabouts of Obergruppenführer Steiner and some of Himmler's personal staff. To his surprise they immediately bundled him into a jeep to go to find Steiner, but because of the chaos on the roads they were unable to get through, and they took Cooper back to Schwerin for the night.

At 0055 hours on 3 May, the Intelligence message log of 2nd British Army recorded the text of a signal from the 'Phantom' liaison team attached to 8 US Division. It read: 'I have with me British man called TH a trooper [*sic*] who states he is int agent and has been sending infm through General FORTUNE. Has been in Germany since 1939. Send instructions for disposal please.'[19] Evidently Cooper had at last found a British officer to report to.

Bizarrely enough, Cooper and the handful of soldiers still 'serving' in the BFC found themselves in the same town at the same time as the BFC rejects from the isolation camp at Drönnewitz. The British liaison officer, Captain Denys Hart MC of the 'Phantom' Regiment (1st GHQ Liaison

Regiment), appears not to have kept a very close eye on Cooper, because he was able to wander off into the town and meet Don Bowler, the Fascist medical orderly from Genshagen, who had been evacuated from Drönnewitz to the Municipal Theatre in Schwerin. There, led by the enterprising Cowie, the ex-BFC men had overpowered and disarmed their guards and gone foraging for food.

Cooper pointed Bowler, who had always resisted joining the BFC, in the direction of the increasingly suspicious Captain Hart, who then decided, because of the seemingly garbled stories that Cooper and Bowler were giving him, to arrest Cooper, Croft and the entire Drönnewitz group, including Sergeant Trinder and Corporal Bowler. At 1330 hours on 3 May, Hart sent the following message to 2nd British Army:

I have now approx 27 heavily armed British here, some of whom appear to be implicated with the British Free Corps also one alleged to be co-broadcaster with William Joyce. The whole set up is suspicious and you may give me instrs as my friends here (8 US Div) do NOT like touching the situation.[20]

The group consisted of Cowie, Futcher, Symonds, Rose, Alexander, Nightingale, Miller, Lane, Chipchase, Wood, Perkins, Martin, Cryderman, Chapman, Van Heerden, Wilson (of the original Luckenwalde group – not John Wilson), Clarke, Leigh, Haynes, Kipling, Dowden and Blackman, who had all been involved in the BFC in one way or another; Maylin, Marshall, Bowler and Trinder from the Genshagen 'staff', and Dillon, a recalcitrant Irish broadcaster.

Despite Hart's precautions, several of this group were able to slip away and join up with British POW transports heading back to Britain where they were arrested over the next few weeks. For Thomas Cooper his adventure was over, and he remained in military custody pending removal to the British Military prison in Brussels, where he was incarcerated until he was brought back to the UK in September to face charges of high treason.

The BFC members who had stayed in Berlin when Mardon took his group to the Oder front did not hang around for long. Miller was, as we have seen, taken to Drönnewitz; Wilson and Barker stayed until 9 April before taking off towards Bremen; and Labuschagne slipped away in the direction of Dresden, there to be 'liberated' by advancing US forces.

John Leister, who had by now gone through a form of illegal marriage with his old schoolfriend Lena Jürgens, was attached to the 'Kurt Eggers' Regiment's 'Skorpion West' operation. Lena, who worked in the Zehlendorf headquarters of the regiment, forged two rail passes to get them to Italy and the couple set off on 9 April. They arrived at their destination, Milan, twelve days later, having managed to pick their way through the chaos of Germany in total collapse. When they arrived it was to find a warrant waiting for Lena's arrest and return to Berlin, but amidst the confusion of a partisan attack they were able to draw a small allowance from the SS headquarters and head for the hills – Leister dumping his BFC uniform on the way. They hid out in the town of Bressanone until the Americans arrived.

For Eric and Annelise Pleasants escape from Berlin was more problematic. Eric switched his BFC uniform for a Wehrmacht one in the cellar of a bakery in north-east Berlin and disguised himself by wrapping bandages around his head, but by the time they attempted to leave the city it was encircled by the Russians. Desperate to get out, they took first to the underground railway tunnels and later the sewers, aiming to get south-east in the direction of Anneliese's parents' home near Dresden. They were lucky, making it out of the city, though during the course of their escape Eric Pleasants was obliged to kill two Russian soldiers with his bare hands when they attempted to arrest him in the southern suburbs. They lay low with Anneliese's parents for some months, surviving the depredations of American occupation troops who were, in Pleasants' opinion, more brutal towards local populations than either the Germans or the Russians.[21] But then they found that the Americans were pulling out and the Russians taking over. They stayed on in the Russian zone, Eric Pleasants eking out a living doing a strongman act to entertain the occupying forces, until in early 1946 they were arrested on suspicion of spying. After a quick trial Eric Pleasants was sent to the 'Inter' camp at Vorkuta in the Russian Arctic where he remained for seven years; he neither saw nor heard from Anneliese again.

For the broadcasters of the Concordia Büro and the Reichsrundfunk, the collapse of Germany assumed a more measured pace. The bombing of

Berlin led, in February 1945, to the evacuation of Concordia's non-essential staff, like the broadcasters themselves, to Helmstedt, where they continued making programmes almost to the very end. The 'Germany Calling' team, including the reconciled Joyces, were sent in March to Apen, on the Dutch border, from where they transmitted programmes for rebroadcasting along the telephone lines to Hamburg.

For most of the broadcasters the end came suddenly. Concordia broadcasts continued until the Americans occupied Braunschweig, only a few miles from their location, at which point Hetzler issued false identity cards, divided up the contents of the station's cash-box amongst his staff and told them to scatter.

For the Joyces, proceedings were more prolonged. On 7 April the Propaganda Ministry in Berlin directed that they should be kept out of Allied hands at all costs. Plans centred at first around a scheme to smuggle them from Bremen to Southern Ireland by U-Boat but it soon became clear that this was impractical – there were few boats available, and the RAF and Royal Navy had such absolute command of the air and sea around Germany that there was little hope of getting a submarine through. Instead Joyce was given identity documents in the name of Wilhelm Hansen, a schoolteacher born in Galway, and a plan was worked out to get him to Sweden. In the meantime he continued to broadcast, making his last recording, drunk, on 30 April 1945; it was never broadcast.

Later on the same evening a car appeared at the Hamburg studios to take the Joyces to Flensburg on the Danish border, as the first stage in their journey to Sweden. They reached Flensburg but the plan was already breaking down – there was no vehicle to meet them there – and they were lucky that their driver from Hamburg, an SS Funkschutz soldier, was permitted to take them over the border to Abenra. There they waited for news for four days before it became clear that there was no prospect of going further – Danish resistance fighters were taking control of the country in conjunction with British Special Forces – and they decided to go back to Flensburg, capital of Admiral Dönitz's provisional government. They stayed on there until 11 May – at the same time, coincidentally, as Heinrich Himmler who was attempting to get himself a job in the administration – but the town was becoming overcrowded and eventually they were forced to leave. By chance they headed for Wassersleben, a nearby village, where Joyce discovered that Edwin Bowlby had holed up with his girlfriend Helge Dietze. The Joyces stayed with Bowlby for a nigh., and the next day obtained lodgings with an elderly English widow who lived in the area. They remained undetected for two weeks.

On Monday 28 May the Joyces went into the village of Kupfermühle to buy food, and to their delight found that bacon was on sale. They decided to walk home through a forest, gathering firewood on their way, but they had an argument and Joyce became sulky. After they had eaten their lunch, he apologized to Margaret and offered to take her for a walk, but it was her turn to do the washing-up and she declined. Joyce nevertheless decided to go alone. After walking for a while, he sat down and dozed off in some woods near Wassersleben. When he woke he realized that Margaret would be worried about him and he set off for the road in order to get home quicker. Looking about him as he walked, he noticed two British officers apparently looking for firewood. As he passed them he said, 'Here are a few more pieces' in French and, as the officers straightened up, repeated his advice in English. To one of the officers, Captain Alexander Lickorish, the voice sounded familiar: 'You wouldn't happen to be William Joyce, would you?' he asked. In reply Joyce started to reach inside his coat pocket to fetch out his papers but he was forestalled by the other officer, Lieutenant Perry, who, thinking that Joyce was reaching for a weapon, drew his own .38 revolver and shot Joyce in the right leg, felling him immediately.

The last of the renegades to fall into Allied hands was James Brady, the young Irish member of Otto Skorzeny's Jagdverbände. After the 'rescue' of Admiral Horthy his unit returned to Berlin until January 1945, but the imminent arrival of the Soviets meant that even special forces had to be thrown into the battle as standard infantry, and along with the rest of his company Brady found himself holding the Schwedt bridgehead against powerful Soviet attacks. They hung on until the end of February when they were evacuated to a position on the Oder, where a couple of days later Brady was wounded during a Russian counter-attack. Whilst he was convalescing he was attached to a training team teaching policemen how to use anti-tank weapons, before returning to the Oder on 25 March where he was promoted to Sturmmann. Two days later his unit was all but wiped out in a Russian attack and Brady himself was wounded in the head, causing him to be evacuated to Grunau where he remained until the Soviets arrived. Not keen to be captured by the Russians, he escaped from Grunau and made his way to Berlin where he was given the rank of Rottenführer and took part in the last battle for the capital of the Reich.

During the Berlin fighting, Brady received his third and final wound in the service of the Waffen-SS when he was hit in the legs by shrapnel, injuries that put him in a German military hospital until 10 May. Even so, he was able to escape from Russian captivity and he went underground for over a year, living on his wits and with the help of other SS veterans, until he turned himself in to the British authorities in Berlin in September 1946, sixteen months after the end of the war.

13

The Reckoning

Other than the orders that were given by MI9 in London for the elimination of Harold Cole in 1942, no serious consideration was given by
the intelligence services to the question of what to do with the other
renegades until planning for the invasion of Europe in 1944 began in
earnest. When it began to take into account the need to have some
organization to deal with British defectors, there were two strong candidates: MI5, the Security Service, whose role was the countering of
threats to British national security; and MI9, a service set up at the start
of the war to assist in the evasion of British servicemen from occupied
Europe and to exploit the intelligence potential of British POWs abroad.
Both were to become deeply involved.

Prior to the invasion, investigation of the renegades was little more
than an interesting sideline for the intelligence services. There was natural
concern about the broadcasting activities of Joyce, Amery and the secret
stations, but as the threat of invasion receded it was recognized that their
propaganda had no significant material impact and that MI5 had more
important matters to worry about. Similarly with the British Free Corps:
although John Brown's messages from Genshagen in the autumn of 1943
had created quite a stir and there were genuine fears that a British unit
fighting on the Eastern Front might create a rift with the Soviets, when
the scale of the BFC became apparent the British authorities were able
to breathe more easily.

Nevertheless, with the opening of a 'second front' in France in June
1944, the problem of the renegades again raised its head. The threat that
the traitors posed (or at least *could* have posed) was very real; it would

be a simple matter to put a Free Corps member in a British uniform and infiltrate him across the front line as a spy or saboteur. In consequence, from the beginning of 1944 measures were taken to counter this threat.

The first task for MI5 was the drafting of what became known as the 'British Renegades Warning List'. This was a central register of all those suspected of having aided the Germans in continental Europe, giving, it appears,[1] their names, dates of birth and descriptions. The first draft of the list was drawn up by Roger Hollis[2] of the counter-subversion division (F Division) in the summer of 1944, using information gleaned from such diverse sources as MI9's POW camp correspondents, a repatriated former Rundfunk broadcaster (Denyss Chamberlain Wace, who was killed by a German bomb in June 1944), and an Irish spy who had been captured in Eire after landing by parachute in 1943 – he turned out to have broadcast on the Rundfunk's Irish service.

The first draft was not terribly well received by its customers, who probably failed to appreciate the difficulty of producing such a document with no direct evidence at all to rely upon; but in the months that followed it was added to and amended and began, much more, to fulfil the purpose for which it had been intended. The list itself was issued to the field security units of the British 21st Army Group, and to British diplomatic personnel in neutral and liberated countries who were thought most likely to encounter renegade Britons in the course of their work. Information was also expected to be collected by the field arm of MI9 – IS9 (WEA) – which deployed to France after the invasion with the task of retrieving escapers and evaders, and supervising the repatriation of liberated POWs.

The first recapture of renegade Britons provided MI5 with a windfall of intelligence material. Courlander and Maton, who gave themselves up in Brussels on 4 September 1944, had both been prominent broadcasters on the secret stations before joining the British Free Corps, for which Courlander was the chief recruiter. In consequence, the statements made by the two men, which were both very lengthy, gave an extremely accurate picture of the situation within these two principal groups of traitors. Having added this to information received through MI9 sources, Lieutenant-Colonel Vivian Seymer of MI5 was able to compile a preliminary report on the British Free Corps and the Concordia Büro, which was issued on 27 March 1945,[3] and which tentatively identified thirty-nine Britons as members of the BFC and a further fifteen as being involved in radio propaganda for Concordia. Considering the limited sources that he was using, Seymour's report on the BFC was surprisingly accurate in most respects and it formed the basis on which subsequent investigation of the renegade unit was based as Allied troops began to sweep through Germany itself (a copy of this report is reproduced in Appendix 1, p. 200).

Although it was expected that most of the traitors would be picked up by the advancing Allies in the normal course of military operations and by the IS9 (WEA) POW collection centres, MI5 formed a specially selected team of officers to handle their subsequent arrest and interrogation. The men assigned to these duties came from a small group of skilled Scotland Yard detectives who had been seconded to MI5's B Division in 1940 in order to handle special counter-sabotage investigations: the Police liaison section of B57 branch. This group, whose principle members were Leonard Burt, Reginald Spooner and William Scardon, were commissioned in the Intelligence Corps and posted to the MI5 office in Paris in April 1945. From there their task was to travel into Germany and seize documents, photographs and other artefacts relating to the traitors, as well as to interrogate the traitors themselves. They had a busy time of it – most of the traitors were recaptured during the month of May – and in the end they were forced to allow many of the minor renegades to return to Britain to be dealt with by MI5 and Special Branch officers there.

Because most of the traitors 'fell' into British hands quite easily, there were only two 'manhunts' of any consequence. The first was for William Joyce, whose chance capture has already been described; the second was for Harold Cole who proved to be considerably more elusive. Cole's betrayal of the PAT escape line had already made him an assassination target for the British intelligence services as early as 1942, and not surprisingly, as the war came to an end, he sought to make himself scarce. Through a series of lucky coincidences, he was able to represent himself to the advancing US forces in southern Germany at the beginning of May

1945 as a British intelligence officer who had escaped from German captivity – an American officer who had known him as a genuine agent in northern France in 1941 had vouched for him – and he was able to obtain US Counter Intelligence Corps documents identifying him as such. Having done this, he moved himself into the French occupation zone where he set himself up as a war crimes liaison officer with a French regiment in the village of Saulgau.

Cole's purpose appears to have been to obtain money for a long-term getaway. In the month or so that he spent in and around Saulgau, with a motley group of fellow 'investigators', he launched a minor reign of terror against local Nazi officials who he thought might be hiding gold or cash. This culminated in the brutal interrogation and murder of Georg Hanft, a former SS officer, who it appears was designated as the local leader of the Nazi 'Werwolf' resistance movement. (Although there were a few incidents, 'Werwolf' never got off the ground; Germany was too profoundly defeated.)

Cole was eventually arrested through his own overconfidence: in June 1945 he sent a postcard to a former girlfriend in France who showed it to a member of MI9. He was taken into custody by Peter Hope of MI9 on 11 June and transferred to a detention centre in Paris.

Investigation of the renegades continued throughout the summer of 1945 under the capable direction of Burt, Spooner and Scardon, and revealed, if it wasn't obvious already, what pathetic characters the majority were. The excuses that they gave for their actions were depressingly repetitive: most claimed to have changed sides to spy on the other traitors; or to sabotage the German propaganda effort and the British Free Corps. Only a few were prepared, as Joyce was, to face up to the consequences of their actions. Despite the expectations of the press, it was ultimately decided that only a handful would face charges of treason, which carried the mandatory death penalty; the rest would be tried for lesser charges against the 1940 Defence Regulations. The four men who were to go on trial for their lives in the winter of 1945 were William Joyce, John Amery, Walter Purdy and Thomas Cooper.

As the most prominent traitor of the war, Joyce was the first to be tried. He had been interrogated by Scardon on 31 May in his hospital bed at Lüneburg and had proved to be a co-operative subject; he held back nothing from the MI5 officer. However, amongst Joyce's possessions Scardon had found a birth certificate showing that he was born in New York in 1906, and he learnt from the prisoner himself that Michael Joyce, his father, was a naturalized US citizen. The consequence of this was that, when the Director of Public Prosecutions suggested to the Attorney-General, then Sir David Maxwell-Fyffe, that Joyce be tried for treason, he is said to have greeted the proposal with 'incredulity'.[4] Instead the Government hoped to be able to secure a conviction against Joyce under the defence regulations.

Although Joyce was something of a figure of fun in Britain for his 'Haw-Haw' broadcasts, he was also widely detested as the mouthpiece of Nazi Germany in the most bitter war in history. Rumours had already begun to spread that his nationality might enable him to escape the punishment he was thought to deserve, and a campaign developed to press for a treason trial and execution. The Government capitulated, and on 18 June Joyce appeared before the Bow Street Magistrates' Court to be remanded on a charge of high treason. After a series of further remand appearances, he was committed for trial at the Old Bailey on 17 September 1945.

For all that has been written about the trial of William Joyce since, the issues of the case were quite simple. He did not deny the actions that had led to his being charged with treason; he simply denied that they were treason. The three counts against him were that he had committed treason by broadcasting for the Germans between September 1939 and May 1945; that he had committed treason by taking German nationality whilst Britain and Germany were at war; and that he had committed treason by broadcasting for Germany between September 1939 and July 1940, when his British passport expired. The probability that Joyce was an American citizen and that there might not be a case for him to answer surrounded the entire proceedings. The prosecution was led by the new Labour Attorney-General, Sir Hartley Shawcross, and in his case he sought to show that Joyce was a British subject, and therefore a traitor. The only evidence given which outlined Joyce's offences came from his own statement, read in court by Scardon, and from a Special Branch inspector called Hunt who alleged that he had heard Joyce broadcasting the news of the supposed destruction of Folkestone in late September or early October 1939 (he had heard Joyce speak at political meetings before the war and recognized his voice). Otherwise, Shawcross produced evidence of Joyce's claims of British nationality: when he had joined the OTC in 1922; and when he applied for and renewed his British passport during the 1930s.

Gerald Slade KC, for the defence, replied by producing conclusive evidence that Joyce was born and remained a United States citizen until he took German nationality in September 1940. In a dramatic moment on the third day of the trial, the judge, Mr Justice Tucker, ruled that the first two counts against Joyce – those of broadcasting throughout the war and treasonably becoming a German citizen – should be dismissed. As news spread of this ruling, an angry crowd gathered outside the Central Criminal Court in the expectation that Joyce would shortly be released; they need not have bothered.

Thereafter, the trial of William Joyce hinged on one argument. Shawcross maintained that, having fraudulently obtained a British passport, Joyce would nevertheless have received the protection of the Crown had he sought it, and that he therefore owed a corresponding duty of loyalty to the Crown. Slade argued that the only way that Joyce had available to him to leave Britain was to use his fraudulently obtained passport, and that he had no intention whatsoever of calling upon the protection of the Crown having left its jurisdiction. Legal precedent, such as it was, showed only that an alien had a duty of loyalty to the Crown when resident in British territory. The judge ruled that Shawcross was correct and the jury took twenty-three minutes to decide that Joyce was guilty of treason. He was sentenced to hang by the neck until he was dead.

After he had been brought to England, and throughout his trial, Joyce had been kept on remand at Wormwood Scrubs prison in Hammersmith. Now that he was under sentence of death, he was taken to Wandsworth prison which had one of the two gallows remaining in London. (It still does. The death sentence remains in force for treason and Wandsworth prison possesses the only working execution apparatus in Britain. The other gallows at that time were at Pentonville.) However, all was not yet lost for Joyce; in his summing up at the old Bailey, Mr Justice Tucker had admitted that his ruling on the question of Joyce's allegiance might well be wrong, and an appeal was launched immediately after the trial. The Court of Criminal Appeal, with Joyce in attendance, sat on 30 October; the proceedings lasted for three days. Once again the question of whether Joyce's fraudulent use of a British passport required a duty of allegiance was examined in great depth, as was trial by a British court for offences allegedly committed by an alien overseas, but in the end the appeal court came to the same conclusion as Mr Justice Tucker and the verdict stood.

Thereafter, Joyce's last avenue of appeal against conviction rested with the House of Lords, which sat to hear his case on 10 December. Joyce was amused to find himself placed in the 'Diplomatic Box' to observe the proceedings and he was pleased to be served luncheon in the Queen's Robing Room. Once again the question of the passport was examined in fine detail, and once again the appeal was dismissed, although one of the Law Lords found for the appeal on the purely technical grounds that Joyce's continued possession of the passport had not been left to the jury to decide. This decision was announced on 18 December and the execution was set for 3 January 1946.

Joyce faced his last few weeks with courage and equanimity. By now Margaret had been brought over from Germany and lodged in Holloway prison and they were allowed to meet regularly: he also resumed correspondence with his brother Quentin and MacNab. On the morning of 2 January, Margaret travelled to Wandsworth for the last time to see her husband; both were upset that the visit had taken place too early in the day for their final parting, and after she had gone he wrote her an emotional eight-page letter in which he expressed his love for her and his conviction that they would ever meet again. To his brother Quentin who arrived to see him during the afternoon he gave a final anti-Semitic statement to be published after his death and then he sat down to wait.

In the early evening of 2 January the prison doctor offered Joyce a sedative, which he accepted. Unsurprisingly, he slept fitfully that night and got up at half-past six on his last morning. At eight o'clock he took communion with the prison chaplain and then settled to write his last letter to his wife. He completed it at 8.36 and underlined the time at the bottom; he then wrote a brief note to MacNab. At nine o'clock exactly, the condemned-cell opened to permit the entry of Albert Pierrepoint, the hangman. Joyce stood to have his hands strapped behind his back and obediently followed Pierrepoint to the gallows, pausing only briefly to look down at his trembling legs and smile. His ankle were strapped together by Riley, Pierrepoint's assistant, and a white cap was placed over his head; followed immediately by the noose. Pierrepoint pulled the lever and Joyce dropped precisely seven feet and four inches and died.[5]

Amery's trial was an altogether more compact affair. On 28 November, when he appeared in front of Mr Justice Humphreys at the Old Bailey, he pleaded guilty to eight counts of treason. It had been widely expected that his defence would be similar to Joyce's: that he had received Spanish nationality prior to joining the Germans; but this proved not to be the case. John Leister, the young member of the British Free Corps, later claimed that Amery had been offered a deal whilst interned in Italy: if he pleaded guilty he would be reprieved; but there is no evidence to suggest that this might be true.[6] In fact, Amery had taken the advice of his lawyers that he had little chance of escaping conviction, and wishing to spare his family the agony of a long trial, had decided to forestall the proceedings.

Pierrepoint came for Amery on the morning of 29 December. As he entered the cell, Amery rose and greeted him with the words: 'Mr Pierrepoint, I have always wanted to meet you, though not, of course, in these circumstances'. Amery, concluded Pierrepoint, was the bravest man he ever hanged.

Cooper and Purdy were also convicted of treason, but both were reprieved on the grounds that they had been followers in treason rather than leaders. Both had their sentences commuted to life imprisonment. Cooper was released from prison in January 1953 and Purdy in December 1954. Cooper is believed to have gone to live in Japan. Purdy went to live with his 'wife' and child in Germany.

Sentences varied for the lesser renegades. MacLardy, the BFC's ideologue, received a life sentence at his court-martial in Cheshire although this was later remitted to fifteen years. His erstwhile henchman Britten's court martial took place at Colchester in June 1946 and he received a ten-year stretch. Two months later he was found to be suffering from an incurable form of Crohn's disease and he was released. Wilson, who had acted as the senior BFC NCO after Freeman's dismissal, received ten years, but Symonds, who was considerably less mature and even younger than Wilson, got fifteen years. Railton Freeman, who was educated and mature enough to know the consequences of his actions, received ten years' imprisonment, after which he told his lawyer: 'This just shows how rotten this democratic country is. The Germans would have had the honesty to shoot me.'[7] By contrast James Clark, the young son of Frances Eckersley, who had started broadcasting just after Joyce, was merely bound over for two years, and Kenneth Berry of the BFC received a nine-month sentence.

Disparities in the punishments meted out were a simple reflection of the perceived severity of the treason by the courts and courts-martial which heard the cases, and to some extent reflected the differing attitudes of the Commonwealth countries to the crime of treason against the British Crown. The Canadian courts-martial which heard the cases of Galaher, Martin and George Hale, who were all convicted for their activities as informers (Martin was also convicted for his BFC membership), delivered sentences of life, twenty-five years and fifteen years respectively; whereas the South African court which sat in judgement on Mardon, Viljoen and Labuschagne of the British Free Corps acquitted the latter two and fined Mardon £75 for the crime of high treason, commenting that he had committed 'the acts which we have held to constitute the crime of high treason with no wish to injure your own country'.[8] Courlander, the New Zealander, received a fifteen-year sentence of which he actually served seven years (he died in Auckland in 1970 after years spent boasting of his SS membership in local bars and pubs), whilst the Australian soldiers who joined the BFC – Stokes, Chipchase and Williams – do not appear to have been proceeded against.

The last of the renegades to face trial was Fusilier James Brady, late Unterscharführer of the SS-Jagdverbände and one of the tiny handful of Irishmen who were seduced from their loyalty at Friesack special camp. At a court-martial in Curzon Street, Mayfair, in December 1946, presided over by a very senior member of the Ulster protestant ascendancy, he was jailed for twelve years.

A handful of renegades escaped punishment entirely. Harry Batchelor of the British Free Corps was acquitted because his statement had been improperly taken by the detectives who interrogated him; and a few others, including Roy Futcher, Kenneth Lander, Ralph Baden-Powell, Robert Lane and William Miller, were such small fry that, by the time they were tracked down in their civilian occupations in Britain, it hardly seemed worth trying them and they were let go with a warning as to their future conduct. Douglas Berneville-Claye, the SAS officer who tried to take the BFC into battle, staunchly denied any involvement, either as a camp informer or an SS officer, and was let go for lack of untainted evidence (many BFC members recognized him of course). He came to grief within a year as a result of his criminal propensities and was cashiered from the Army and imprisoned for stealing a typewriter and a quantity of coal.

Harold Cole also escaped trial. In November 1945 he managed to walk out of the Paris detention centre, dressed in a stolen American uniform; he immediately went to ground in the teeming metropolis, taking up residence in a room above a bar off the Boulevard Raspail. He maintained a low profile there as the security authorities hunted around Europe for him, but almost inevitably his presence became known to the neighbours and he was reported to the police as a suspected deserter or escaped POW. On 8 January two detectives called at the bar to investigate and quickly went to the upstairs room with the bar's owner. She knocked on the door and called to 'Monsieur Harry', only to be greeted by the sight of her tenant wielding an automatic pistol. In the brief mêlée that followed, Cole fired two shots, slightly wounding one of the policemen; they replied with a volley from their own pistols and Cole was pitched back on to his bed by the impact of several bullets. He died instantly without uttering a word. It was a fitting end for the man described by Reginald Spooner as 'the worst traitor of the war'.

There is a pervasive air of unreality surrounding the story of the British renegades of World War Two. It is difficult to see how even the most intelligent and best educated of them – Joyce, Amery, Baillie-Stewart, Banning – could possibly believe that what they were doing was, as they claimed to believe at the time, in the best interests of Britain, and yet they certainly recognised that they were committing treason through their actions. At the same time, the German officials who sponsored them – Hesse and the England Committee, and the Germanische Leitstelle of SS Headquarters – were deluding themselves that Hitler paid anything more than lip-service to their ideal of a 'Germanic' Europe. In truth, the Führer was never interested in anything much other than reversing the result of the First World War, and he was prepared to go to any length to do so. If his manpower requirements were such that he had to use foreign troops – even from the armies of his enemies – then he was prepared to give them a try. There was no more to it than that.

The renegades were not of real strategic significance during the war, of that there is no doubt; in fact it is quite likely that by diverting resources from more realistic projects they had a marginally negative effect on the German war effort. Nevertheless, they *could* have been important. If German forces had crossed the channel in the summer of 1940, the NBBS could have played a vital part in disrupting lines of communication and diverting resources; if a spy like Duncan Scott-Ford had managed to compromise more shipping movements Britain might have been brought to its knees; if a British SS Brigade had appeared on the Eastern Front to fight and die against the Red Army, Stalin might have refused to co-operate with the western allies. It was for these reasons that Joyce and Amery were hanged and others nearly so. Even so, with the benefit of hindsight, execution is a dramatic overreaction to what these two most prominent traitors actually managed to achieve.

The common denominator if there is one, which was shared by the renegades and their immediate sponsors, was their utterly unrealistic view of the world; whether out of simple stupidity – and the names of several members of the British Free Corps spring readily to mind – or for more complex psychological reasons. It is difficult to imagine, for example, what Frank Axon thought he was gaining when he joined the BFC in March 1945; it is hard to conceive how Alexander Dolezalek might be of the opinion that fake communist riots in Germany might cause Britain and the United States to change sides in the last days of the war.

Only a few of the apparent renegades were able to turn the situation to their advantage: John Brown was able to contrive for himself a comfortable life in Berlin for nearly eighteen months *and* return to Britain as a decorated hero for his undoubted ingenuity in obtaining intelligence for MI9; Tom Freeman disrupted the BFC at a crucial moment in its formative stages and subsequently escaped to continue his fight against Nazi Germany. Others who tried to beat the system did less well: Eric Pleasants left England in 1940 to avoid taking part in a war that he did not agree with: subsequently he was to spend thirteen years being kicked around by the two most vicious totalitarian regimes that the world has seen. Even so, in the course of an interview for this book, he told the author that, given the same circumstances, he would act in the same way.

MI5's Report on the British Free Corps dated 27 March 1945

THE BRITISH FREE CORPS

General History

1. About May 1943 the Germans announced to Prisoners of War the establishment of a Holiday Camp in Berlin, to be known as Stalag IIID/999. About a month later they opened another Camp, Stalag IIID/517 at Genshagen. This was for ORs, the Officers remaining at IIID/999. In October 1943 we heard, by Secret channels, from Ps/W in Germany, that, from the outset, these Camps were regarded with grave mistrust and recognized as what they were, namely, propaganda establishments to subvert the loyalty of British Ps/W. They were almost immediately labelled, by Ps/W, 'The Prop. Camps', by which title they are known today.

2. It does not appear that the selection of the first batch of prisoners to be sent there was cleverly, or even systematically made. For instance no attempt was made beforehand to identify BUF men or prisoners with German pre-war connections. Instead the first batch consisted of a heterogeneous collection, who had mostly been for long in captivity, and very few were volunteers. The only evidence of purpose in selection is that it included a few entertainers (among them a dance band), interpreters, and, whether by accident or design, several men with some experience of journalism.

3. In the event the camps were a failure from the start. The Camp arrangements were incomplete when the Ps/W arrived. The latter was on their guard and obstructive when possible. There was no attempt by the enemy at intensive propaganda, but there was better food then in the ordinary Camps, a library,

and organized recreation (so far as obstruction by Ps/W allowed) including conducted motor coach tours around Berlin, group photographs, and walking out under supervision.

4. At an early stage, probably in October 1943, certain Ps/W were individually sounded as to whether they would join a unit to be called St George's Legion. The purpose of this unit was declared to be to fight Bolshevism, and the inducements were

   (a) that five Colonels and a Brigadier had already joined,
   (b) that the unit had already reached Brigade strength,
   (c) that it would be better to be a fighting soldier than to go to seed as a prisoner,
   (d) that it had the support of the British Government,
   (e) that it would lead to promotion.

   The theme was later, in April 1944, elaborated in a pamphlet widely distributed in all Camps, on the lines that

   (i) Britain had been slow to recognize the Russian peril, and that, in joining, Ps/W would be serving the true interests of their Country.
   (ii) Those who joined would get in on the ground floor of what was bound to become a great British movement.

   In October 1943, the month that all these activities first came to light, the name AMERY, the significance of which was unknown to those approached, was mentioned uncertainly by two Canadian Officers who had been approached to join, as that of the Brigadier associated with St George's Legion.

5. Concurrently with canvassing in Stalags IIID/999 and /517, the Germans sought recruits by another method. At Luckenwalde was a Transit and Interrogation Camp, called Stalag IIIA, for prisoners recently captured. The general policy in this Camp seems to have been precisely the reverse to that in Stalags IIID/999 and IIID/517. To IIIA were sent prisoners, particularly Irish and Indian, who were reported from field interrogation to be likely material. On arrival they found the hardest camp conditions and acute discomfort. The aim was, apparently, to present these to prisoners as the normal camp conditions they would find when sent on to the base Stalags. P/W of weak loyalty would then choose the alternative of enlistment in the Legion. It may have been to widen the appeal that the name was changed from 'St George's Legion' to 'The British Free Corps'. The new title was first reported in December 1943.

6. The uniform of the Legion, first seen at the end of 1943, was an ordinary German field-grey uniform with an embroidered Union Jack on the left arm.

(It is an indication of the scale of German hopes that 800 of these Union Jack badges were made.) Later three leopards were added to the collar, and a Service flash 'BRITISH FREE CORPS' in Gothic lettering was added to the sleeve.

7. The strength of the unit in the early stages is not certainly known. It was probably greatest at the end of 1943 but, in February 1944, we received reliable information that the strength was a mere twenty.

   At present we have no certain knowledge as to the training received by the Corps. We do know that some members of it were armed with revolvers, and also that in the early part of 1944 they were hanging about the barracks at Hildesheim day after day with nothing to do. It may well be that the numbers were never sufficient to justify any military training as a unit.

8. Throughout the early part of 1944 Censorship intercepts from P/W mail provided ample, and often amusing, evidence of the general indignation felt within the Camps, and the persistent efforts made by the Germans to secure recruits, including the sending of men in uniforms to the larger Camps to serve as decoys.

9. Early in 1944 Stalags IIID/999 and /517 were closed owing to the bombing of Berlin, and recruiting then depended on visiting recruiters who were sent to the Camps, including John AMERY himself, and recruits came from two sources:

   (i) Men enlisting to escape the conditions at Luckenwalde,
   (ii) Men enlisting as an alternative to punishment (usually as a result of association with German women while on a Working Party).

10. Early in 1944 certain of the few enlisted members of the British Free Corps were drawn from it, and assigned to other subversive activities, such as broadcasting and SS. Propaganda Units at the Front.

11. The information which follows as to those responsible for founding the B.F.C., how it came into being, and the identity of its members, was obtained from two men, Corporals COURLANDER and MATON, who were themselves members, and who were found in Brussels at the time of its occupation in mid-September 1944. Right up to this time they had been actually serving in the Free Corps.

   Since that date we have received information that the 'Prop' camps had a second lease of life after the first bombing, but were finally closed at the beginning of 1945. At the present time it is, of course, extremely difficult to obtain information as to the existing situation in the Free Corps.

   We know that, as late as September 1944, two recruits named Gnr. NIGHTINGALE and Pte. MILLER were enlisted. There may be others; but it is reasonable, in view of the war situation, to assume that the B.F.C. is now stagnant if it is not disbanded. The members may be used as orderlies and messengers.

12. It will be seen that the first recruits for the B.F.C. came from the 'Prop. Camps', Stalags IIID/999 and /517. These Camps also provided a number of broadcasters, some of whom were also, at one time or another, members of the B.F.C. It would probably be inaccurate to assume that those two, and other, subversive activities were born out of the propaganda camps and owed their existence to them. Prisoners of War would certainly have been used for broadcasting propaganda and probably the B.F.C. would also have been formed, whether the propaganda camps had existed or not. Renegades of categories other than Ps/W were broadcasting long before the Camps were formed, and the British Free Corps is, after all, an old idea, being analogous to the Irish Brigade which Casement tried to form in the last war. What is true is that the propaganda camps were a convenient foundation for subversive activities, and were used to nourish them. The German effort was quite a large one. The completeness of its failure is the more remarkable. The details of the effort, and who was behind it, serve to support the foregoing remarks.

The exact scene of these activities is irrelevant to this note, but it is important to realize

(a) that Stalag IIID is a generic title which includes all P/W establishments in the Berlin region, which were all administered from H.Q.
(b) that Stalag IIID/999 was situated in Zohlondorf West, and Stalag IIID/517 at Genshagen.
(c) that in June 1944, the B.F.C. was in an old monastery building near Michaclisplatz at Hildesheim. Connected with this, in Berlin, was a house in the Grunewald district where recruits were received and issued with clothing.

Personnel

13. When Stalag IIID/517 was opened, of the cadre staff of five Servicemen who were already there to receive the first batch of Ps/W, the four in the executive positions are reported to have had pre-war B.U.F. sympathies. The German in charge was Sonderführer Oscar LANGE, an ex-New York docker, who, in spite of his low rank, was allowed considerable initiative and had also to do with the recruiting arrangements in Luckenwalde (scc 5 above). LANGE, therefore, was concerned both with the propaganda camps as such and with the plan for forming the Free Corps. He was under the direct control of Hauptmann BENTMANN. This Officer was in charge of the Wehrmacht

propaganda section of Oberkommando der Wehrmacht (O.K.W.), and was interested in the formation of a British Unit, but only for propaganda purposes. BENTMANN and LANGE are to be regarded as soldiers, responsible for implementing the policy of higher authority, so far as that policy was to be applied to Service Ps/W; but it appears that the higher authority was shared between the Foreign Office, Propaganda Ministry, and S.S., all of whom had a hand in the programme. This divided authority later led to friction and discord and was partly responsible for failure in recruiting at the Camps.

14. Looking at this higher authority, on present information it seems likely that the idea of the propaganda camps originated with the German Foreign Office, while the prime mover in starting the Free Corps was John AMERY, the British civilian renegade. The latter's name was given to a recruit by LANGE as early as August, 1943, as 'now forming a unit to fight against Communism'. The relations at that time between AMERY and the Foreign Office are not known, and on them depends how far he may also have been responsible for the idea of the propaganda camps. What is known, however, is that the Foreign Office was actively interested through the persons of HESSE, ZIEGVELD, ADAMI and SCHMIDT.

Dr HESSE, who was German Press Attaché in England before the war, worked through ZIEGVELD, who was a student in England at the outbreak of the last war, and was interned. ZIEGVELD is reported to have been a foundation member of the 'link' and the author of the book named 'England at the Cross Roads'.

ADAMI is believed to have been keeping an eye on the activities of AMERY on behalf of the Foreign Office.

Of these men, ZIEGVELD came into direct contact with Ps/W.

The S.S. representative was Haupsturmführer Hans Werner ROEPKE, who was to take direct command of the B.F.C. as a Waffen S.S. Unit. Some influence in the shaping of the B.F.C. was also exercised by Major HEIMPEL, who was security officer and as such held the Gestapo brief.

Besides AMERY, another notorious British civilian renegade was directly involved in the B.F.C. This was Vivian STRANDERS. This man is reported to have become an acknowledged member of the N.S.D.A.P. some time before assuming German nationality. He was appointed to succeed ROEPKE in command of the B.F.C. in August 1944.

Something is known of several other German characters associated with the propaganda camps and the B.F.C., in varying degrees, but those mentioned are sufficient to illustrate the set-up.

15. The known membership of the British Free Corps at various times consisted of the following:

(1) Cpl. COURLANDER, R.N., New Zealand Army; the son of a Baltic jew, may have had genuine anti-Russian leanings.

(2) Cpl. MATON, F.P., R.A. and Commandos, whose make-up is fertile ground for Nazi ideas with which, on his own admission, he is impressed. He has a good Military record and was NOT an enrolled member of the B.U.F.

(3) COOPER, T., a civilian with German connections and sentiments. A very active member of the B.F.C.

(4) Sgt. MacLARDY, F., R.A.M.C.; pre-war District Secretary of B.U.F.

(5) MINCHIN, A., Seaman P/W; recruited three other members; was one of the first to join the B.F.C. himself; motive uncertain.

(6) Sgt. WILSON, J.; believed a weak character, entered B.F.C. via Luckenwalde – perhaps under duress.

(7) Pte. MARTIN, E.; Canadian Army; little known; employed previously by Germans at Luckenwalde Interrogation Camp; boastful, brutal type; ambitious.

(8) LEWIS, J., Seaman P/W; convinced Fascist; vain.

(9) Pte. BRITTON, K.; Nazi by temperament; B.U.F. member.

(10) 'REID' – an alias, unidentified P/W; Luckenwalde recruit, but not an unwilling one.

(11) 'DAVIS' – an alias, a Battalion Signaller; a Luckenwalde; real sympathies in doubt.

(12) LANE, 'Sandy', unidentified P/W; recruited at Luckenwalde; really anti-German; now left B.F.C.

(13) 'ROGERS' – an alias; picked up by Germans in Austria; really anti-German; now left B.F.C.

(14) 'FRAZER' – an alias. South African; came with 'ROGERS', linguist; true identity and background unknown.

(15) 'Aussie No. 1', Australian P/W; recruited at SCHWERIN (? to dodge trouble).

(16) 'Aussie No. 2', Australian P/W; (same as 15).

(17) 'Aussie No. 3'; Australian P/W; came with 'ROGERS'; anti-German, intends to escape.

(18) 'BARKER' – an alias; Australian seaman P/W; recruited early by MINCHIN.

(19) BERRY, K. Ships Boy P/W; taken prisoner at age of 14, now 19–20; recruited at St. Denis; we have evidence that he now regrets it.

(20) 'CAMERON' – an alias; out and out Nazi; nothing else known about him.

(21) PLEASANTS; civilian; recruited by MINCHIN.

(22) LEISTER; civilian.

(23) Sgt. ROSE, N.: Regular soldier P/W; recruited Luckenwalde, B.F.C. storekeeper; anti-German.

(24) 'BROWN' – an alias. Regular soldier P/W; probably got into trouble and joined to avoid punishment; believed to own petty criminal record.

(25) 'The International Brigade man'; identity unknown.

(26) 'The New Lad'; identity unknown.

(27) 'Sailor'; identity unknown.

(28) 'Ukraine Joe'; identity unknown.

(29) 'COWARD' from Marienbad'; identity unknown.

(30) Gnr. NIGHTINGALE, H., R.A.; joined September 1944 to avoid punishment for intercourse with German woman.

(31) RUSSLER, Wilhelm; may be German stool-pigeon to the Corps.

(32) Lieut. SHEARER, W.A.W.; the only Army Officer recruit; was to have taken his place as British Officer in unit; believed psychological case; considered by Germans too unbalanced for intended employment; returned to Camp and now repatriated.

(33) SCHMETTERLING; British; origin unknown; joined voluntarily.

(34) PHILLPOTTS, Joe; British; reported to have joined voluntarily as a means of obtaining permission to marry girl he had met on a working party.

(35) 'The Corps Tailor'; nothing known about him; may be identical with any of 25–29.

(36) STURMER; German; presence unexplained.

(37) Pte. JACKSON, E.; P/W; nothing further known.

(38) Pte. MILLER, W.; P/W; joined like No. 20 to avoid punishment.

(39) Lieut. PURDY, W., R.N.R; P/W; now seconded for radio duties.

Radio

16. The principal subversive activity other than the B.F.C., nourished by Stalags IIID/999 and /517, was to add to the staffs of the secret broadcasting stations of which Radio National (music and talks), Workers Challenge (talks to appeal especially to the working class) and Empire Senders (for Dominion and Colonial audiences) were examples. All the above stations were pretended to be operating secretly within the countries to which the propaganda was directed. This enterprise, which employed more civilians than Service renegades, was under the joint control of the Foreign Office and Propaganda Ministry, and was known as the Bureau Concordia. After some discord it was ruled that the Foreign Office should exercise political control over all foreign propaganda, and in this capacity should censor material submitted by the

Propaganda Ministry. It is unnecessary in this note to explore the details of this organization and its control, though the Security Service has considerable information on the subject (which is contained in a memorandum by Mr Shelford). There is a present interest, however, in those characters with whom British prisoners came in touch, and those prisoners themselves.

17. The headquarters for the Foreign Office department for controlling the activities of the Bureau Concordia, and the recruiting of renegades for it, appears to have been run by Professor HAFERKORN. ADAMI (see 14 above) assists HAFERKORN and has visited P.W. Camps to obtain recruits.

18. There are Englishmen, resident in Germany before the war, who are concerned in the organization and some of whom took a parallel interest in the formation of the B.F.C. A P/W who is almost on an equal footing with some of these men, such as JOYCE, BAILLIE STEWART and AMERY, is Pilot Officer FREEMAN, whose case is peculiar in that, though without earlier German connections, he has worked his way so far as to be a fully accepted member of the German control.

19. In addition to a number of British civilians, the following Service renegades have been employed in editing, writing scripts, and broadcasting for the enemy, and in certain cases the same men are also employed in journalism: (One of them, for instance, Pilot Officer FREEMAN, recently wrote the leading article in the chief Nazi organ 'Angriff' under his own name).

> Sgt. CHAPPLE, Arthur, R.A.S.C.
> Cpl. COURLANDER, R.N., NZ Forces, in addition to a permanent position in the B.F.C. and service later in the Waffen S.S. he, at one time, broadcast for Empire Senders. (Since repatriated).
> P/O FREEMAN, B.R.M., R.A.F.
> Rfn. HOSKINS, C., K.R.R.C.
> Sgt. HUGHES, R.D., R.A.F.
> Cpl. MATON, F.P., Commandos – as for COURLANDER above.
> Lieut. PURDY, W., R.N.R. (also a member of the B.F.C.)
> L/Cpl. SPILLMAN, R., K.R.R.C.
> Gdsmn. GRIFFITHS, W.H., Welsh Guards.

All these men received payment varying from 1000 RM a month for FREEMAN down to 400RM.

M.I.5.

27.3.45

V. H. SEYMER

Lieut.-Col.

Table of Comparative Ranks of the British Army, German Army and the Waffen-SS

British Army	German Army	Waffen-SS
Private	Schütze/Oberschütze	SS-Schütze/SS-Oberschütze
Lance-Corporal	Gefreiter	SS-Sturmmann
Corporal	Obergefreiter	SS-Rottenführer
Sergeant	Unteroffizier/Unterfeldwebel	SS-Unterscharführer/-Scharführer
Staff-Sergeant	Feldwebel	SS-Oberscharführer
Warrant Officer Class Two	Oberfeldwebel	SS-Hauptscharführer
Warrant Officer Class One	Stabsfeldwebel	SS-Sturmscharführer
Second Lieutenant	Leutnant	SS-Untersturmführer
Lieutenant	Oberleutnant	SS-Obersturmführer
Captain	Hauptmann	SS-Hauptsturmführer
Major	Major	SS-Sturmbannführer
Lieutenant-Colonel	Oberstleutnant	SS-Obersturmbannführer
Colonel	Oberst	SS-Oberführer/-Standartenführer
Brigadier	Generalmajor	SS-Brigadeführer
Major-General	Generalleutnant	SS-Gruppenführer
Lieutenant-General	General	SS-Obergruppenführer
General	Generaloberst	SS-Oberstgruppenführer
Field-Marshal	Generalfeldmarschall	No equivalent

German Army and Waffen-SS ranks of the Second World War did not precisely correspond with the Anglo-American system in terms of the appointment that the rank would carry; it was not uncommon, for example, in the final months of the war, to find brigades and divisions being commanded by Majors and Oberstleutnants and their Waffen-SS equivalents. The table given here, therefore, merely illustrates the respective positions in the hierarchies.

Appendix 3

John Amery's Proclamation of the Legion of St George

BRITISH NATIONAL REPRESENTATION

PROCLAMATION TO ALL BRITISH SUBJECTS INTERNED

FELLOW COUNTRYMEN:

150,000 of our fellow countrymen are in prison in the home country, because they have declared themselves against this fratricidal war. In violation of the Habeas Corpus Act and the fundamental laws of our constitution these men have never been brought to trial or even allowed to see a lawyer.

American troops have not only occupied Ulster but are arriving in increasing numbers in England.

Naval bases and Colonies have been handed over to Mr Roosevelt's administration.

BEYOND ALL THIS

This war has ceased to be a war of nations but has become a war of

CONCEPTION

Europe and our country, your wives and children at home are menaced by the invasion of the HORDES OF BOLCHEVICK BARBARITY.

For this reason I have approached the German Government with the proposal to form

A BRITISH LEGION AGAINST BOLCHEVISM, to be known as the LEGION of ST GEORGE.

I appeal to all Britishers to answer this call to arms for the defence of all the principles that we Englishmen have been the first to proclaim in the world.

THE DEFENCE OF OUR HOMES, OF OUR CHILDREN AND OF ALL CIVILISATION AGAINST THE DRAGON OF ASIATIC AND JEWISH BESTIALITY.

The St George Legion will fight only against the Communists and on NO OTHER FRONT!

All men will commence in their present rank and promotion will be open to all men alike, without any distinctions or qualification, political or otherwise.

Within the limits of the military possibilities the Legion of St George will fight at the junction of the German–Finnish front, beside the troops of the undaunted liberty loving Finnish people.

The British Representation in Berlin formally guarantee to all ranks: A PERMANENT WELL PLACED JOB IN THE BRITISH ADMINISTRATION OR A PRIORITY IN ANY OTHER EMPLOYMENT THEY SHOULD DESIRE ONCE PEACE IS SIGNED, OR THE POSSIBILITY TO FORM THE ELITE IN THE NEW BRITISH ARMY.

Hundreds of soldiers have volunteered to join this Legion.

Men who have escaped to England have come to join us.

Three Royal Air Force aeroplanes have come over to us so far with their arms and equipment.

It is up to you civilians to give a hand to show that we intend to take our responsibilities to maintain THE INTEGRITY OF OUR EMPIRE, by giving the world proof that we have not all sold out to the JEW OR PLUTOCRAT.

I ASK YOU TO OPT NATIONAL

The British Representation which is a 100% British organisation will take no steps whatever of intimidation against the persons who do not opt, BUT fellow countrymen the world is watching us, EUROPE EXPECTS THAT EVERY CIVILISED MAN WILL DO HIS DUTY, National England desires that you will show yourselves worthy of Nelson's immortal signal:

'ENGLAND EXPECTS THIS DAY EVERY MAN WILL DO HIS DUTY'

Your place is with us Nationalists . . . . Your duty is to opt NATIONAL under the glorious banner of St George we are going to write a new page in the History of the British Empire: more, WE SHALL SAVE THE BRITISH EMPIRE FROM COMMUNISM AND AMERICAN RAPACITY.

We shall show the world that free Englishmen:

NEVER, NEVER WILL BE THE SLAVES OF A JEWISH PLUTOCRATIC TYRANNY, THAT WE ARE WORTHY DESCENDANTS OF THE YEOMEN THAT DICTATED MAGNA CHARTA.

Pay no attention to waverings or opposition: the first to opt will be the examples of bravery and courage to those that now waver or are against us but who will have to join us one day when they realise all the truth.

In these fatal days when we are before the bar of civilisation: I beg, I demand, that you put aside all hesitations, all the prejudice, all the lies that have led you where you are . . . that you take this IMMENSE OPPORTUNITY THAT I HAVE OBTAINED AND WITH ME, WITH ALL THOSE THAT HAVE ALREADY JOINED.

YOU WILL OPT NATIONAL . . . FOR ENGLAND AND ST GEORGE!

PARIS 20–4–43   John AMERY

Appendix 4

The Free Indian Legion

Although the two thousand or so members of the Free Indian Legion of the German Army (and later the Waffen-SS) were technically British subjects and were recruited by the Germans from units of the British Indian Army, I did not include them in the main body of the text because the circumstances in which they became 'renegades' were fundamentally different to those of the native Britons who changed sides. It could be – and indeed has been – argued that the Indians' move was made within the context of a legitimate struggle to be rid of an oppressive colonial power, and that any loyalty they owed to the British Crown was the result of many years of coercion. Nevertheless, the story of the Indian Legion is a fascinating example of how far the supposedly 'Aryan' German Armed Forces – and more particularly the Waffen-SS – were prepared to stretch their own racial requirements in order to attract more soldiers; and, as it happens, I also found that a British renegade did serve with the unit in a junior capacity throughout its existence. In consequence, I have decided to outline the history of the unit briefly in this appendix.

The Free Indian Legion was the brainchild of Subhas Chandra Bose, one of the Mahatma Gandhi's chief rivals for the leadership of the Indian independence movement. In contrast to Gandhi, Bose advocated a more aggressive confrontation with British imperialism, and he saw the outbreak of war in Europe as an opportunity to capitalize on British weakness. In January 1941 he left his residence in Calcutta, where he was under virtual house arrest, and travelled via Afghanistan to Moscow where he hoped to be able to raise support for armed insurrection in India. Instead, the Soviets passed him on to Berlin where he arrived at the beginning of April. He began discussions with the German propaganda and foreign ministries almost immediately.

By coincidence, shortly after Bose's arrival in Berlin, the 3rd (Indian) Motorized

Brigade was captured, largely intact, by Rommel's Afrika Korps at El Machili in Libya. Bose and his German sponsors decided that this offered an opportunity experimentally to canvass support for an Indian unit within the German Armed Forces, and a Major of the Luftwaffe was despatched to talk to all English-speaking ranks of the Brigade on 15 May. As a result of this, a party of twenty-seven officers were moved to Berlin by air where they arrived four days later, and the Germans began to organize the move of the rest of the Brigade to a special camp at Annaburg.

For the next six months Bose and his assistants conducted an intensive recruiting campaign amongst Indian POWs, with the result that in January 1942 the Propaganda Ministry announced the formation of the 'Indian National Army' (Jai Hind) in Berlin – at this time the unit consisted of just eight firm adherents. Whilst the political leadership of the Indian unit was operating in Berlin, the Germans moved the most likely 6000 candidates for membership of their new unit to a new training centre in Frankenburg – designated as 'Arbeitskommando Frankenburg' for security purposes – and began to give them military training; although they maintained a fiction that the prisoners were to be used as a labour battalion.

At the end of July 300 volunteers were removed from Frankenburg and taken to yet another camp at Königsbrück where they were issued with German Army uniforms bearing a badge on the right arm which showed a leaping tiger superimposed on an Indian tricolour, surmounted by the legend 'Freies Indien'. The men were then officially designated the 'Free Indian Legion' and an attestation and oath-taking ceremony was held for them on 26 August. In the months that followed, several hundred more prisoners were recruited by various means – including outright force – and by the middle of 1943 the unit consisted of about 2000 men organized into three battalions. At around this time it became known as Infanterie Regiment 950.

One of the oddities of the Free Indian Legion was that the working language used by both the German and Indian personnel within the unit was English. To this end, in July 1942 an English interpreter, Frank Chetwynd Becker, had been posted on to the strength of the unit from a Wehrmacht interpreter unit in Dresden. Becker had been born in 1915 in Essex, the son of a German-born but naturalized British father and an English mother. His mother died just after he was born and his father in 1924 and he had then been taken to live in Germany by an uncle although he retained his British nationality. In 1935 he returned to England to work on behalf of a German company and he remained, living in Croydon, until August 1939, when he went to Germany for a holiday. Trapped by the outbreak of war, Becker reported himself to the authorities and was given the opportunity – because of his mixed background – of working for Germany as a non-combatant or going into internment. He decided to opt for the former and was given a job as a 'Sonderführer'.

In May 1943 the Indian Legion was moved to garrison duties on the Dutch North Sea coast where they were mainly used for the construction of coastal defences, and from there they were sent, in August, to France. There they continued with normal occupation duties, occasionally tangling with French resistance units, until August 1944 when, as a result of the successful Allied landings and their rapid advance, it was decided to evacuate them to Germany. During this period resistance attacks on retreating German units were greatly stepped up, and three members of the Legion, Unteroffizier Kalu Ram, Leutnant Ali Khan and Gefreiter Mela Ram, were killed during ambushes.

The Indian Legion was initially based near Hagenau in Alsace, well away from any fighting, until, with the approach of US forces, they were again evacuated to Heuberg in the south. At this time, in the autumn of 1944, the Wehrmacht handed over control of the unit, in line with the policy on foreign legions, to the Waffen-SS who were thereafter responsible for their administration. The changeover to SS control had no material effect on the way the legion was organized and the German personnel and the legionaries' uniforms were unchanged. As the war came to a halt in April 1945, the legion found itself in American custody in the Lake Constance area.

The Indian Legion never fought as a unit and did nothing materially to aid the German war effort during its short existence. The fact that many, probably a majority, of its membership were tricked or forced into joining meant that discipline was always a serious problem – one of the Legion's most enthusiastic members, Unteroffizier Mohammed Ibrahim, was actually shot by his own men – and this was compounded by the Germans' ignorance of Indian military customs and of caste and religion. As a result, the British colonial authorities took a lenient view of the Indian renegades and only a handful of ringleaders were tried by courts-martial. Subhas Chandra Bose travelled to Japan by submarine in March 1943 to organize the 'Provisional Government of Free India'; he died in an air crash in the last days of the war there.

Notes

Introduction
1. Rebecca West, *The Meaning of Treason*, p. 174.

1. Mosley, Joyce and Fascism in Britain
1. Bullock, *Hitler and Stalin: Parallel Lives*, p. 77.
2. Taylor, *English History 1914–1945*, p. 57.
3. Stanley Baldwin.
4. Mosley, *My Life*, p. 49.
5. Mosley's grandfather had died in 1915, naming his grandson as heir to his fortunes and estates.
6. Mosley, op. cit., p. 70.
7. 27 March 1924.
8. Skidelsky, *Oswald Mosley*, p. 97.
9. Ibid., p. 97.
10. Ibid., p. 125.
11. Ibid., p. 133.
12. Ibid., p. 177.
13. Ibid., p. 252.
14. Cole, *Lord Haw-Haw*, p. 23.
15. Cross, *The Fascists in Britain*, p. 57.
16. Cole, op. cit., p. 34.
17. Cross, op. cit., p. 65.
18. Skidelsky, op. cit., p. 319.
19. Cole, op. cit., p. 68.
20. Ibid., p. 77.
21. Ibid., p. 71.
22. Ibid., p. 82.

23. Hinsley *et al.*, *British Intelligence in the Second World War*, vol. 4, p. 15.

24. Rebecca West, in *The Meaning of Treason*, suggested that there was 'a long and complicated and illicit series of events' behind Joyce's move to Berlin and that 'William Joyce had found a port at which there was either a breakdown of routine fantastically fortunate for him, or another traitor, working with him on the same pattern of treachery'. Both of these suppositions are pure fantasy on her part (as is much of the rest of her book).

2. Germany Calling

1. Cole, op. cit., p. 108.
2. Ibid., p. 108.
3. David Niven, *The Moon's a Balloon* (Hamish Hamilton, 1971).
4. West, op. cit., p. 204.
5. Home Office. HO45/25787.
6. Ibid.
7. Cole, op. cit., p. 113.
8. Ibid., p. 115.
9. Ibid., p. 118.
10. Selwyn, *Hitler's Englishman*, p. 117.
11. Joyce, *Twilight over England*.
12. Ibid.
13. *The Times*, 3 May 1991.
14. Sproat, *Wodehouse at War*, p. 56.
15. Ibid., p. 125.

3. Black Propaganda

1. Höhne, *The Order of the Death's Head*, p. 238.
2. PRO. HO45/25827.
3. Ibid.
4. Cole, op. cit., p. 160.
5. BBC Monitoring, 20 July 1940.

4. John Amery

1. Taylor, op. cit., p. 327.
2. West, op. cit., p. 191.
3. Littlejohn, *Foreign Legions of the Third Reich*, vol. 1, p. 117.
4. L. S. Amery, *The Empire at Bay: Diaries 1929–1945*, p. 1072. This book contains a short and poignant appendix written by Leo Amery to explain his son's conduct.

5. Home Office. HO45/25773.
6. Ibid.
7. Ibid.
8. Ibid.
9. It may be remembered that Plack was P. G. Wodehouse's Hollywood contact who persuaded the writer to make his ill-judged broadcasts on prison-camp life.
10. HO45/25773.
11. Ibid.
12. Ibid.
13. John Amery, *John Amery Speaks* (Berlin, 1943).
14. Ibid.
15. HO45/25773.
16. USNA, Microcopy T-120, roll 715, frames 327976–7.
17. HO45/25773. Amery's claims of support from England were, of course, untrue.
18. Ibid.
19. Ibid.
20. Ibid.

5. The Lost Boys

1. PRO. HO336/2.
2. PRO. FO369/3172 (an official had noted 'rubbish!' in the margin).
3. PRO. HO45/25805.
4. Ibid.
5. Höhne, op. cit., p. 419.
6. PRO. HO45/25836. Statement of R. R. Futcher.
7. PRO. HO45/25805.
8. Ibid.
9. Ibid.
10. Ibid.
11. Ibid.
12. See Masterman, *The Double-Cross System*, and Hinsley *et al.*, op. cit., vol. 4, *Security and Counter-Intelligence*.
13. Höhne, op. cit., p. 307.
14. In July 1944 Berger reported to Himmler that there were 1200 Irishmen at Buchenwald, and that they were resisting all attempts to influence them. USNA Microcopy T-175, frame 2450460.

6. Our Flag Is Going Forwards Too!

1. USNA, Microcopy T-120, Serial 1168, roll 715, frame 327968.
2. Ibid., frame 327969.
3. Höhne, op. cit., p. 22.
4. Ibid., p. 39.
5. Ibid., p. 134.
6. Ibid., p. 411.
7. Felix Steiner, article in *Wiking Ruf*, no. 4, 1955.
8. Buss and Mollo, *Hitler's Germanic Legions*, p. 16.
9. Stein, *Waffen-SS: Hitler's Elite Guard at War*, p. 153.
10. Buss and Mollo, op. cit., p. 18.
11. Ibid., p. 18.
12. Höhne, op. cit., p. 461.

7. John Brown and the Genshagen Experiment

1. Material on Hillen-Ziegfeld comes mostly from de Slade's *The Frustrated Axis*, where he is called by the alias 'Hidding-Bockau'.
2. Brown, *In Durance Vile*.
3. PRO. HO45/25805.
4. Brown, op. cit., p. 84.
5. PRO. Crim 1/485.
6. Ibid.
7. Ibid.
8. Private information.
9. Brown, op. cit., p. 99.
10. De Slade, op. cit., p. 101.

8. Luckenwalde

1. PRO. HO45/25805.
2. *Manchester Guardian*, 5 Sept. 1945.

9. Fellow Countrymen

1. PRO. HO45/25805.
2. Ibid.
3. Private information.
4. Private information.
5. Private information.
6. PRO. HO45/25805.
7. PRO. CRIM/485.
8. Interview, Eric Pleasants, Dec. 1992.

9. Ibid.
10. Ibid.
11. PRO. HO45/25805.
12. 'They put these men in villas in various pleasant parts of Germany, and dressed them in German uniforms with flashes with the letters B.F.C. and the Union Jack to show that the wearers were British soldiers, and let them go rotten with idleness and indiscipline and debauchery.' Rebecca West, op. cit.
13. Hans W. Roepke, letter to the author, 13 Aug. 1982.
14. Interview, Eric Pleasants, Dec. 1992.
15. PRO. HO45/25805.
16. Ibid.
17. Private information.

10. Other Traitors: Other Treasons
1. Much of the information on Freeman is derived from the file opened on him by the SS when he was commissioned as an Untersturmführer in 1944. The file survived the war and is held at the Berlin Document Center.
2. Private information.
3. Private information.
4. BDC file: B. R. M. Freeman.
5. Private information.
6. In the film *The Great Escape* Bushell was called 'Bartlett' and his part was played by Richard Attenborough.
7. Private information.
8. Private information.
9. Private information.
10. Private information.
11. Private information.
12. Ibid.
13. Ibid.
14. Ibid.
15. Ibid.
16. Ibid.
17. BDC. File on B. R. M. Freeman.
18. Private information.
19. Ibid.
20. HO45/25763.
21. Murphy, *Turncoat: The True Case of Traitor Sergeant Harold Cole*, p. 24.
22. Long, *Safe Houses are Dangerous*, p. 87.

23. Langley, *Fight Another Day*, p. 105.
24. Murphy, op. cit., p. 189.

11. The British Free Corps in Dresden
1. Private information.
2. PRO. HO45/25805.
3. Alexander MacKinnon, interview with James MacLeod, Nov. 1991.
4. Private information.
5. Interview, Eric Pleasants, Dec. 1992.
6. Alexander Dolezalek, letter to author, 11 Feb. 1990.
7. Ibid., 31 Mar. 1990.
8. PRO. HO45/25836.
9. Alexander MacKinnon, interview with James MacLeod, Nov. 1991.
10. Before leaving, Cowie and Futcher burnt as many BFC documents as they could find, together with a collection of photographs. This is one of the principal reasons why there is such a dearth of photographic and documentary material relating to the unit.
11. Interview, Eric Pleasants, Dec. 1992.
12. Ibid.

12. The End Game
1. Private information.
2. South African Transcripts.
3. Private information.
4. South African Transcripts.
5. Bender and Taylor, *Uniforms, Organisation and History of the Waffen-SS*, vol. 2, p. 34.
6. George Croft, statement to Military Police, May 1945.
7. Alexander MacKinnon, interview with James MacLeod, Nov. 1991.
8. Private information.
9. HO45/25803
10. PRO. HO45/25803.
11. 'Tanky' Smith, telephone conversation, Apr. 1993.
12. PRO. HO45/25803.
13. Private information.
14. Private information.
15. Alexander MacKinnon, interview with James MacLeod, Nov. 1991.
16. Ibid., July 1993.
17. Ibid., July 1993.
18. Private information.

19. PRO. WO171/4649.
20. PRO. WO171/4649.
21. Interview, Eric Pleasants, Feb. 1993.

13. The Reckoning

1. The British Renegades Warning List remains classified. Nevertheless there are numerous references to it in open files, particularly those in the HO45 group at the Public Record Office.
2. Later Sir Roger Hollis, controversial Director of MI5 in the 1960s.
3. A copy of this report can be found in WO311/42 in the Public Record Office.
4. Selwyn, op. cit., p. 167.
5. PRO. PCOM9/2122.
6. Interview, Eric Pleasants, Mar. 1993.
7. West, op. cit., p. 111.
8. South African National Archives. Trial of D. C. Mardon, p. 116.

Bibliography and Notes on Sources

Unpublished Sources

The great majority of material in 'Renegades' has been derived from archive sources held by a number of governmental organizations, both British and foreign. Of these, the most important have proved to be: firstly, in the Public Record Office (PRO) at Kew, London, the HO45 class, under the heading 'War', the group: 'Renegades, and persons suspected of assisting the enemy'; and secondly, the US National Archives (USNA) microfilm holdings of the records of the Reichsführer-SS, and of the German Foreign Minstry. All documents have been noted in the text when directly quoted.

Published Sources

In addition to archive material I have also consulted a number of published works; these are listed below. One of the principal sources of information for this book was the many contemporary newspaper reports of the trials of the renegades; as with the archive and published material, these have been noted when directly quoted.

Adamson, Iain. *The Great Detective*, Frederick Muller, 1966.
Bender, Roger James, and Taylor, Hugh Page. *Uniforms, Organisation and History of the Waffen-SS*, 5 vols, R. J. Bender Publishing, 1969.
Brown, J. H. O. *In Durance Vile*, Robert Hale, 1981.
Bullock, Alan. *Hitler and Stalin: Parallel Lives*, HarperCollins, 1991.
Buss, P. H., and Mollo, A. *Hitler's Germanic Legions*, Macdonald & Jane's, 1978.
Cole, J. A. *Lord Haw-Haw and William Joyce: The Full Story*, Faber, 1964.
Coogan, Tim Pat. *The IRA*, Fontana, 1980.

Cross, Colin. *The Fascists in Britain*, Barrie and Rockliff, 1961.

Foot, M. R. D., and Langley, J. M. *MI9: Escape and Evasion 1939–1945*, Bodley Head, 1979.

Höhne, Heinz. *The Order of the Death's Head*, Secker and Warburg, 1969.

Hinsley, F. H., *et al*. *British Intelligence in the Second World War*, 5 vols, HMSO, 1975.

Langley, J. M. *Fight Another Day*, Collins, 1974.

Littlejohn, David. *Foreign Legions of the Third Reich*, 4 vols, R. J. Bender Publishing, 1977.

Long, Helen. *Safe Houses are Dangerous*, William Kimber, 1985.

Masterman, J. C. *The Double-Cross System 1939–1945*, Yale UP, 1972.

Murphy, Brendan. *Turncoat: The True Case of Traitor Sergeant Harold Cole*, Macdonald, 1987.

Rolf, David. *Prisoners of the Reich: Germany's Captives 1939–1945*, Leo Cooper, 1988.

Selwyn, Francis. *Hitler's Englishman: The Crime of Lord Haw-Haw*, Routledge & Kegan Paul, 1987.

Seth, Ronald. *Jackals of the Reich*, NEL, 1972.

Skidelsky, Robert. *Oswald Mosley*, Macmillan, 1975.

Slade, Marquis de. *The Yeomen of Valhalla*, privately published, 1970.

—— *The Frustrated Axis*, privately published, 1978.

Stein, George H. *Waffen-SS: Hitler's Elite Guard at War*, Cornell UP, 1966.

Taylor, A. J. P. *English History 1914–1945*, Oxford UP, 1976.

West, Nigel. *MI5*, Bodley Head, 1981.

West, Rebecca. *The Meaning of Treason*, Macmillan, 1949.

Ziemke, Earl F. *Stalingrad to Berlin: The German Defeat in the East*, Military Heritage Press, 1968.

INDEX